Science
& Nature

Publications International, Ltd.

Contributing Writers
Joel E. Arem, Ph.D., Lynne Hardie Baptista, Jennifer Boudart, Gary Dunn, Toni Eugene, Martin F.J. Flower, Ph.D., Donald F. Glut, Alice Jablonsky, Karolyn Kendrick, David R. Kristovich, Ph.D., Francis Reddy, Scott Weidensaul, Elissa Wolfson

Contributing Consultants
Isaac Abella, Ph.D., Richard Block, Bruce A. Bolt, Ph.D., Todd A. Culver, Peter Dodson, Betty Lane Faber, Ph.D., Robert W. Grumbine, Ph.D., Howard E. Lawler, Ellis D. Miner, Mark A. Rosenthal, W.R.C. Shedenhelm, Deborah Simmons, Robert Lee Wallace, Steven Webster

Picture Credits
Front cover: **Ted Levin/Earth Scenes; FPG International:** Herbert Lanks, Michael Simpson, Jeffrey Sylvester; **Richard Pharaoh/International Stock Photography; U.S. Geological Survey; Paul Chesley/Tony Stone Images, Inc.**

Back cover: **FPG International:** Lee Kuhn, Elizabeth Simpson, Ulf Sjostedt; **Anna E. Zuckerman/Tom Stack & Associates**

Heather Angel Photography; Animals Animals: Doug Allan, Anthony Bannister, G. I. Bernard, M. A. Chappell, Bruce Davidson, E.R. Degginger, Steve Earley, K. Gillett, Richard Kolar, John Lemker, Zig Leszczynski, C. C. Lockwood, Alan G. Nelson, Oxford Scientific Films, Peter Parks/Oxford Scientific Films, Donn Renn, L.L.T. Rhodes, Tim Rock, Carl Roessler, Charles & Elizabeth Schwartz, Dr. Nigel Smith, G.H. Thompson, Lewis Trusty, Anne Wertheim, Fred Whitehead; **Archive Photos; Joel E. Arem; Donald Baird; Biofotos:** Bryn Campbell, J.W.H. Conroy, C. Andrew Henley, Soames Summerhays; **Bruce Coleman, Inc.:** James H. Carmichael, Kjell B. Sandved, Sullivan & Rogers; **Ken Carpenter; Comstock; Kent & Donna Dannen; Dinosaur National Monument/National Park Service; Gary A. Dunn; Eagle River Media Productions:** Glenn M. Oliver; **Earth Scenes:** E.R. Degginger, John Eastcott/YVA Momatiuk, Michael Fogden/Oxford Scientific Films, Michael P. Gadomski, Richard Kolar, Patti Murray, Fritz Prenzel; **Entomological Society of America/Ries Memorial Slide Collection; Field Museum of Natural History; Clayton A. Fogle; Robin White/Fotolex Associates; FPG International:** Barbara Adams, William D. Adams, Age Fotostock, Laurence B. Aiuppy, Jade Albert, Paul Ambrose Studios, Lee Balterman, Jose Luis Banus, James Blank, Jon Brenneis, Jay Brenner, M. Bruce, Chan Bush, Bruce Byers, Carmona Photography, Nancy Cataldi, Willard Clay, F. Cooler, Ed Cooper, Duane Davis, Floyd Dean, Paul Degreve, Art Montes De Oca, D. Dietrich, Jeff Divine, David Doody, Charles Feil, Charles Fitch, Gerald L. French, John Gajda, Kenneth Garrett, Gebhardt, A. Giampiccolo, Michael Goldman, John E. Gorman, Robert Graham, Larry Grant, Mark Green, Farrell Grehan, Peter Gridley, Dennis Hallinan, Hansen Planetarium, Richard Harrington, Michael Hart, Steve Hix, Randall Hoover, Max & Bea Hunn, George Hunter, Icon Communications, M.P. Kahl, S. Kanno, Bernd Kappelmeyer, Michael S. Kass, Alan Kearney, Michael A. Keller, Keystone View Company, W. Kina, Michael Krasowitz, Lee Kuhn, Richard Laird, H. Lanks, Latin Stock, Franz Lazi, L & M Photo, L.O.L. Inc., Bill Losh, D.C. Lowe, Dick Luria, Guy Marche, Court Mast, James M. Mejuto, Joachim Messerschmidt, Jeffry W. Myers, NASA, Neil Nissing, David Noble, Stan Osolinski, Diane Padys, John Pearson, Patricia Pomtili, Terry Qing, Gary Randall, Ross Rappaport, Steve Raye, Scott Rea, Robert Reiff, Carl Roessler, Martin Rogers, Luis Rosendo, Barry Rosenthal, K. Rothman, Ron Rovtar Photography, Leonard Lee Rue III, Len Rue, Jr., A. Schmidecker, Herbert Schwarte, Gail Shumway, Jerry Sieve, Eric Silberg, Michael Simpson, Dean Siracusa, Jedidiah Smith, C. Smith, John Stevens, M. Stoklos, M. Sutton, Jefferey Sylvester, J. Taposchaner, Bob Taylor, Telegraph Colour Library, Ron Thomas, Tom Tracy, John Terence Turner, August Upitis, U.S. Navy, Larry West, L. Willinger, Marv Wolf, Toyohiro Yamada, Earl J. Young/NASA, Jack Zehrt/ESOC, Zeismann, Nikolay Zurek; **Brian Franczak; Steve Fuller; Galen Gates; Peg Gerrity; Ray Gudas; Douglas Henderson; Steven Holt; Blair Howard; The Image Bank:** Harald Sund**; Images of Nature:** Thomas D. Mangelsen; **International Stock Photography:** Wayne Aldridge, George Ancona, Tom Carroll

Photography, Peter Russell Clemans, James Davis, Chad Ehlers, Warren Faidley, Bob Firth, Dennis Fisher, M. Freeman/ Telegraph Colour Library, Frank Grant, Michele & Tom Grimm, A. Howarth, Michael J. Howell, Miwako Ikeda, Peter Langone, Steven Lucas, Kit Luce, Ronn Maratea Photography, Frank Maresca, Buddy Mays, John Michael, Donald L. Miller, Steven S. Myers, NASA, Wilson North, Tom O'Brien, Horst Oesterwinter, Dario Perla, Richard Pharaoh, Phyllis Picardi, Len Rhodes, Robert C. Russell, Lindsay Silverman, Robert Slack, Elliot Smith, Bill Stanton, Telegraph Colour Library, Tom Till, Michael Von Ruber, Peter Walton, White/Pite; **Bob Jones; Lou Jost; R.Y. Kaufman/Yogi; Steven C. Kaufman; Howard Lawler; Zig Leszczynski; Scott Lewis; Kenneth Lorenzen; Charles W. Melton; Pablo Montes O'Neill; NASA/JPL; National Center for Atmospheric Research; National Geophysical Data Center; Gregory S. Paul; Peter Arnold, Inc.:** Luiz C. Marigo; **Photo/Nats**: Cheryl Kemp, John F. O'Connor, David M. Stone, Kim Todd, Muriel V. Williams; **Photri:** M. Long, Leonard Lee Rue III; **Rainbow:** T. Broker, Bob Curtis, Christiana Dittman, Michael J. Doolittle, T.J. Florian, Jean Kepler, Coco McCoy, Dan McCoy, Hank Morgan, Glenn M. Oliver, Paul Skelcher; **Gary Retherford; Lorie Robare; Ann Ronan Picture Library; Gregory K. Scott; Jeffrey Scovil; Paul Sereno; John Sibbick; Marty Snyderman; Tom Stack & Associates:** Nancy Adams/E.P.I., Rod Allin, Walt Anderson, D. Holden Bailey, Paulette Brunner, John Cancalosi, M. Hall Clason, Mary Clay, Gerald & Buff Corsi, Chris Crowley, Ken W. Davis, David M. Dennis, Dave B. Fleetham, Jeff Foott, Warren Garst, Dick George, John Gerlach, Manfred Gottschalk, Kerry T. Givens, Thomas Kitchin, Larry Lipsky, Joe McDonald, Bob McKeever, Gary Milburn, Mark Newman, M. Timothy O'Keefe, Brian Parker, Patrice, Don & Esther Phillips, Rod Planck, Milton Rand, Edward Robinson, Rick Sammon, Kevin Schafer/Martha Hill, Wendy Shattil/Bob Rozinski, John Shaw, Richard P. Smith, Doug Sokell, Diana L. Stratton, Spencer Swanger, Jack Swenson, Dennis Tackett, Larry Tackett, Roy Toft, Don & Pat Valenti, Greg Vaughn, Barbara Von Hoffmann, F. Stuart Westmorland, Anna E. Zuckerman; **Tony Stone Images, Inc.:** Paul Chesley, David Leah, Dennis O'Clair, Charles Thatcher; **Tyrell Museum of Paleontology; U.S. Geological Survey; VIREO:** S. Bahrt, A. Carey, Allan & Helen Cruickshank, W. Greene, C.H. Greenewalt, B. Henry, M.P. Kahl, A. Morris, O.S. Pettingill, D. Roby, B. Schorre, Ned Smith, F.S. Todd, B.K. Wheeler, J.R. Woodward; **Visuals Unlimited:** Hank Andrews, A.J. Copley, John D. Cunningham, Carlyn Galati, Arthur R. Hill, Bill Kamin, Daphne Kinzler, Glenn Oliver, Jay Pasachoff, SIU, Richard Walters; **Bob Walters; Kathy Watkins; Weatherstock:** W. Balzer, Keith Brewster, J. Christopher, Warren Faidley, M. Laca, Gary McCracken, NASA, David R. Olsen, Lawrence M. Sawyer, Joe Towers, John W. Warden, Kent Wood; **The Wildlife Collection:** Tim Crosby, Ken Deitcher, Michael Francis, Robert Franz, John Giustina, Charles Gurche, Martin Harvey, Chris Huss, Ken Keitcher, Tim Laman, Robert Lankinen, Dean Lee, Clay Myers, Jo Overholt, Robert Parks, Michael Rothman, Gary Schultz, V. Siegel, Vivek R. Sinha, Jack Swenson; **Robert Winslow; Norbert Wu**

CONTENTS

OUR NATURAL WORLD continued

PHYSICAL SCIENCES

We take much of our everyday world for granted. We see the sun in the sky, but we rarely wonder what makes it shine and how its light reaches our eyes. We walk down the street, never asking ourselves why we don't float above the Earth rather than standing firmly on it.

Scientists have studied many of these everyday mysteries and solved quite a few. We now have a greater understanding of the gravity that keeps our feet on the ground, the waves that carry light to our eyes, and many other unseen aspects of our world.

Explore the many mysteries around you and you'll find that your everyday world is more complex and exciting than you ever imagined!

Energy & Work

The ideas of "energy" and "work" are closely related to each other. *Work* has a very particular meaning in science. Work is done whenever a force moves an object in the direction of the force. For example, work is done by an electric motor when you ride in an elevator, or by your muscles when you climb the stairs or drive a nail into a piece of wood. As the force of the electric motor pushes upward, the elevator moves in that direction. When you walk up the stairs, your muscles exert upward force and you move up.

According to this way of thinking about work, a weight lifter does work when lifting a set of barbells up, but not while holding them steady and not while moving them across the room at a constant height. Carrying packages or groceries takes effort but no work is done because your lifting force is pushing upward but you are moving forward.

Energy is the capacity or ability to do work. The energy needed for lifting an elevator comes from an electric motor. Climbing the stairs requires muscles fueled by energy from the food we eat.

Energy comes in different forms, but it is itself not a substance. Instead, energy is an ability of substances. Fuels, such as wood, gas, and oil, contain or store energy. Batteries and certain chemicals, such as explosives, are materials that release energy when we need it. But none of these materials *are* energy. They simply contain it.

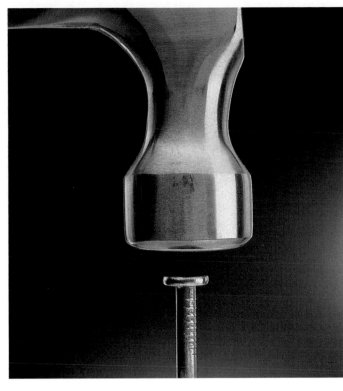

As you hammer a nail, you exert a downward force on the nail, and the nail moves down.

Someone trying to push a huge boulder may feel exhausted, but no work is done if the rock never moves.

Wood is a fuel. It contains energy that is released when it burns. This car battery is a device for storing energy so that we can use it when we need it.

Energy & Work

The sun heats the oceans and causes their currents.

Nuclear power plants use nuclear fuels, such as uranium, that generate energy by nuclear fission.

We can never use all the energy in a fuel for producing motion.

A car engine heats up when it runs. The engine transforms fuel into energy with the goal of moving the car forward. The engine's heat is a by-product of this process.

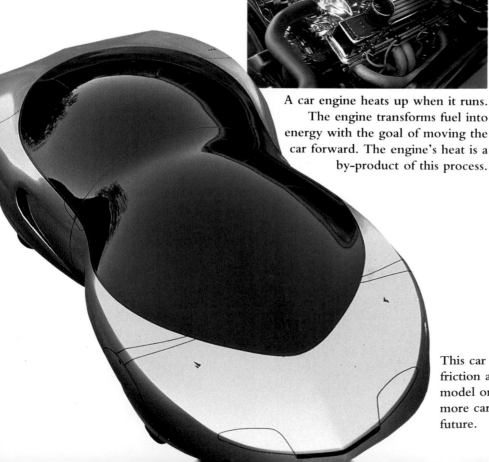
This car was designed to create as little friction as possible. You won't see this model on the streets now, but maybe more cars will look like this in the future.

The sun is a major source of energy. It warms the surface of the Earth and heats the oceans. This heat causes currents that move the air and power the planet's weather. Winds may propel a sailboat or turn a windmill to pump water from the ground.

Coal, gas, and oil are made up of material from great forests that existed million of years ago. These forests got their energy from the sun. So the sun is the original source of the energy we get from coal, oil, and gas.

Heat is often one of the *by-products* of energy transformation. A by-product is something that is produced by a process but that is not the goal of the process.

Heat is produced because moving objects rub against other objects, or against the air through which they move. This force is called *friction*. It converts some of the useful energy, that would otherwise go into motion, into waste heat. Jet aircraft and automobiles experience friction, or "drag," when they move through the air. Friction prevents us from getting full use of the energy we spend.

Efficiency is the word we use to describe how much useful work is done compared to the amount of energy used. Because of things like friction, we always use energy at less than 100 percent efficiency. That means that some energy always gets wasted on by-products like sound and heat.

Kinetic and Potential Energy

Objects in motion have *kinetic* (kuh-NE-tik) energy, the energy of motion. When a car accelerates, the force of the engine through the wheels does work in the form of kinetic energy. If you turn the engine off, a rolling car will continue to move until all the kinetic energy is converted by friction to heat.

Another form of energy is *stored* or *potential* (puh-TEN-shuhl) energy. There are many forms of stored energy, including fuels, electric batteries, and chemicals. A compressed spring is an example of *mechanical potential energy*. It does nothing while at rest. But when released, the spring can shoot an object into the air.

A pendulum is an example of a system that is constantly converting potential energy to kinetic energy and back again. At the top of the swing, the weight is at a specific height above the ground and the energy is all potential. But, at the bottom of the swing, some of the stored energy is converted into kinetic energy, which carries the pendulum back up to the top of the return swing.

Hydroelectric (hy-dro-i-LEK-trik) power plants convert the kinetic energy of falling water into electricity. A large dam is built on a river, forming a deep lake behind the dam. Water from the lake falls through tubes behind the dam, turning the blades of machines called *turbines* (TER-buhnz). The turbines convert the energy from the moving blades into electricity.

Energy is converted from the stored chemical energy of gasoline to the energy of motion of the car.

Energy comes in many forms and can be converted from one form to another.

When the mechanical potential energy in the coiled spring is released, the mousetrap will be sprung.

Dams harness the kinetic energy of falling water. It is then transformed into electrical energy by turbines.

9

Internal & Chemical Energy

Even in solid matter, atoms and molecules are constantly vibrating and turning.

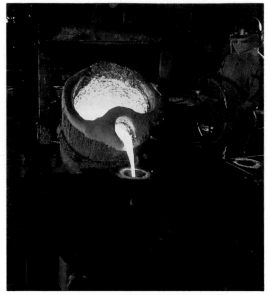

When extreme heat is applied, the internal energy becomes so great that a metal's solid structure fails and it melts.

You can't see it, but everything around us vibrates with the *internal energy* of atoms and molecules. These particles make up the smallest units of matter found under ordinary conditions. The motions and the forces between the individual atoms and molecules of a substance create an internal energy.

The internal energy of a substance changes as its temperature changes. Heating a piece of metal makes its temperature rise. The metal has absorbed heat—its atoms are bumping into each other more rapidly than before and its internal energy has increased.

Chemical energy comes from making or breaking chemical bonds that link atoms and molecules together. Chemical energy is the driving force behind all life. Our bodies release the energy contained by the chemical bonds in the foods we eat.

Coal burns in the presence of oxygen, producing carbon dioxide gas and releasing its chemical energy as heat. Coal's chemical energy can be converted into electrical energy and stored or transmitted.

Similar processes formed coal, oil, and gas deposits. Oil, gas, and coal are called *fossil fuels* because of their link to the ancient forests.

Long ago, green plants found a way to make chemical energy from the energy sources around them. Green plants contain a chemical that absorbs light energy from the sun. The plant uses the sun's energy to make its own food.

Today, we rely on the sunlight captured by ancient plants for the energy we use. About 300 million years ago, great forests grew all over the world. As plants lived and died, thick blankets of plant matter were buried on the forest floor. Over time, this matter was compressed and it chemically changed into coal and gas.

Electromagnetic Waves

Light is a pure form of energy that can be emitted and absorbed by matter. It is the visible part of a more general form of energy, called *electromagnetic waves*. Examples of invisible electromagnetic energy are radio waves, microwaves, X rays, and gamma rays.

Scientists believe that electromagnetic waves are emitted in small bundles of energy called *photons* (FO-tahnz). These photons stream outward from light sources in vast numbers. Photons have no mass.

All electromagnetic energy travels at the speed of light in empty space. Light is the fastest thing in the universe, traveling at 186,000 miles a second in space.

Electromagnetic waves are given off by atoms and molecules as a result of energy changes that often occur within atoms. Atoms are made up of a center, called a *nucleus* (NOO-klee-uhs), and particles called *electrons* that orbit the nucleus just as the planets orbit the sun. Sometimes electrons gain and then lose energy. When this happens, they emit photons.

A heated piece of metal gives off light through a process called *incandescence* (in-kuhn-DE-suhns). As the metal's temperature increases, the motion and the kinetic energy of the atoms and electrons increase. The orbiting electrons pick up some extra energy by bumping into each other and then quickly lose it, emitting photons.

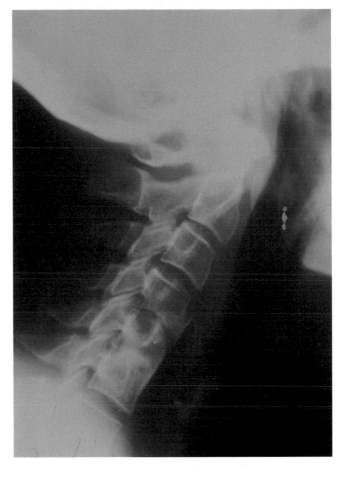

X rays are a very useful form of electromagnetic energy. They can be used to take pictures of our bones.

Light is a kind of energy wave that human eyes can detect.

Light takes about eight minutes to reach us from the sun.

One example of incandescence is the filament lightbulb. It has a thin wire called a *filament* (FI-luh-muhnt). When an electric current runs through the filament, it heats to a white-hot glow.

11

Electrical Energy

Lightning is the electrical discharge resulting from air and cloud friction.

We depend on electricity and the energy carried with it for many things. Computers, telephones, refrigerators, and more depend on a reliable and steady supply of electrical energy.

The electron carries electrical energy in wires. It is the basic electric particle in nature: All matter contains electrons that normally orbit around the nucleus of an atom. In some materials, however, the electrons are loosely held, so simple friction can remove the electrons' electrical charge.

Electrical energy we can use comes from batteries or electrical energy generating plants. A battery contains materials that go through chemical reactions. The chemical energy of the materials is transformed into electrical energy that can be used to power many devices, from flashlights to cars.

Electrical power plants produce electric currents in a completely different way. They use a process called *induction* (in-DUHK-shuhn) and *magnetic fields*. A magnetic field is an area of force around a magnet or around coils of wire with electricity running through them. In induction, the electrons in a metal wire are forced to move when a magnetic field changes, or when a wire moves in a magnetic field. Power generating stations use high-pressure steam to spin electrical turbines, which are wire coils inside magnetic fields. As the wires move in the magnetic field, electrons are forced to flow and electricity is generated.

Just think of the ways we use electricity: lighting, cooking, heating, food storage, transportation, communication, and more.

Turbines are part of machines called *generators*. Generators like those in the photo generate electricity.

Nuclear Fission & Fusion

One of the most recently discovered ways of generating energy is *nuclear fission* (NOO-kleer FI-zhuhn). This process has given humans the ability to release vast amounts of energy.

Atoms of certain elements, such as uranium or plutonium, are naturally unstable and are easily broken apart. These elements have many particles called *protons* and *neutrons* in their nuclei. When a fast-moving neutron from the outside collides with a nucleus of the element called uranium 235, the nucleus breaks into several pieces. The result of the break-up is atoms of different elements, more free neutrons, and the release of energy. The free neutrons can go on to collide with other uranium 235 nuclei and continue the process of fission. The energy released can be transformed into electricity.

A second nuclear process is *nuclear fusion* (NOO-kleer FYOO-zhuhn). In nuclear fusion, atoms whose nuclei contain few protons and neutrons combine to form larger atoms. As this happens, energy is released.

However, colliding nuclei strongly resist combining with each other. One way to make them combine is to subject them to extremely high temperatures. This process is called *thermonuclear fusion*. It takes place naturally deep inside the sun, where the temperature is 27 million degrees Fahrenheit.

Nuclear power plants operating today use nuclear fission to generate energy.

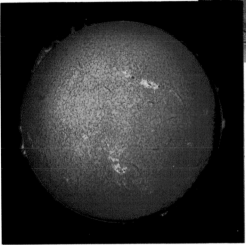

Nuclear fusion powers the sun. Scientists have not yet found a practical way to get energy from nuclear fusion here on Earth.

The changes that produce nuclear energy take place inside the nuclei of atoms.

Fusion could be a useful energy source for the future. The fuel for fusion can easily be extracted from seawater, while the waste products would be less dangerous than those of fission plants.

13

Petroleum

Oil companies must drill holes to reach the oil and pump it to the surface.

Some of the oil in the United States is found in desert regions in California and Nevada. This oil derrick is in Utah.

Oil refineries, like this one, are built near places where oil is found. This is where oil is transformed into fuel for cars and other machines.

Petroleum (puh-TRO-lee-YUHM) is one of the most frequently used sources of energy in the world. Most people call petroleum by its common name, oil. Oil is found underground. It collects in the holes, or pores, of rocks buried deep in the Earth.

Oil is used to make thousands of products. One product is fuel. Cars, airplanes, ships, and many other machines run on fuel made from oil.

These fuels also create heat and electricity for homes and businesses. Oil is also turned into other forms that go into things like carpets, plastics, and even toothpaste!

There are some problems with our use of oil for energy. First of all, the search for oil is expensive. Roads must be built so people can reach the places oil is found. Houses must be built for the workers. Food, water, machines, and tools must be shipped in. And once the oil is collected, it must be transported to the places where it is used.

More importantly, oil takes millions of years to form. Once it is turned into something else, it is changed forever. Someday, the world's oil supply will run out. Other sources of energy will have to take its place.

14

Renewable Energy Sources

Renewable (ri-NOO-uh-buhl) energy sources are those that will not run out. Solar energy is one example of a renewable energy source.

Rocks buried deep in the Earth are very, very hot. Underground water flowing through these rocks turns into steam. The steam remains trapped under the Earth's surface.

People drill beneath desert surfaces to reach steam trapped underground. They are also making their own steam by piping water down to the hot rocks. The steam is used to turn machines called turbines. This process generates electricity.

Energy from the Earth's heat is called *geothermal energy* (JEE-o-THUR-muhl EN-ur-jee). People are working hard to make geothermal energy easy to use.

The winds are also used for energy. The wind turns windmills. The windmills turn turbines that pump water or make electricity.

Solar energy, geothermal energy, and wind energy make good replacements for oil. Their supplies will not run out, as oil is expected to. And, unlike oil, these forms of energy cause little or no pollution.

Some areas also have natural gas trapped deep below the surface. Natural gas pollutes less than oil. But its supplies are limited, too. In the future, people will have to learn to rely less on energy from oil and natural gas. They will have to use more energy from sources that never run out, like the sun, the wind, and the Earth's heat.

Deserts are great places to collect solar energy. The sun shines there almost all the time.

Above: Solar energy collected from a 20-mile area of desert can supply about a million homes with electricity! Right: The sun's energy is collected by solar panels like these. Then it will be transformed into electricity.

Thousands of windmills collect the energy of the wind. Like solar energy, wind energy will never run out.

15

Sound Vibrations

The sound of an airplane taking off is enough to make you run for cover, while a bird's song might make you want to move closer and listen. Both sounds are produced by waves traveling through the air.

Sounds are waves that travel through the air, just as ripples travel across a quiet pond after a stone is thrown into the water.

Although they behave in similar ways, sound waves moving in air are different from water waves. Water waves are called *transverse* (trans-VERS) waves. They cause the water to move up and down. You can make transverse waves by tying down one end of a rope and giving the other end a quick jerk up and down. As the wave pulse travels along the rope, it moves up and down with the wave's movement.

All the sound we hear, from the rustling of leaves to the roar of a jet engine, is caused by vibrations in some substance.

Sound waves do not travel this way through air. When a sound wave travels through a substance, the particles that make up the substance are briefly squeezed together and then spread apart. Places where the particles are more crowded than they would be without the wave are called *compressions* (kuhm-PRE-shuhns). The areas where particles are more spread out are called *rarefactions* (rar-uh-FAK-shuhns). This is called a *longitudinal* (lawn-juh-TOOD-nuhl) wave because the particles move back and forth in the same direction as the wave's motion. To picture this type of wave, imagine giving a quick push-pull to the end of a spring. A tight pulse of

These rippling waves are transporting energy that will eventually affect areas very far away from the original disturbance.

coils moves down the spring (compression) followed by a few coils spaced farther apart than those along the rest of the spring (rarefaction).

Sound can move through any substance, whether it's a solid, liquid, or gas. It travels fastest through the materials that most resist being compressed. This means that sound has the highest speed in solids. It moves more slowly in liquids and slowest of all through gases such as air.

The actual speed of sound in any location depends on the temperature, pressure, and humidity of the air. Sound travels much more slowly than light.

What effect does this speed difference have on the way we perceive things? Across the distance of a soccer field, for instance, it means there is a moment's delay between seeing something happen—such as a player kicking the ball— and hearing the sound it produces. This delay gets longer as distances increase. Although light reaches us almost instantly, sound takes about five seconds to travel one mile. This delay can be used to figure out the distance to the sound's source.

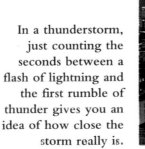

The branch of science that deals with the study of sound is called *acoustics* (uh-KOO-stiks). The study of acoustics affects our lives in many ways. It's important in understanding how people speak and hear. The behavior of sound waves affects the performance of music and the construction of speakers and recording equipment. Companies that build vehicles use acoustics to reduce engine noise. The study of sound is everywhere!

In most weather conditions, sound waves travel through the air at speeds of about 760 miles per hour.

Sound cannot travel through space because there is no material for the waves to squeeze together.

Acoustics is very important in the design of theaters.

In a thunderstorm, just counting the seconds between a flash of lightning and the first rumble of thunder gives you an idea of how close the storm really is.

Looking into Sound

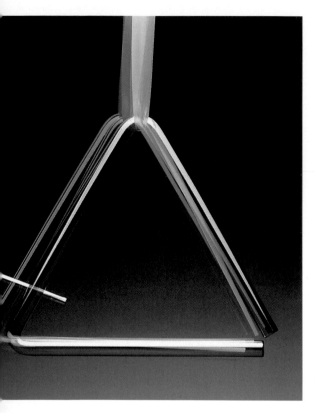

We picture sound waves by looking at the vibrations that make them.

If you strike a musical triangle, you can see the vibrations that produce sound waves in the air.

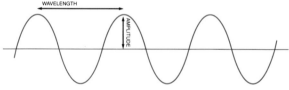

The sound of the space shuttle taking off is so loud it could damage your ears. The takeoff produces sound waves with a huge amplitude.

We know that sound travels through a substance as a series of compressions of that substance. This type of wave is difficult to imagine. But you can picture a way to draw a sound wave.

Many musicians keep their instruments in tune by checking them against the standard tone produced by a *tuning fork*. This small, U-shaped metal bar produces a pure tone when made to vibrate by a gentle tap. Its vibrating prongs set the air into motion, creating the sound we hear. Imagine that we attach a pen to one of the prongs of a tuning fork. While the fork vibrates, we move the pen straight across a piece of paper. The tuning fork draws a wavy line that charts its own vibrations. It's a picture of the back-and-forth movement that makes the sound waves we hear.

Let's look at this line more closely. The height above or below the center of each wave is called the wave's *amplitude* (AM-pluh-tood). At first, the tuning fork's prongs are moving back and forth a great distance; the waves have a large amplitude. The sound is also at its loudest. As the vibration fades, the amplitude of the sound waves decreases and we hear a softer tone.

The distance between the tops of the waves is exactly the same even though the amplitude gets smaller. This distance is called the *wavelength* of the sound.

18

Another aspect of sound waves is called *frequency* (FREE-kwuhn-see). Frequency is measured as the number of complete wave cycles that pass by a single point every second. A sound with a frequency of one wave cycle per second has a frequency of 1 hertz (Hz). The lowest tone on a piano keyboard has a frequency of 27 Hz, while the highest vibrates at 4,200 Hz.

A sound's frequency and wavelength are related. A sound with a long wavelength has a low frequency and a low pitch. A sound with a short wavelength has a high frequency and pitch. It's natural to arrange the sounds the human ear can detect in the same way

as a piano keyboard is set up—from the lowest frequency to the highest.

The range of frequencies we can hear is quite impressive, but many animals can hear sounds we cannot. Frequencies higher than those we can hear are called *ultrasound*. Frequencies lower than the limit of human hearing are called *infrasound*.

Like all waves, sound waves can be reflected and absorbed by the obstacles they run into. People who design theaters and concert halls must pay careful attention to the way sounds bounce around. For example, the ground and audience at outdoor concerts absorb so much sound that bands and orchestras often play inside a shell-shaped structure that reflects sound back to the concert-goers.

Dogs can hear frequencies higher than 30,000 Hz.

Elephants make sounds of far lower frequency than we can detect, although no one knows exactly why.

Human ears can pick up frequencies between 20 Hz and 20,000 Hz.

Even a band shell isn't always enough for a large crowd, and today microphones and speakers are usually used to amplify the sound.

19

Music Makers

Membranophones ("skin sound") are instruments played by striking a skinlike covering stretched over the opening of a hollow object. Most membranophones are drums.

Musical instruments are often classified based on how their vibrations are produced.

All stringed instruments are classified as *chordophones,* a word that means "string sound." Chordophones include the violin, harp, and piano.

Aerophones ("air sound") are wind instruments such as the saxophone. Their sound comes from a vibrating column of air set into motion when someone blows into the instrument.

Musical instruments range from the human voice to electronic synthesizers. Noise is made up of a jumbled mixture of sound frequencies. Musical notes, however, consist of one strong fundamental frequency plus other frequencies that give a unique "color" to the sound of each instrument. For example, no one would confuse a violin with a trumpet, even when both play the same note.

Most musical instruments have two things in common—a vibrating source that actually produces the sound and an object called a *resonator* (RE-zuhn-ay-ter) that helps amplify and color the sound.

The sounds from the vibrating source in many instruments are actually not very strong. The sounds are made louder by *resonance* (RE-zuhn-uhns). Resonance is a way of getting a large vibration with a small effort.

All objects tend to vibrate at certain natural frequencies. An object's natural frequency is also called its *resonant frequency.* If an object can be made to vibrate at its resonant frequency, the amplitude of its vibrations increases dramatically with only a little additional effort. Anyone who has tried out a playground swing has used resonance. To get a swing to go as high as it can, you push it at the right time and in the right direction to match its resonant frequency.

Most musical instruments amplify their sounds by the same principle. *Resonators* are often large solid or hollow objects attached to the source of the vibration in a musical instrument. They amplify and prolong the sound from an instrument. They also add distinctive tones by emphasizing some frequencies over others. This gives the sound from each instrument a unique color.

The main resonator for all wind instruments is the column of air within them. The air within the hollow body of a guitar or violin has one resonant frequency, while the body itself has another. Both are important in amplifying the very faint sound of vibrating strings.

The sound of the human voice comes from an organ called the *larynx* (LAR-inks), or "voice box," which is located in the tube that connects the lungs to the throat. The largest part of the larynx forms the "Adam's apple," a ridge on the neck just above the collarbone. You can feel vibrations from the larynx by lightly touching this bump as you speak.

The human voice benefits from resonance, too. The throat, mouth, nasal sinuses, and chest all influence the final sound. Each of these cavities has a resonant frequency that depends on two things—the volume of air it contains and the size of any openings to the outside. Only the mouth can change both of these properties.

The human voice is an instrument almost anyone can use for making music.

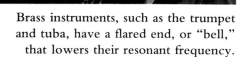

The human voice is a unique and very flexible music maker.

Brass instruments, such as the trumpet and tuba, have a flared end, or "bell," that lowers their resonant frequency.

You can enjoy a guitar's music because resonance amplifies its sound. Without resonance, the sound of the strings would be too faint to hear from more than a few inches away.

21

Earworks

The Ear

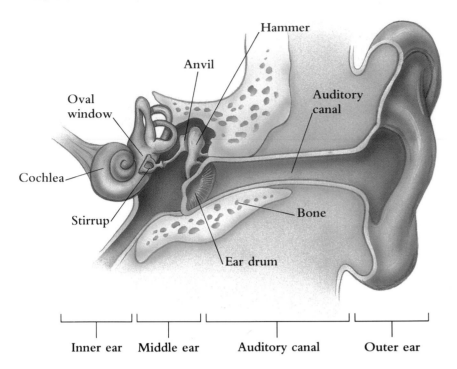

Labels: Hammer, Anvil, Oval window, Auditory canal, Cochlea, Stirrup, Bone, Ear drum

Inner ear | Middle ear | Auditory canal | Outer ear

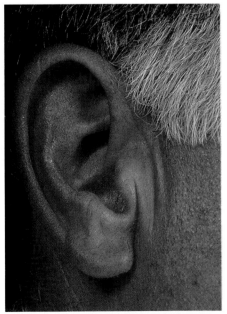

Only mammals have an outer ear.

Your ears detect the vibrations in the air that your brain translates into sounds.

The ear translates the tiny vibrations of the air into electrical signals that are sent to the brain. We hear the amplitude of sound waves as loudness: The greater the amplitude, the louder the sound. We hear the frequency of sounds as *pitch,* the highness or lowness of a tone. The higher the frequency, the higher the pitch. And we hear particular mixtures of frequencies as tone. This quality helps us tell the sounds of musical instruments apart, even when they play the same note.

There is much more to the ear than meets the eye, but the part we do see is called the outer ear. The size and shape of the outer ear help collect and funnel sound waves into the opening of the ear. This opening leads into the *auditory canal,* a tube about one inch long. The other end of the auditory canal is sealed off by the *eardrum,* a thin membrane that vibrates as sound waves strike it.

On the other side of the eardrum, in what is called the middle ear, lies a chain of three tiny bones. Nicknamed the "hammer," the "anvil," and the "stirrup" because of their shapes, the bones rattle whenever the eardrum vibrates. They carry sound vibrations to the inner ear. The last of the bones, the stirrup, rests against a membrane-covered opening, called the *oval window,* in the wall of the inner ear.

The inner ear consists of a snail-shaped, fluid-filled organ called the *cochlea* (KOHK-lee-uh). This organ translates waves of pressure into nerve impulses to the brain.

The *audio spectrum*—the range of frequencies the ear can detect—lies between 20 Hz and 20,000 Hz, although most people cannot hear a pure tone at either extreme. The ear is not very sensitive to sounds lower than 100 Hz. This probably helps us ignore sounds produced in our bodies, such as heartbeats and blood rushing through veins. The ear is very sensitive to sounds near the resonance frequency of the auditory canal, between 3,000 Hz and 4,000 Hz.

One useful scale scientists and engineers use to measure sound is called the *decibel* (DE-suh-bel). Since the ear actually hears sound by detecting changes in pressure, the decibel scale measures the amount of pressure sounds put on the ear. The softest sound the human ear can detect is 0 decibels. You begin to feel pain in your ears when you hear a sound at about 130 decibels. In between, the average background noise in a home is about 40 to 50 decibels, heavy street traffic is about 80 decibels, and a rock concert is about 120 decibels. A jet engine running at full power is a painful 160 decibels.

The sounds received by each ear are not exactly the same. Some sounds may arrive at one ear before the other. High-frequency sounds seem softer to the ear farthest from the source. The brain combines the sounds heard from both ears and uses these differences as clues to tell us what direction the sounds came from.

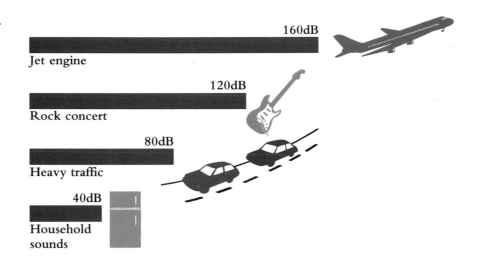

160dB
Jet engine

120dB
Rock concert

80dB
Heavy traffic

40dB
Household sounds

A "loudness spectrum" illustrates how much sound energy it takes to make the human ear take notice.

Sound travels much faster in water, so scuba divers hear none of the differences that help us tell where a sound comes from.

A jet engine at full power can rupture eardrums.

Waves of Light

No spacecraft today can even come near the speed of light.

Like sound, light is a form of energy that travels in waves. It's a special kind of energy called *electromagnetic* (i-lek-tro-mag-NE-tik) energy. But light waves do not move by shifting matter back and forth. Light waves are electric and magnetic waves that actually move most quickly where there is no matter. Our eyes can detect only a small part of the electromagnetic waves that surround us. Radio waves, heat, and X rays are all types of electromagnetic waves invisible to our eyes.

Light is the fastest thing in the universe. It travels about 186,000 miles per second! The sunlight we see has been traveling for about eight minutes, and light from the nearest star takes over four years to reach our eyes.

Light from the moon takes about 1.3 seconds to reach us.

Light energy can come from different sources. Most often, light comes from energy changes within individual atoms.

When astronomers view a distant galaxy, they are seeing light that has been traveling many *millions* of years.

Each atom consists of a center, called a *nucleus* (NOO-klee-uhs), and particles called *electrons* (i-LEK-trons) that orbit the nucleus. Some electrons have orbits close to the nucleus, and others have larger orbits that take them farther from the nucleus. When an electron gains energy, it jumps out to a higher level or orbit. The electron must lose energy to fall back to a lower orbit. When an electron loses energy, it emits a small amount of light energy called a *photon* (FO-ton).

24

A common source of light is the glow from a heated piece of metal. As the temperature of the metal rises, the atoms and molecules within it move faster and faster. They bump into one another with greater speed. Each collision gives energy to the electrons and forces them into higher orbits around their atoms. When they fall back, they send out photons of light. At first, this light is invisible to us. Then, as the metal gets hotter, electrons absorb greater amounts of energy, leap to higher orbits, and give off more energy.

A lightbulb contains a piece of glowing metal. In this case, the metal is a thin wire called a *filament* (FI-luh-muhnt). When the lamp's switch is turned on, an electrical current runs through the wire. The current heats the wire and jiggles the electrons in the wire. The electrons gain energy and move into higher orbits. When they fall back down to their original levels, the electrons give off light photons.

Both the lightbulb and the heated metal are examples of *incandescence* (in-kan-DE-suhns), light given off by materials brought to a very high temperature.

Some materials can be made to give off light without being intensely heated. This process, called *luminescence* (loo-muh-NE-suhns), comes from atoms and molecules that have gained energy without much heating and that release this energy as light.

As a metal is heated, it will look red, then orange, yellow, and finally yellow-white.

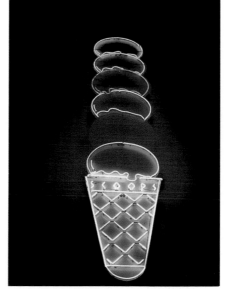

When electricity flows through the tubes, the neon and other gases in this sign give off light.

Many living things, such as fireflies, produce their own light through chemical reactions.

Many lightbulbs have filaments made of a metal called tungsten.

More than Light

We are surrounded by many kinds of electromagnetic radiation that our eyes cannot detect.

Natural electricity, in the form of lightning, can make the unpleasant bursts of radio noise we call static.

In a microwave oven, the water molecules in the food absorb energy and heat up. But a plastic or ceramic dish that contains the food is not affected.

Radar antennas send out microwaves to measure distances to far-off objects.

What we call "visible light" is actually part of a more general energy system called *electromagnetic radiation*. In fact, visible light is only a small part of the *electromagnetic spectrum,* the whole range of electromagnetic radiation. Visible light and waves in other parts of the spectrum are different in three ways: They have different frequencies, different wavelengths, and photons with different amounts of energy. Waves of higher frequency, such as X rays, have shorter wavelengths and photons with higher energy. Lower frequency waves, such as radio waves, have long wavelengths and weak photon energy.

Radio waves are the longest of the spectrum. Radio and television broadcasts aren't the only use for radio waves. Very short radio waves, called *microwaves,* can be used to measure distances to faraway objects. A transmitter sends out a pulse of microwaves. Some of them may bounce off objects such as airplanes, and then return to their source. Because the waves all travel at the speed of light, measuring the time between the pulse and the returned signal will give the object's distance. This method is called *radar.*

Many people cook their meals with microwaves. In a microwave oven, radio waves about 4.7 inches long have different effects on water molecules in the food and other molecules in the food containers. The food is heated but the containers stay cool.

Waves that are much shorter than microwaves, but still longer than red light, are called *infrared*. We feel infrared waves as heat. About 60 percent of the sun's electromagnetic waves occur in the infrared part of the spectrum.

Ultraviolet waves have wavelengths that are shorter than violet light. Ultraviolet wavelengths carry a great deal of energy, enough to break apart many of the molecules found high in the Earth's atmosphere. Most of the sun's ultraviolet light is absorbed in this way by the ozone in the atmosphere.

X rays are even more energetic and actually pass through many materials. They are used in medicine to see inside the body. These waves are also given off by the hottest gases in the sun and stars, but none reach Earth's surface because the atmosphere absorbs them. X rays are more dangerous than ultraviolet light because they can more easily break up molecules and damage cells in the body.

Gamma rays are the most powerful and penetrating electromagnetic waves. Gamma rays are given off only when the nucleus of an atom changes its energy. Gamma rays are very damaging to living tissue. Diseased cells are more sensitive to them than healthy cells, so gamma rays are sometimes used to treat cancer. Although our atmosphere screens out gamma rays from space, satellites have detected them from exploding stars and distant galaxies.

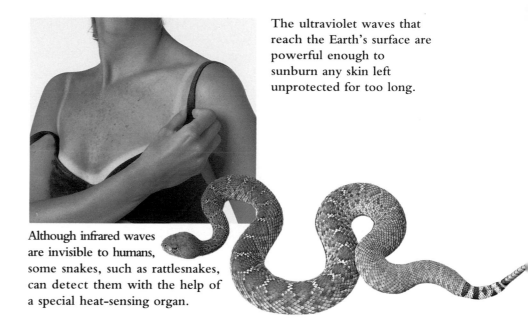

The ultraviolet waves that reach the Earth's surface are powerful enough to sunburn any skin left unprotected for too long.

Although infrared waves are invisible to humans, some snakes, such as rattlesnakes, can detect them with the help of a special heat-sensing organ.

Most incandescent materials—such as a lightbulb or lava from a volcano—actually give off more heat than light.

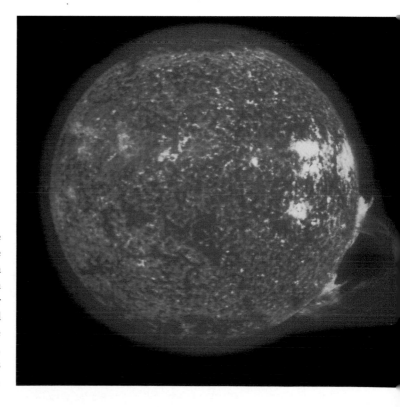

Gamma rays are given off in the cores of stars, such as our sun, in nuclear power plants, and in particle accelerators, powerful devices that smash atoms.

`Using Light

We know that photons are the basic bits of light energy. X-ray and gamma-ray photons carry enough energy to break up molecules or alter the chemicals that make up living cells. Visible-light photons usually aren't powerful enough to make such changes, but there are several important exceptions.

One of the most familiar is photography. Photographic film is coated with one or more layers of light-sensitive chemicals. When a camera takes a photograph, the photons absorbed by these chemicals produce invisible changes in them. When film is processed, the portion of film exposed to the brightest light turns darkest, and the portion exposed to the least amount of light remains clear. It takes another process using light-sensitive paper to make the pictures we pick up at the photo store.

Right: Photos are often processed in a special room called a darkroom. Below: This image is called a *negative* because it is the opposite of the scene that was photographed—the dark areas look light and the light areas look dark.

Green plants found a way to use light energy billions of years ago.

Green plants use light energy to drive the chemical cycles that make their food. They absorb the energy in sunlight and then use it to power chemical reactions that turn raw materials into food for the plant. This process is called *photosynthesis* (fo-to-SIN-thuh-suhs).

In one way or another, most of the life on Earth depends on photosynthesis. From water and carbon dioxide in the air, plants make a kind of sugar. It provides food not only for the plant but also for any animals that eat the plant. Plants release oxygen, the other product of photosynthesis, into the atmosphere. Animals breathe in oxygen to process the foods they eat.

Green plants contain the pigment *chlorophyll* (KLOR-uh-fil), a light-sensitive chemical. This chemical is used in photosynthesis.

Our modern machines rely on the sunlight captured by ancient plants. Hundreds of millions of years ago, great forests grew all over the world. As plants lived and died, thick blankets of leaves, branches, and other plant matter were buried on the forest floor. Over time, this matter was compressed by the newer layers of plant material and by mud and rock that settled on top of it. This process continued for hundreds of millions of years, and today much of this plant matter has been chemically transformed into coal. Similar processes formed oil and natural gas from ocean plants. Oil, gas, and coal are called fossil fuels because of their connection to ancient life. Most of our energy comes from the burning of fossil fuels.

Devices called solar cells can convert light directly into electricity. They work because some materials, like silicon, can absorb incoming photons of light. This causes the silicon's electrons to change in such a way that they can conduct electricity.

How practical is solar energy as an energy resource on Earth? There are some problems. The efficiency of devices that convert solar energy into electricity is only about 15 percent. This means that it takes many solar panels to produce useful amounts of electricity. But scientists are studying ways of improving methods of using solar energy. The sun seems like a good bet for a practical, pollution-free energy source for the future.

Machines as different as a calculator and NASA's Hubble Space Telescope are powered by solar energy.

All the energy in fossil fuels comes from sunlight captured by plants in the forests of the Earth's past.

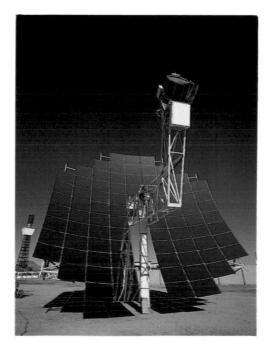

Large areas have to be covered with solar collectors to capture enough sunlight to generate much electricity.

Seeing Clearly

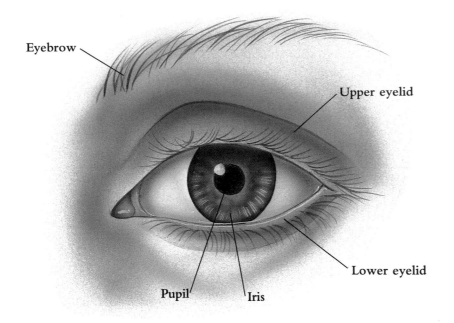

Eyebrow

Upper eyelid

Lower eyelid

Pupil   Iris

Vision is the sense we depend on most in our day-to-day lives.

The eye translates the vibrations of visible light waves into electrical signals that are then sent to the brain. We can see the wavelengths of light because light-sensitive chemicals line the inside surface of the eye.

A clear, dome-shaped layer called the *cornea* (KOR-nee-uh) first bends light waves as they enter the eye. It works like the lens of a camera, bending light waves so that they will come together as a focused image at the back of the eye.

Not all of the light passing through the cornea actually enters the eye. Behind the cornea is a colored ring of muscles called the *iris* (I-ruhs). When people mention the color of your eyes, they are really talking about the color of your irises. At the center of the iris is a hole called the *pupil.* Light actually enters the eye through the pupil. The iris changes the size of the pupil to help the eye adjust to changes in brightness.

After entering the pupil, light waves next reach the *lens* of the eye. Although the cornea does most of the work to focus incoming light, it needs some help bending the light from objects closer than about 20 feet. Tough muscles pull on and flatten the lens when the eye concentrates on a distant object. When the eye looks at something closer than about 20 feet, the muscles reduce their pull on the lens. As the muscles ease up, the lens becomes slightly thicker and better able to bend light.

The iris expands or contracts in response to changes in the brightness of light.

Once through the lens, light passes through a jellylike fluid that fills the interior of the eyeball. Light penetrating even this far into the eye still has not been "noticed"—the eye hasn't *seen* anything. Light must strike a layer of cells at the back of the eye before it is actually detected. This layer is called the *retina* (RE-tuhn-uh).

The wafer-thin retina is made up of about 130 million light-sensitive cells, called rods and cones, plus other cells that send nerve impulses. Cones can see colors, but they work well only in bright light. Rods are very sensitive to weak light and outnumber cones 17 to 1. But rods cannot tell colors apart. Night scenes seem colorless to us because the light entering our eyes is too faint to stimulate the cones. In some animals, such as dogs, the layer behind the retina is very shiny. Light striking this layer is bounced back through the retina's cells to give the dog's light-sensitive cells a second chance of seeing it. This gives dogs and other animals very good vision in darkness.

Rods and cones contain chemicals called *pigments* that undergo changes when light strikes them. The stimulation of these pigments throughout the retina results in electrical signals that are flashed to the brain. Different parts of the brain deal with different features of the images we see, such as color, movement, and shapes. Each eye sees a slightly different image, which the brain merges into a single three-dimensional view.

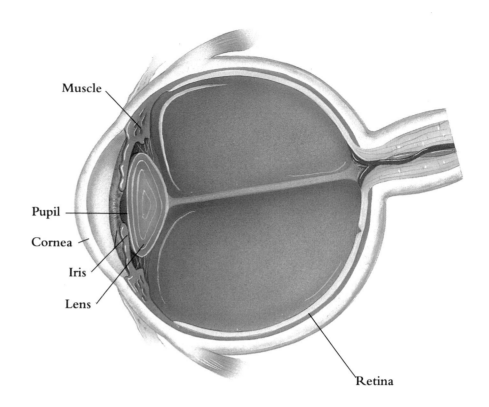

Muscle

Pupil

Cornea

Iris

Lens

Retina

Possibly as much as two-thirds of the activity in the brain is involved in studying information that comes from the eyes.

Light bouncing back through the retina makes the eerie "eye glow" you sometimes see from animals at night.

Insects have *compound eyes,* honeycomb-shaped clusters of lenses.

Reflection

If everything reflected all the wavelengths of light equally, then the world would lack color and we would see only shades of gray.

Clouds, fresh snow, and the paper on this page look white because they reflect nearly all the light of every color that falls on them.

Each paint reflects different wavelengths of light. We see the colors of light that are reflected by the paints.

This building's windows are made reflective by a special coating on the glass. But the windows are not mirrors. If you stand close enough, you can see inside the building.

Whenever light encounters the surface of any substance, some of the light is absorbed, some goes through if the substance is transparent, and some bounces off. The last of these is called *reflection*. We see objects because our eyes detect the light that reflects off them. Transparent substances, such as air and clear glass, reflect and absorb little light.

In order for a substance to look colored, it must have a different effect on some of the wavelengths of light. Grass absorbs red and blue light, so the only color left to be reflected is green. Flowers, dyes, and paints absorb some wavelengths and reflect the ones that make up the colors we see.

Metals are very good reflectors. The first mirrors were simply polished pieces of metal. The familiar bathroom mirror is a combination of metal and glass—a thin film of reflective metal coats the back of a glass plate.

Light reflected from a very smooth surface goes in a definite direction that depends on the direction of the original waves. Light striking the shiny surface of a mirror bounces off it at an angle equal to the angle at which it hits the surface. The reflected light behaves as though it were coming from a point behind the mirror and traveling through a clear window. Your image in a flat mirror always seems to be as far behind the mirror as you are in front of it.

Waves can be concentrated or spread out by curved reflectors. A *concave,* or bowl-shaped, mirror causes the light reflected to come together at a focus. Magnifying mirrors, or the bowl of a spoon, are concave. Concave shapes do the same for sound waves, too. Satellite dishes are concave and concentrate radio waves to a focus.

Dome-shaped, or *convex,* mirrors spread out their reflected light. The image reflected in the back of a spoon looks smaller—as though it were very far away from the reflector. For this reason, the convex rear-view mirrors that come with many cars have a warning written on them: "Objects in mirror are closer than they appear." The weird images made by fun-house mirrors come from changing the shape of the mirror surface.

Reflections are useful to some animals. Dolphins, insect-eating bats, and other animals use sound reflections in a way that's similar to radar. They send out pulses of ultrasound at frequencies higher than 50,000 Hz. The waves reflect off obstacles and carry information about the animal's surroundings, especially the location of food.

Sound waves striking a smooth wall reflect in much the same way. If you shout at a wall, say in a tunnel, the sound reflects back to you. The sound returns to you delayed by exactly the amount of time it would take if it really had been made by someone next to the tunnel wall. This is an echo.

Reflected radio waves have been used to make images of the hidden surface of the planet Venus. Light cannot penetrate the thick clouds that cover Venus, but the clouds do not interfere with radio waves.

Bats use echoes to locate objects.

We use radar to detect distant objects by sending out pulses of radio waves and sensing the waves reflected back.

If you stand some distance from a cliff and shout, the sound reflects off the cliff just as though someone on the other side had shouted to you at the same time.

Refraction

Right: People far from an explosion may hear it clearly while people nearby may not hear it at all.
Below: The light waves that reach our eyes from the pencil change directions when they cross the water, the glass, and then the air.

All waves can experience refraction, but the most familiar examples are those involving light.

Waves traveling through one substance may change their path when they pass into another substance. Whether or not the waves bend from their original path depends on the speed of the waves in each substance. If the waves traveling through the first substance travel faster or slower through the second substance, then the direction of the waves will change. This is called *refraction* (ri-FRAK-shuhn).

The speed of sound in air depends partly on the air's temperature. Sound waves from a loud source, such as an explosion or thunder, travel at different speeds when they encounter air at different temperatures. Under the right conditions, waves traveling up and away from the ground can be refracted so that they head back down toward the ground. A sound could be more easily heard farther from its source than close by.

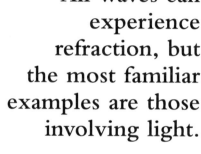

Light can also be affected by changes in the air. Changes in air density can cause light to bend. Air is thickest at the bottom of the atmosphere and becomes thinner higher up. When we look at a sunrise or sunset, we're seeing light that has traveled through many miles of the thickest air. The atmosphere bends light from the top edge of the sun so it looks higher than it really is—but the thicker air closer to the ground bends light from the sun's bottom edge even more. The result is a sun that looks not round but oval!

When the sun hovers at the edge of the horizon just before sunset, we can see it because of refraction. If the light from the sun were traveling in a straight line, the sun already would have disappeared from sight.

Refraction also helps us see more clearly. The shapes of different lenses affect the way light passes through them. Concave lenses, which are thicker on the ends than in the middle, spread out light waves. People who are nearsighted use concave lenses to help them see clearly. Convex lenses, which are thicker in the middle than at the ends, bring light rays together. People who are farsighted use convex lenses to correct their vision.

All the wavelengths in visible light are not refracted equally. Red light is bent the least, and violet light is bent the most. This lets us use refraction to separate the colors of "white" light. If you shine a beam of white light through a wedge-shaped piece of glass, or *prism,* the colors of the rainbow fan out from it. The prism shape refracts each color of light by a different amount.

Rainbows themselves are created by a combination of refraction and reflection. Sunlight striking a drop of water refracts as it enters, then reflects off the inside of drop, and finally refracts again as it leaves. The two refractions separate the colors of sunlight, and the reflection sends the light back toward the sun—and us.

Telescopes look outward into space. They use either a large lens (refracting telescope) or a large concave mirror (reflecting telescope) to collect light. The largest refracting telescope has a lens that is 40 inches across.

Convex lenses can be used as magnifying glasses.

In order for you to see a rainbow, a curtain of water drops must be in front of you and the sun must be behind you.

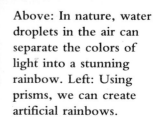

Above: In nature, water droplets in the air can separate the colors of light into a stunning rainbow. Left: Using prisms, we can create artificial rainbows.

Interference

For two waves to be canceled out completely, both must have the same frequency and amplitude.

Water waves may combine to make a calm sea.

It's tempting to think that when waves come together the result will be bigger waves. But when waves from different sources exist at the same time in the same substance, what happens will depend on how their vibrations match up.

What happens when waves combine? It's possible for sound waves from different sources to combine and make silence.

Suppose two identical stones are thrown into a calm pond at the same time. If the two waves meet as each reaches the high point of its vibration (the crest of the wave), they will join together to make a double-high wave. But if they meet in the opposite way, with one wave at its crest and the other at its low point, they simply will cancel each other out. The low point of one wave is just as deep as the crest of the other is high. So when they are added together, the result is no wave.

The meeting of waves is called *interference,* and it happens in all waves. *Constructive interference* occurs when waves meet in such a way that they combine to make a larger wave. *Destructive interference* occurs when the waves cancel one another out.

Something even more interesting occurs when two sounds with slightly different frequencies interfere. The combined sound rises and falls in amplitude. We hear this as a beat, a periodic change in the sound's loudness. Because the sounds do not share exactly the same frequency, destructive interference cannot completely cancel them. All it can do is change the loudness of the sound. The beats become longer and slower as the difference between the two frequencies decreases.

Light is a different story. Visible light is a mixture of frequencies. But light waves from two different sources cannot interfere with one another (except for lasers). This is why we don't notice interference patterns between streetlights or floor lamps. The only way to make light interfere is to split up the light from one source into separate beams. This is what happens when you see colors swirling over a soap bubble or an oil slick on water.

When light strikes a thin, transparent substance such as a soap bubble, it can be reflected at least twice—once by the outer surface and once by the inner surface of the bubble. Often the light is reflected many times. Whether light goes though constructive or destructive interference depends on the thickness of the film and the wavelength of the light. At any given point on the soap film, some wavelengths of light show constructive interference and other wavelengths show destructive interference. Because white light is made up of wavelengths of all colors, taking away some wavelengths and increasing others results in a colorful display.

The pearly, shimmering colors of mother-of-pearl also result from interference. Mother-of-pearl comes from the shells of oysters and abalones, which secrete thin layers of material on the inside surfaces of their shells.

The beautiful, swirling colors on a soap bubble are caused by interference. If you look at a bubble close up, you can see the many colors of light.

Except for lasers, light waves from different sources cannot interfere with one another.

Mother-of-pearl is the shiny, colorful lining of an abalone or oyster shell. Interference is the reason for its changing colors.

Polarization

The light given off by the sun and other incandescent sources—such as a candle flame—is always unpolarized. Its vibrations have no preferred direction and go every which way.

Bees use partly polarized light from the sun as a compass to help them find their way around.

Our eyes cannot see the difference between polarized and unpolarized light.

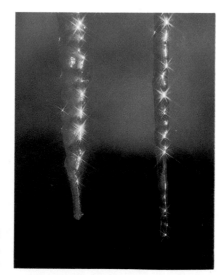

Many minerals—including snow and ice—can polarize light.

Have you ever wondered what polarized sunglasses are? The answer to this question has to do with the way in which light waves travel and their vibrations from side to side. You might imagine light waves traveling along side by side and all vibrating in the same direction. This is not the case. The truth is that light waves vibrate in many different directions perpendicular to their direction of travel. This means that if you could actually see individual light waves coming directly toward you from the sun, you would notice that some of them would be vibrating up and down, others would be vibrating side to side, and still others would be vibrating at all different angles. When light passes through certain kinds of matter, the waves can be made to vibrate all in the same direction. We say that the waves become *polarized* (PO-luh-reyezd).

Bees and some animals can see the difference between polarized and unpolarized light. The light from the sun becomes partly polarized when it is scattered by gas molecules in the atmosphere. Bees can use the polarized light to figure out the location of the sun even on cloudy days.

Polarization was first discovered in minerals. Calcite and quartz can split one light beam into two polarized beams. Other substances, such as the mineral tourmaline and quinine crystals, can absorb light vibrating in one direction much more strongly than light vibrating at right angles.

So how does polarization help us? The most common use for polarized light can be found in sunglasses. While sunlight isn't polarized, it can become partially polarized after reflecting off certain surfaces. These reflections can create a harsh glare that makes you squint. Polarized sunglasses reduce the reflections by absorbing the polarized light. At the same time, they allow normal sunlight through.

With the help of polarized sunglasses, you can see examples of double refraction in frost. On a clear day, look through a frosted window while you rotate the sunglasses in front of your eyes. Polarized light from the sky passes through the tiny ice crystals and is bent by an amount that depends on the light's wavelength and direction of vibration. The frost will seem to be painted with faint splashes of color. If you put a few layers of cellophane tape on a clear surface, you will see the same effect.

Photographers also use polarizing filters. Light from the clear sky can be partly polarized. Photographers use a polarizer to reduce the polarized light from a scene. This makes the sky look darker in the photograph, but it does not darken the clouds by the same amount, so they stand out more.

And what about sound waves? Because sound waves in air are longitudinal, rather than transverse, there is only one possibility for vibration. This means that sound waves do not have the property of polarization.

You can see the effect of polarization on a hot highway in the "puddles" of light that seem to appear in the distance. The puddles are actually polarized reflections of the sun's light.

When you wear polarized sunglasses, you can still see objects around you, but the glare from the reflections is dimmed.

If you look at frost on a windowpane through polarized sunglasses, you can see the effects of double refraction.

Laser Light

One of the most common lasers uses a combination of helium and neon gas—it makes the red light of the supermarket scanner.

Inside a laser tube, electrons are excited by an electrical current or a flash from a bright light.

"Laser" stands for "light amplification by stimulated emission of radiation."

Lasers have many uses in industry. They are very precise tools for cutting, welding, and many other operations.

Lasers produce a beam of light that is compact and intense, scientifically interesting, and very useful. In fact, you've probably seen a laser in action—it's the web of red light that scans bar codes at the supermarket checkout. Lasers are also used in compact disc players, so you may own one without knowing it.

What makes laser light so special? Unlike light from other sources, the light produced by lasers has only one very pure wavelength. Many gases and even solids and liquids can be used in producing laser light.

The light waves from lasers move together in a way that light from ordinary sources cannot. The sun or an incandescent lamp, for example, does not give off light as a steady stream of waves but rather in random bursts. The unique property of lasers is that their light waves move along in step—the light is said to be *coherent* (ko-HEER-uhnt).

At the heart of every laser is a tube containing some material whose atoms must first become excited. That is, the atoms must be placed in a state where their electrons are in high orbits and ready to give off photons by falling back to lower levels. Once in a high-energy state, the electrons would normally just give off their light and return to the lowest orbit. But under the right conditions, the presence of light can force the electrons to do this much sooner than normal. Light is amplified, or made stronger, by this process.

The material in the tube gives off one wavelength of light. Some of the waves strike a mirror at the end of the tube, which reflects them back into the material. As they travel along the tube, the reflected waves stimulate more atoms to emit radiation. A beam of coherent, amplified light builds up in the tube. When the beam reaches the front of the tube, a special kind of mirror lets some waves escape as an intense beam of light. Those that don't escape bounce back through the tube, exciting more atoms.

Because light vibrates so much faster than radio waves, lasers can be used to carry great amounts of information. Telephone and cable television companies pipe laser light through special fibers that trap the light inside by internal reflection. A 144-fiber cable can carry 40,000 telephone conversations at once!

Lasers have found uses in construction and surveying because they make a perfectly straight line. And since the beams travel at the speed of light, which is constant, they can be used to measure distance. Astronomers have used such "laser ranging" to determine the moon's distance from Earth. In manufacturing, laser beams can melt, weld, cut, or drill.

Even more remarkable, lasers can record three-dimensional images called *holograms*. A laser beam can be split into two halves by a mirror. These two halves are used to record a hologram of an object on photographic film.

Lasers and fiber optics can carry much more information than electrical currents in wires.

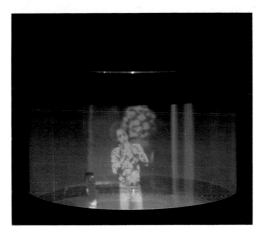

You've probably seen a special kind of picture called a hologram.

Above: Today you can find holograms on credit cards, jewelry, and magazine covers. Right: Lasers are used for storing and retrieving information on compact discs.

41

Light & Energy

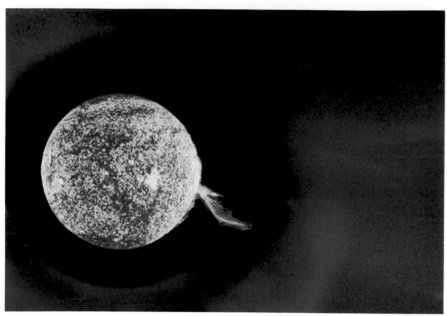

Visible photons arrive from the sun in great numbers, bringing in vast amounts of energy.

The study of light is a very powerful tool indeed.

Photons can hit a specific molecule on a piece of photographic film to produce an image. This is something particles can do.

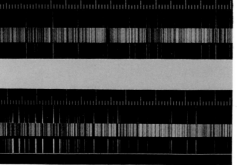

A spectrum, like this one, helps scientists study the colors of light coming from a distant star. This information helps them determine what makes up a star millions of miles away.

Light is one of the purest forms of energy that we encounter in our world. Photons are the basic bits of light energy. The energy of a photon of visible light is very tiny. On the other hand, a single gamma ray, which is a high-frequency photon, is quite energetic and can be detected easily. Gamma rays, like light, are part of the electromagnetic spectrum.

Photons are hard to define. In some ways they behave like waves, but in other ways they behave like particles. Photons give rise to interference, just as waves do. They also have wavelength and frequency measurements, just like waves. In certain experiments, however, scientists have found that photons can act as particles. For example, they can scatter or make a particle of mass move by bumping into it. The important things to remember about photons is that they have no mass and that they always travel at the speed of light.

A photon is emitted when changes take place within the atoms of a substance. The color of a photon depends on the substance that emitted it. For example, we know that sodium puts out a specific shade of yellow photons. Scientists often use light to study chemicals. The colors of light emitted by a substance can show us exactly what the substance is made of. That's how we know what the sun, the stars, and the intergalactic gases are made of. Scientists have studied the light these objects emit.

The energy in light also can be transformed into other forms. If you've ever walked on an asphalt driveway in bare feet on a sunny day, you know how hot the asphalt gets. You've also probably heard someone saying that you could fry an egg on the hood of a black car parked in the hot sun. This is partly because visible light from the sun is totally absorbed when it encounters a black surface. The visible solar light energy is transformed to heat energy. Infrared rays from the sun also add heat.

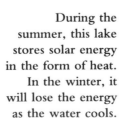

Solar light energy cannot normally be stored except indirectly. Water in a lake heats up over the summer as it absorbs solar energy. When winter arrives, the warm lake makes the weather milder near the shore. The sun's energy is stored in the water as heat, and then the heat is slowly lost over the winter. Solar cells convert solar energy into electrical energy that is stored in batteries. In photosynthesis, the energy of light is stored in the chemical bonds of the plant's food to be used later as energy. In all these cases, the light itself vanishes, transformed into a new state.

Light's energy can be transformed and used in many ways.

A tree captures the sun's energy and transforms it into the chemical energy the tree needs to survive and grow. This giant sequoia has been collecting and using solar energy for centuries.

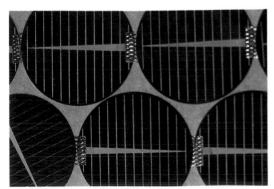

Solar cells can collect energy from the sun and convert it into electrical energy. The electrical energy can be stored in batteries.

During the summer, this lake stores solar energy in the form of heat. In the winter, it will lose the energy as the water cools.

43

Light & Energy

Above: Like our sun, the stars probably generate their energy by the process of thermonuclear fusion. Right: Today we rely on oil from deep beneath the Earth's surface for much of our energy. In the future, controlled fusion could take over as the main source of energy for our homes and cities.

Once fusion has begun, the process keeps itself going.

Nuclear fusion can be very destructive if it is not controlled. The hydrogen bomb is an uncontrolled release of vast amounts of nuclear energy.

The sun is the source of our light on Earth. But how is the sun's energy generated? Scientists believe that a process called *thermonuclear fusion* (ther-mo–NOO-kleer FYOO-zhuhn) occurs deep inside the hot sun, where the temperature is about 27 million degrees Fahrenheit. Under these extremely high temperature conditions, the nuclei of hydrogen atoms are smashed together with great force. They stick together to form the nuclei of helium atoms. This process releases energy and maintains the intense high temperature. Some of the sun's matter is converted to energy.

If it takes high temperature to continue the process, how does it start? Astronomers tell us that stars, such as our sun, originally evolved from large clouds of hydrogen gas drifting in space. These clouds got heavier, and the force of gravity caused them to start becoming smaller. This process releases gravitational energy in the form of heat. At some stage in the process, the temperature became high enough to begin fusion.

The goal of much energy research during the past 50 years has been to make a practical controlled fusion process on Earth. If scientists succeed with this goal, we will have 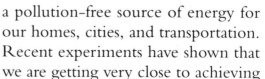 a pollution-free source of energy for our homes, cities, and transportation. Recent experiments have shown that we are getting very close to achieving this goal.

The Doppler Effect

One important feature of both sound and light is the effect motion has on the waves. This is called the *Doppler effect*.

You can hear the Doppler effect as a drop in pitch as a car speeds past. As the car comes toward you, the waves press up closer to one another. This results in a shorter wavelength and a higher frequency. The opposite happens when the car has passed by: The waves get more stretched out.

The same thing happens with light. Approaching objects, such as stars, cause shorter wavelengths, so the light they emit goes farther into the blue part of the light spectrum. This is called the *blue shift*. Objects moving away cause a shift to longer wavelengths, or the *red shift*.

Doppler radar uses this principle to look at moving objects. When radar microwaves reflect off the targets, they are Doppler-shifted in frequency. Wave detectors can determine how fast the target is moving.

Scientists have used the Doppler effect to find that light from all galaxies is red-shifted. This means that all the galaxies and stars are moving away from us. Scientists see this as evidence that the universe is expanding. By figuring out how fast the universe is expanding, we can backtrack to estimate the age of the universe.

You have probably experienced the Doppler effect. You hear it in the quick change in pitch of a train horn or police siren as it rushes past you.

In order for us to see the Doppler effect on light with the naked eye, an object must be traveling at least one percent of the speed of light. Nothing humans have invented can move that fast!

Baseball pitchers often have their pitches clocked by hand-held Doppler radar "guns" behind the plate.

Doppler radar can be used to track the progress of a tornado.

Building Blocks of Matter

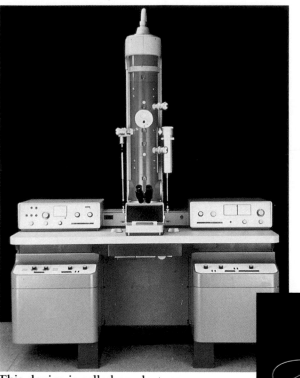

This device is called an electron microscope. It is used to study particles too small for a normal microscope to detect. Some very powerful electron microscopes can detect individual atoms.

Scientists use special microscopes and computers to detect atoms.

This model shows the way an electron orbits an atom's nucleus.

Gold is a chemical element. It is made up of just one kind of atom.

Everything around us—from the farthest star to our own body—is made of matter. Matter is simply any substance that occupies space and possesses mass. All matter around us is composed of great numbers of tiny particles called atoms and molecules.

Each different type of atom represents one tiny piece of a very basic substance called a chemical *element*. No chemical process can break an element down into simpler materials. The molecule in table salt, for example, can be split into atoms of sodium and chlorine, but sodium and chlorine cannot be broken down into other materials. They are chemical elements.

An atom is the smallest piece of matter that can be considered to be a chemical element. It is too small even to be seen by a normal microscope. A piece of solid matter the size of a sugar cube contains a trillion trillion atoms.

But atoms can be broken into even smaller pieces. The atom is actually built from three very different particles. At the atom's center is the *nucleus* (NOO-klee-uhs), which is formed when two kinds of particles—called *protons* and *neutrons* (NOO-trahns)—bind together. Clouds of negatively charged particles called *electrons* forever swarm around the nucleus.

The makeup of an atom's nucleus determines which element it is. If an atom loses or gains a proton, it becomes another element.

46

When two or more atoms join together, they form a molecule. The atoms may belong to the same type of element. For instance, two identical oxygen atoms bond together to form the oxygen molecules in the air we breathe. In more complex molecules, atoms from different elements come together. Glucose, a simple sugar made by many plants, contains 24 atoms—6 each of carbon and oxygen plus 12 atoms of hydrogen. A single molecule of rubber may hold tens of thousands of carbon and hydrogen atoms.

Whenever two or more different elements chemically join together, the resulting molecule is called a *compound*. Glucose, rubber, and water are compounds because they contain different elements, but oxygen is not because it's made from a single element. Chemical compounds are very different from the individual elements within them. Table salt, made up of sodium and chlorine, is edible. But sodium is a highly unstable metal and chlorine is a poisonous gas.

Most substances we come across every day are not pure elements or compounds, but *mixtures*. A mixture is made of two or more elements that are not chemically joined, which means that each element keeps its own characteristics. A mixture contains different substances that can occur in any amounts, and each substance can be removed from the mixture without a chemical change. Milk, air, paint, clouds, smoke, and cement are all mixtures.

Paint is a mixture. The substances that make it up can be separated without changing their individual chemistry.

Water is a chemical compound. Seawater is a mixture of salt and other materials mixed with water.

Table salt, which contains sodium and chlorine, is a compound.

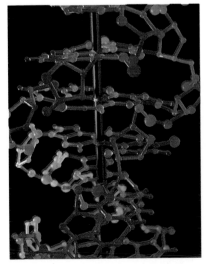

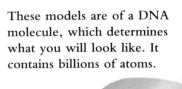

These models are of a DNA molecule, which determines what you will look like. It contains billions of atoms.

Three States of Matter

Copper, like most metals, is a solid made up of crystals.

The differences between the states of matter have to do with how the atoms and molecules in a substance are packed together.

Although they are built up from the same atoms, diamond and graphite are very different simply because of the way their atoms are arranged.

The matter around us comes in three basic forms, or states—solid, liquid, and gas. Under the right conditions any substance can occur in any of these three states.

The atoms or molecules in solids are packed most tightly. The distances between the atoms or molecules in a solid cannot change very much, so solids have a very rigid structure. They also have a definite shape that will not change unless it is forced to do so.

The particles that make up most solids occur in a regular pattern called a *crystal,* which repeats itself throughout the substance.

Diamond and graphite are both *crystalline* (KRIS-tuh-luhn) forms of the element carbon. (Crystalline means that they are made up of crystals.) But their properties are so different that you'd never guess they are made of the same stuff. Graphite is the soft, dark, slippery-feeling material used in pencils. It's easily cut or broken. A diamond, on the other hand, is the hardest substance known. It's transparent, cannot conduct electricity, and will cut into other substances.

The atoms and molecules in solid materials cannot move around much, but they can vibrate and spin. The hotter the solid becomes, the more freely its particles move. At a certain temperature, called the *melting point,* solids lose their shape and their internal structure, becoming liquid.

The molecules or atoms in liquids have enough energy to flow, but not enough to rise out of a container. Because their particles are not arranged in any fixed pattern, liquids have no shape of their own. Although the molecules or atoms in a liquid have more freedom than those in solids, they still remain very close to one another.

The surface of every liquid behaves as though it has an invisible skin. This can be seen by filling a cup of water to the brim, and then carefully adding water until the cup just overflows. A close look at the water's surface shows that it's actually higher than the rim of the cup. The "invisible skin," called *surface tension,* occurs because the particles in a liquid attract one another. A molecule beneath the surface feels an equal pull from other molecules in all directions. But a molecule at the surface feels only the pull of molecules beneath and beside it, not from above. This imbalance pulls the surface molecules inward.

Liquids mix readily with other liquids, solids, and even gases. Carbonated drinks, such as colas or sparkling water, are mixtures that contain carbon dioxide gas dissolved in a liquid. They are also solutions, a type of mixture in which the ingredients mix uniformly and cannot be easily separated. Seawater is a solution of salt and water. Not all substances will form solutions, though, not even all liquids. For example, alcohol and water will not mix with gasoline.

Water is the most common liquid.

The oil and vinegar in a salad dressing will not form a solution. When shaken they will mix temporarily. But later, both ingredients will separate.

When enough heat is applied to most solids, they melt, changing from a solid to a liquid.

A liquid reacts to gravity by flowing into the bottom of a container and taking on its shape—whether the container is a glass, a lake, or the great basins that hold the Earth's oceans.

49

Three States of Matter

The amount of water vapor in the air changes with the weather and location on Earth. Sometimes we can see it as fog.

At room temperature, air molecules race around at over 1,000 miles per hour on average!

As the particles in liquids vibrate and bump into one another, some of them may gain enough energy to break their bonds. These atoms or molecules may leave the liquid and mix with the particles that make up the air. These escaped particles have become a gas, the thinnest form of matter. The higher the liquid's temperature, the greater the number of atoms or molecules that can hop out of it.

The molecules of gases are the most widely separated and have the greatest freedom of movement. They collide with one another—and with everything around them—at all possible angles and move at very different speeds. At any given instant some particles may be close to standing still while others are zipping off at tremendous speed following a collision.

Gases are considered *fluids* (FLOO-uhdz)—they can flow from place to place and change their shape whenever a force acts on them. Gases have no definite shape and rapidly expand to fill any available space. Unlike solids and liquids, gases can be easily compressed because there is so much space between the particles. Pumping up a bicycle tire compresses air by squeezing it into smaller space.

The air around us is a solution of many gases. One gas, nitrogen, makes up 78 percent of what we take in with every breath. Oxygen molecules make up about 21 percent of the total molecules in the air.

When the temperature climbs to the liquid's boiling point, all of its particles have enough energy to become a gas, or to evaporate.

The pressure of the air or helium inside the balloon makes it fill and stretch.

Forces in Our World

Forces are constantly acting on everything around us. The most familiar of these are *gravitational* (gra-vuh-TAY-shuh-nuhl) forces. The Earth's gravity attracts us to the planet's surface. Without it, we would float off into space. Earth's gravity also tugs on the moon so it stays close.

Many forces we encounter often act in pairs. They are in delicate balance so everything stays in place. If you set a glass of milk on a table, it presses down on the table by force of gravity, but the table pushes back with an equal force. At the same time, the table presses on the floor while the floor pushes back on the table's legs.

Every object feels the pull of gravity toward the Earth's center. Gravity causes all freely falling objects to fall at the same rate. These objects fall toward the ground at an ever-increasing speed. When speed increases (or decreases), we use the word *acceleration* (uhk-se-luh-RAY-shuhn) to describe the change in speed.

The pull of gravity on all objects on the Earth gives the same acceleration, but the force is different for heavy and light objects. The reason for this has to do with the mass of an object, a measure of the total quantity of matter in it. Mass is a constant quantity—the mass of an object is always the same no matter where the object is located. But gravitational force or weight can vary depending on location.

The sun's gravity attracts the Earth and all the planets, keeping them in orbit around the sun.

A person who weighs 120 pounds on Earth would weigh 20 pounds on the moon.

Accelerator pedals speed up cars by giving more gas to the engine. We use the brake pedal to slow a car down, but technically both changes in speed are called accelerations.

The table presses upward on the glasses with the same amount of force that the glasses exert pressing downward. Nothing moves because the forces are balanced.

51

Forces in Our World

In scrap metal yards, cranes with giant electromagnets use magnetic force to pick up tons of scrapped steel.

Electrical forces and magnetic forces are used by many household appliances.

Mass also affects another quality of motion called *inertia* (i-NER-shuh). An object's inertia is the measure of how much it resists change by any kind of outside force. The greater an object's mass, the greater its resistance to change of motion and the smaller its acceleration when a force acts on the object.

Not all forces and motion are produced by gravity. Other important forces also exist. *Electrical forces* are at work in moving charged particles, called electrons, through wires in homes and factories, TV sets and computer screens, so we can work, play, and study. *Magnetic forces* attract metal in steel mills and scrap yards and hold notes or pictures on refrigerator doors at home.

The electrical force has its origin in electric charges. You can create an electric charge by rubbing your feet on a carpet in winter, and getting a big shock when you touch the doorknob. Batteries store electric charges. To start a car, a current flows from the battery through the starter motor. This current is produced by electrical forces.

Magnetic forces are used in many ways too. Magnets attract metal, and can even keep metal objects from falling to the ground in response to gravity's pull. An electromagnet is a special kind of magnet that can be turned on and off by switching an electric current. A special kind of crane uses an electromagnet to lift and move heavy objects.

Electrical forces produced by the battery start the car engine.

In a TV picture tube, electrons starting in the back of the tube are accelerated and steered by electrical forces until they make a dot of light on the screen. Thousands of colored dots make up the image.

Newton's Laws

In 1686, Sir Isaac Newton, a great English scientist, discovered three simple laws of motion.

Newton's first law of motion deals with inertia. It says that any object that is not moving will stay put until an outside force acts on it. The law also states that a moving object will keep moving without changing direction or speed unless an outside force acts on it. Objects cannot just start moving on their own. Once moving, they will not turn or stop on their own.

Although this law sounds very simple, it isn't so obvious in the everyday world. For instance, if you slide a book across a desk, the book slows down and stops before it travels far. The sliding book slows down because a force *is* acting on it—a force called *friction*. Friction happens whenever moving objects rub against matter, and it takes away some of the objects' energy.

There is no friction in space, so the motion of the planets should be a good example of Newton's first law. Since the planets move in curved paths, then some force must be tugging on all of them at every instant, so they cannot move in a straight line. We know this force is the pull of the sun's gravity. What would happen if the sun's gravity were magically turned off? According to the first law of motion, the planets would stop moving in curved paths and start moving at a constant speed in straight lines.

Even air creates a frictional force. Engineers try to reduce this force on cars by designing them with rounded surfaces that slip through air more easily. Cyclists use special helmets designed to reduce friction.

Newton's laws explain the ways in which force, matter, and motion are related.

Without the sun's pull, the planets would simply zoom off into space.

Newton's Laws

The principle of Newton's third law allows this jet airplane to take off.

The third law of motion is often stated like this: For every action, there is an equal and opposite reaction.

Newton's second law of motion is the most important one. It describes exactly how a force will change the motion of an object. If we know the force and mass of an object, we can predict the acceleration. The second law states that an object will always accelerate in the same direction as the force pushing it. Gravity, for example, pulls objects toward the Earth's center. So when you drop a glass, gravity makes it accelerate downward, toward Earth's center, until it crashes to the floor.

The second law also states that the same force will change the motion of a small mass faster than it will a larger mass. You feel the effects of this all the time. If you throw a baseball, you will get more motion than if you throw a bowling ball with the same amount of force.

The last of Newton's three laws of motion states that every force applied by one object on another object creates an opposing force in the second object that is equal to the force but acting in the opposite direction. So every object that exerts a force on another object is always affected in turn by a reaction force.

This principle hurls the space shuttle into space. A rocket engine produces hot gases that escape through a nozzle at the bottom of the engine. As the gases blast out of the rocket, they create a powerful reaction force that lifts the rocket into the air.

Pool players apply Newton's third law to control the direction balls will travel on a pool table after they collide.

Newton's second law can tell us how much force is needed to make a bowling ball roll fast enough to knock over the pins.

ASTRONOMY

Have you ever wished you could climb into a spaceship and take a trip through the universe? Many strange and fascinating sights would await you beyond Earth's sky.

Our planet is part of a solar system of nine planets orbiting around the star that gives us light. Our sun is just one of millions of stars in the galaxy we call the Milky Way. And our galaxy is just one of many scientists have been able to detect with telescopes.

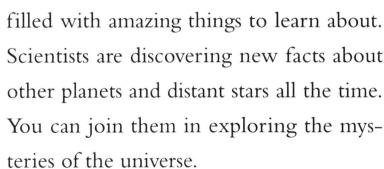

The universe is huge beyond our imagining and filled with amazing things to learn about. Scientists are discovering new facts about other planets and distant stars all the time. You can join them in exploring the mysteries of the universe.

Galaxies

There are billions of galaxies in the universe, and each galaxy contains from millions to hundreds of billions of stars. Most galaxies, like stars, cluster together in groups. Groups of galaxies are called clusters.

Top: A cluster of galaxies in the constellation Hercules. Center: This spiral galaxy looks much like our home galaxy. The Milky Way Galaxy is also a spiral galaxy.

Left: A nebula is made up of gas and dust. This nebula is called the Trifid Nebula.

The thousands of twinkling stars that you see in the sky on a clear night are part of our galaxy. If you look closely, you might also see fuzzy glowing patches in the sky. They are masses of interstellar gas and dust. People hundreds of years ago named these glowing patches nebulae, from the Latin word for cloud.

Other glowing patches in the sky are whole systems of stars far out in space. Stars cluster together in systems or groups called galaxies. Galaxies are vast, swirling communities of stars—like neighborhoods of stars.

The stars in a galaxy are held in place by gravity. Everything in a galaxy—all the bits and pieces of rocks and stars—revolves, or moves around, the center, called the nucleus.

The star we know best, the Sun, is part of the community of stars called the Milky Way Galaxy. The Milky Way is Earth's home galaxy. Scientists once thought the Milky Way was the only galaxy, but now we know that the Milky Way is one of about 20 galaxies that make up our home cluster, or local group.

Scientists have divided the many billions of galaxies into three types. The Milky Way is shaped like a spiral. It is called a spiral galaxy. A spiral galaxy is shaped a bit like a pinwheel. It has long, curving arms of stars, gas, and dust. From Earth, which is in the Milky Way, we cannot see all of the galaxy.

What we see of the spiral arms looks like a hazy cloud that arcs across the sky. Some spiral galaxies have tightly wrapped arms, and others have loosely wrapped arms. The center of a spiral galaxy is reddish because old red stars are located there. Most of the light comes from young, bright stars in the disk.

The second type of galaxy is called an elliptical galaxy. Elliptical galaxies do not have arms. They range from nearly round shapes to ovals that are shaped a lot like footballs. Elliptical galaxies seem to have mostly old stars. Unlike spiral galaxies, elliptical galaxies have little gas and dust.

The third type of galaxy is called an irregular galaxy because it has no special shape. It is a formless collection of stars and gas.

One irregular galaxy is called the Large Magellanic Cloud. It looks like an enormous fuzzy swarm of stars. The Large Magellanic Cloud and its near neighbor, the Small Magellanic Cloud, are the closest galaxies to our Milky Way. But they are still far away—it takes a beam of light from the Large Magellanic Cloud 175,000 years to reach Earth. These two irregular galaxies are visible only from the southern hemisphere, the part of Earth that lies below the Equator.

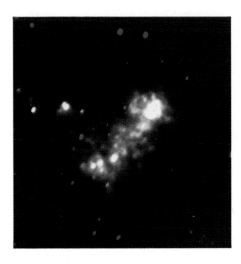

The closest galaxies to our Milky Way Galaxy are the Small Magellanic Cloud (above) and the Large Magellanic Cloud (right).

The billions of galaxies beyond the Milky Way, whatever their shapes, lie in the outer reaches of space—in deep space. Scientists learn more about our galaxy and other neighbor galaxies every year.

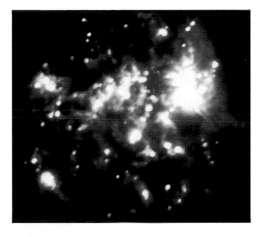

A neighbor galaxy to the Milky Way, the Great Galaxy in Andromeda, is a spiral shape. The Andromeda Galaxy is one of the few galaxies we can see without a telescope. It looks like a thin cloud about twice as big as our Moon. But Andromeda is very big and bright. It is brighter than 20 billion suns. Andromeda seems small because it is far away.

The Milky Way

Galaxies are gigantic. It takes a beam of light 100,000 years to travel across the Milky Way. Until 1924, scientists thought the Milky Way was the only galaxy. Now we know that there are billions of galaxies.

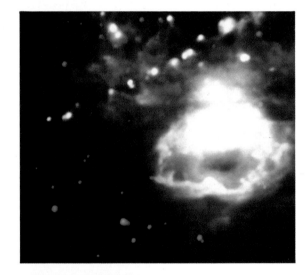

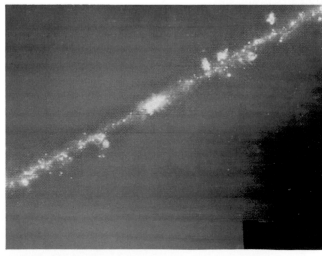

Top: Star systems in the Milky Way. Center: A star forming in the Milky Way. Left: A photograph of the central part of the Milky Way taken by the spacecraft IRAS.

There are billions of galaxies in the universe, and each contains millions of stars. The Sun, the Earth, the planets, and the stars we usually see in the sky each night are part of a family of stars called the Milky Way Galaxy. For us on Earth, the Milky Way is our home galaxy. Everything in the Milky Way revolves—or moves—around the center of the galaxy. The Sun is our most important star in the Milky Way. The Earth and all the other planets, their moons, and other space rocks revolve around the Sun.

The Milky Way has spiral arms of stars that wrap around it. In the spiral arms of the Milky Way, there are extremely hot blue-white stars. They are giant stars, much hotter than the Sun. The center of the Milky Way Galaxy, where the four parts of a pinwheel join together, glows orange red. That glow comes from red giant stars—old stars that are not as hot or as bright as they were billions of years ago. Within the pinwheel of the Milky Way are deep red patches. These glowing patches are called nebulae. They are vast areas of gas and dust where new stars are born.

Huge collections of stars form balls like loosely packed snowballs that surround the center of the Milky Way. These huge balls of stars are called globular clusters. There are more than 100,000 different globular

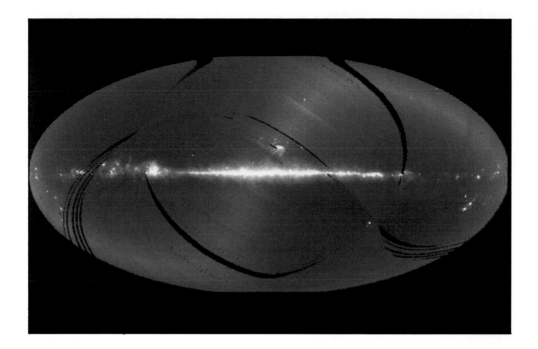

The Milky Way is only a small part of the universe. And our entire solar system— the Sun and all the planets—is just a small part of the Milky Way.

clusters surrounding the center of the Milky Way. Each cluster contains more than 100,000 stars. In the Milky Way there are billions of bigger and brighter stars than our Sun, and billions of stars smaller and dimmer. The Sun is so important to us on Earth because it is the center of our solar system.

The Sun and the planets of our solar system, including Earth, are in a large spiral arm of the Milky Way. That arm of the galaxy is called the Orion Arm. Our solar system is about two-thirds of the way from the center of the Milky Way in the Orion Arm. Our Sun, with its family of planets, moves around the center of the Milky Way all the time. It moves very fast, but the Milky Way is so big that from Earth we don't even notice that we are moving. The Milky Way is so big that it takes the solar system 230 million years to circle around it one time.

Above: A full view of the Milky Way Galaxy taken by the spacecraft IRAS.

Above and left: Because our solar system is part of the Milky Way, we cannot see what the Milky Way looks like. We are too close to see all of our home galaxy. What we do see of the Milky Way from Earth is a hazy band of clouds that arc across the sky.

Stars

Stars are different colors. Old stars are redder than younger stars, which are white or blue. Can you spot an older star in this star system?

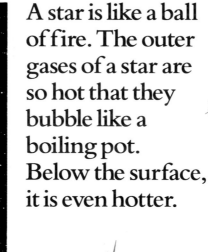

A star is like a ball of fire. The outer gases of a star are so hot that they bubble like a boiling pot. Below the surface, it is even hotter.

Right: Nebulae, such as the Horsehead Nebula in Orion, are where stars are born.

At the middle of a star—the core—temperatures and pressure are so great that particles ram each other so hard that they stick together. This process is called fusion, which produces energy in the form of light. Fusion makes a star shine.

Stars are different colors. The hottest stars shine with a blue-white light. They are young stars. Some stars shine with a red light. Red stars are cooler than blue stars and are usually older. Some stars seem to glow yellow or orange—they are in the middle of their lives. The color of a star depends on how hot it is, how big it is, and how much energy it produces.

The rate at which a star produces energy is called luminosity. Stars are different sizes, and some have more gases than others. The more massive a star is, the more luminous it is. Each star has a different brightness. How bright a star appears from Earth is called apparent brightness or apparent magnitude. But stars are not all the same distance away, so it is difficult to compare their real brightness.

Scientists rate stars as if they were the same distance from Earth. That measurement of brightness is called absolute brightness or absolute magnitude. The absolute magnitude of a star far from Earth is greater than its apparent magnitude.

Stars are formed—or born—in nebulae. A globe of matter called a protostar grows in the spinning cloud of dust and gases. The gravity

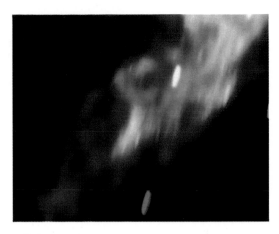

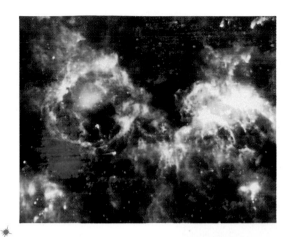

This is the beginning of two new stars!

of the protostar attracts more matter, and the protostar grows. As it gets bigger, it grows hotter and brighter. Its gravity continues to draw more material, which gets packed tighter and tighter. The protostar core heats up and glows red. It gets so hot and pressure increases so much that fusion occurs, and the star begins to shine, giving off energy as light.

After millions—or even billions—of years, a star begins to burn its heavier gases. Over time, it sends out less energy and begins to cool. Less massive stars shine longer than more massive stars, but all stars will die.

Some stars are so special that they stand out. Supergiants are very large, massive stars that are very bright. One of the most famous supergiants is called Betelgeuse. It is about 520 light years from Earth. Betelgeuse is a red supergiant. Betelgeuse is very bright, but it is cooler than some stars because its surface is so gigantic that lots of energy can be released all the time. Betelgeuse is about 800 times bigger than our Sun. Rigel is a star 900 light years away that shines so brightly we can see it even without telescopes. Rigel is a blue supergiant.

Right: A ring nebula. Below: Both Betelgeuse and Rigel are part of the constellation Orion at the bottom of the picture. The three evenly spaced stars that are between Betelgeuse and Rigel are called Orion's belt.

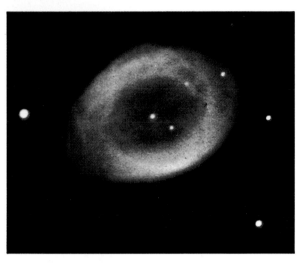

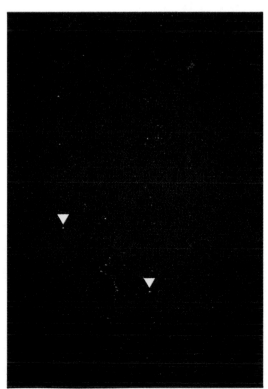

Betelgeuse   Rigel

Tonight, look out your window at home. Can you spot Betelgeuse or other famous stars? Stars are one of the many wonders of our universe.

Earth's Sun

Right: The Sun is so big that it holds objects in our solar system around it by a force called gravity. Earth, the other eight planets, asteroids, and comets move around the Sun because of its gravity. Below: During a solar eclipse, the corona of the Sun is visible. Usually, the brightness of the Sun makes the corona invisible.

Every day, whether it is a bright, hot day or a cold, rainy day, the Sun shines light on Earth. Sometimes daylight is bright. Sometimes clouds hide the light, but there is still light from the Sun. The Sun is a star.

Of billions of stars in the universe, the Sun is the star closest to Earth. It is the star we know best. A lot of what we know about stars, we learned from studying the Sun. The Sun is 93 million miles away from Earth. A beam of light could travel that distance in eight minutes and twenty seconds.

The Sun is by far the largest thing in our solar system. Everything else in the solar system is very small compared to the Sun. And of all the stars in the universe, the Sun is only a medium-size star.

The Sun formed about 4½ billion years ago. Scientists believe it formed from a whirling cloud of dust and gases. Like all stars, the Sun spins—much as a top spins when you twirl it. And the Sun, like all stars, is always changing. Nuclear explosions occur constantly inside the Sun.

The Sun is made mostly of a gas called hydrogen. Scientists have found that the Sun is formed of four layers. The outer layer is called the corona. It glows. Usually, the Sun is so bright that we can't see the corona. If you can watch the Sun when the moon is passing in front of it, you can see the glow of the corona.

The Sun is very powerful. It makes our daylight, makes our weather, and makes our crops grow. Without the Sun, there would be no life on Earth!

The Sun's symbol

The next layer of the Sun is the lower atmosphere. It is also called the chromosphere. The chromosphere is always exploding. Violent eruptions like huge volcanoes occur all the time. Some of the largest of these explosions are called solar flares.

The surface of the Sun, the part we see most easily from Earth, is called the photosphere. The fourth—and last—layer of the Sun is called the core. It is the middle of the Sun, where all the heat and light we feel and see on Earth is produced.

The heat and light that the Sun produces are two kinds of energy. Both the heat and light come out of—or radiate from—the Sun. This heat and light radiation travels in waves. Just as the waves in the ocean come in different sizes, radiation from the Sun travels in waves of different sizes.

The only light we can see travels in wavelengths that make up a rainbow. A rainbow has bands of color —red, orange, yellow, green, blue, and violet. These are the colors our eyes can see.

Other forms of light—or radiation —reach Earth from the Sun. We cannot see these forms of light. We feel infrared rays as heat. When you sit out on the beach and get hotter and hotter, infrared rays from the Sun are making you hot. That same day at the beach, you will get either burned or tanned. The rays that tan or burn you are called ultraviolet rays.

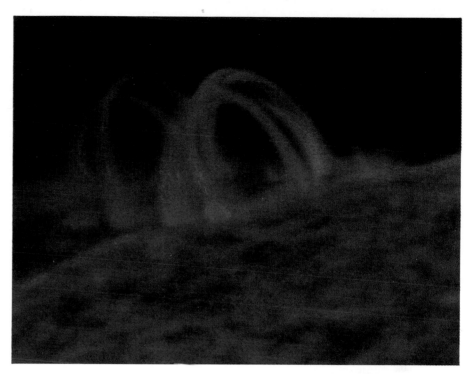

Skylab took this picture of a solar flare—a giant loop of hydrogen gas that erupts on the Sun. Some solar flares can cause magnetic and electrical problems on Earth.

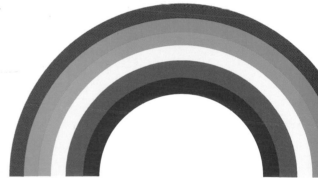

The Ulysses spacecraft will be studying the Sun and interstellar space.

The Sun gives off energy that can make a rainbow, make you hot, and tan your skin.

The Solar System

Earth is a planet that moves around the Sun. The Sun is a star. Its light gives us day, and when that light is not shining on our part of the Earth, we say it is night. The Sun makes life here possible. Without the Sun, it would be too cold to live on planet Earth.

The Earth is only one of many objects held in place by the Sun's gravity. Other objects revolve around the Sun, too. All these objects make up the solar system. The word "solar" means Sun. The solar system is the family of objects that revolve around the Sun.

The Sun has 99 percent of all the material in our solar system. It is the biggest object in our solar system. Including the Earth, there are nine planets in the solar system.

The planet nearest the Sun is Mercury. Then comes Venus, Earth, and Mars. Beyond these four inner planets are a band of large chunks of rock and metal called asteroids.

Thousands of asteroids revolve around the Sun beyond Mars. This band of rock and metal chunks is called the asteroid belt.

Sometimes asteroids ram into each other in space and break into smaller pieces. Comets also break up, and the pieces are called meteoroids. Meteoroids sometimes approach Earth and appear as bright streaks in the night sky. The meteoroids that get close enough to glow in our sky are called meteors. The few

Just as your family is made up of separate people who are related, the solar system is made up of different objects that are related to the Sun.

Above: Earth is the only planet in our solar system that we know has life on it. Left: The Sun is the center of our solar system.

64

meteors that reach the surface of Earth are called meteorites.

Beyond the belt of asteroids lies the biggest planet in the solar system —Jupiter. Jupiter is a ball of gases. So are the next planets: Saturn, Uranus, and Neptune. They are called the gas giants.

The farthest planet from the Sun is Pluto. It is the smallest known planet, and is different from the other four outer planets. Pluto is an icy ball smaller than Earth's Moon.

Beyond Pluto, at the edge of our solar system, comets also revolve around the Sun. Comets are ice and dust. There are millions of comets circling the Sun, but they only can be seen when they get close enough to the Sun that its heat makes them glow. The gravity of other comets and planets can change their path so that they come into the inner portions of the solar system, where we can see them. Eventually, comets evaporate and become grains of dust.

Scientists think the solar system formed about 4½ billion years ago. A huge swirling cloud of dust and gas—a nebula—grew smaller and smaller. Over millions of years, the innermost pieces drifted toward the center and became hot and formed our Sun. The more distant parts of the cloud contained what would become the rest of the solar system.

Jupiter is one of the gas giants.

All the planets, their moons, asteroids, and comets revolve around the Sun. They are all a part of our fascinating solar family called our solar system.

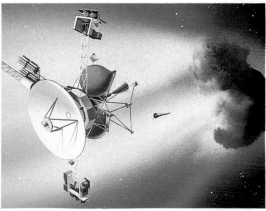

Above: Comets are also held in our solar system by the Sun's gravity. Left: Scientists are constantly trying to learn more about our solar system. They plan to send a spacecraft that will meet up with a comet to study it.

65

Mercury

Mercury, the planet closest to the Sun, is also the fastest planet in the solar system. Mercury revolves around the Sun in only 88 days compared to Earth's 365-day year.

Mercury revolves quickly, but its rotation is very slow. It takes the planet 59 Earth days to complete one rotation. Because of the slow rotation and the fast revolution around the Sun, sunrises occur only once every 176 Earth days.

The long days on Mercury and its nearness to the Sun help make it one of the coldest and hottest planets in the solar system. The side of Mercury facing the Sun bakes in daylight at more than 800°F. On the night side of the planet, temperatures drop to minus 274°F. No other planet has such a wide temperature range.

Mercury is one of the hottest and coldest planets in our solar system!

Mariner 10 took this recent picture of Mercury's rocky, cratered surface.

Mercury is a bare and rocky ball covered with deep holes, called craters. The craters formed when meteorites crashed into Mercury billions of years ago. The biggest crater is called Caloris. It is 800 miles across —bigger than the whole state of Texas.

Mercury has no satellites of its own. It is a world with almost no atmosphere, or air. There are no rivers and no oceans. Almost nothing has changed on the planet since shortly after the solar system formed billions of years ago.

Mercury was named after a Roman myth. Mercury was the fast messenger of the gods.

Mariner 10 traveled nearly 100 million miles through space before it got close to Mercury. The trip took 146 days. Mariner 10 passed close to Mercury three times. Each time it photographed and mapped the planet. Television cameras on the spacecraft sent the pictures through space back to Earth.

Mariner 10 discovered that huge, steep cliffs up to two miles high cut through Mercury's rocky surface. The cliffs slice right across the walls of craters and are hundreds of miles long. Lava from old volcanoes has created wide plains on one side of the planet, and the entire surface of Mercury is covered with a thick layer of dust. Scientists have known for a long time that Mercury is very dense —that the material it is made of is tightly packed together so it weighs a lot. (A rock the size of your lunchbox weighs a lot more than your empty lunchbox. The rock is denser.) Mariner 10 proved that Mercury has a very large core of iron, which makes it very dense. It is almost as dense as Earth, but contains less than a tenth of the material of Earth.

About 14 times every hundred years, Mercury passes right between the Earth and the Sun. It ● moves from east to west. Scientists call this crossing a solar transit. Then Mercury looks like a small black dot against the bright circle of the Sun.

On this January morning in 1984, four planets could be seen in the sky. The largest glowing object is Venus. Below and to the left, just above the orange sunrise, is Jupiter. If you look very closely, to the left of Jupiter is a small white object, that is Mercury. Antares, a red star, is straight to the right of Venus. To the top right of the picture is Saturn.

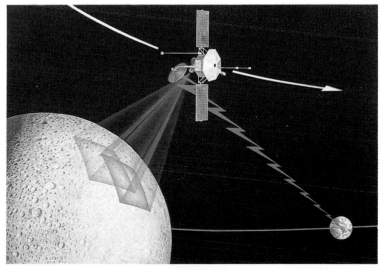

Mariner 10 was the first spacecraft to explore Mercury.

Mercury was fast because of his winged sandals. The planet is also quick; its planetary year is 88 Earth days!

Venus

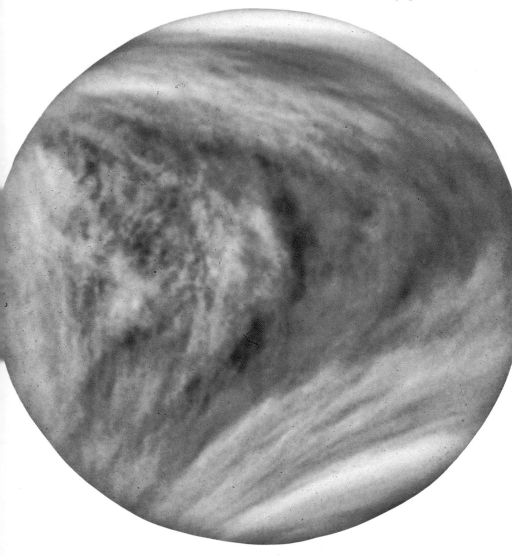

Venus is unbelievably hot, but it is also cloudy. Only a little light gets through the deep clouds that cover the planet. There is no water and no oxygen. Life on Venus is impossible for humans.

Not long ago, people thought Venus was like Earth. They called it Earth's sister planet. It is like Earth in size, mass, and density. But it is also very different.

The orbit of Venus is nearly circular. It is twice as big as the orbit of Mercury, so scientists can see Venus outside of the Sun's glare. Venus completes one revolution in 225 Earth days.

The rotation of Venus is the longest in the solar system. It takes Venus 243 Earth days to complete one rotation. So Venus's day is longer than its year! And Venus rotates backward. Earth rotates the same direction as its revolution around the Sun. Venus rotates opposite to its revolution around the Sun. Scientists call this retrograde—backward— rotation.

The thick clouds that cover Venus make it bright. They reflect the light of the Sun. Those same clouds make it hard to study Venus. They are so thick that they completely hide the surface. Scientists finally got good looks at Venus when spacecrafts bounced radar off the surface and sent back the information to Earth.

Lightning flashes across the sky and thunder booms almost all the time on Venus, the second planet from the Sun.

Venus was named for the Roman goddess of love and beauty. The sign of the planet is the hand mirror the goddess used to admire herself.

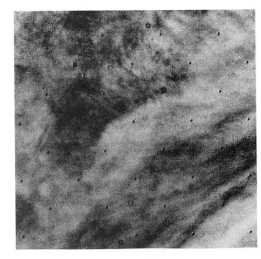

Mariner 10 took this close-up picture of the clouds covering the surface of Venus.

In 1974, Mariner 10 found that Venus was very dry and sizzling hot. Pioneer Venus 2 sent back information about three blankets of clouds around the planet. The upper layer is poisonous. The clouds are made of sulfuric acid, and they swirl at almost 200 miles an hour. The thin, hazy upper layer of clouds is 15 miles thick. Below it, another layer of clouds 40 miles thick covers the surface of the planet. The atmosphere at the surface of Venus is almost all carbon dioxide. (Humans breathe in oxygen and breathe out carbon dioxide.) The atmosphere of carbon dioxide is very heavy.

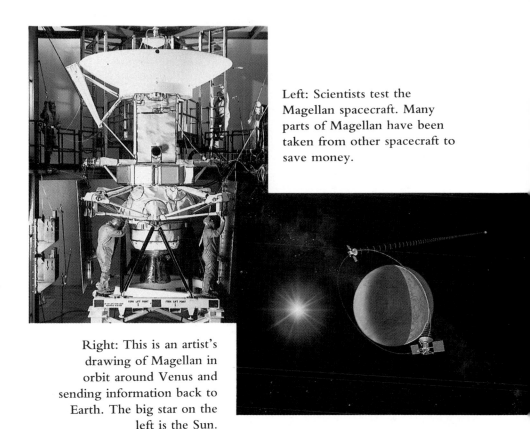

Left: Scientists test the Magellan spacecraft. Many parts of Magellan have been taken from other spacecraft to save money.

Right: This is an artist's drawing of Magellan in orbit around Venus and sending information back to Earth. The big star on the left is the Sun.

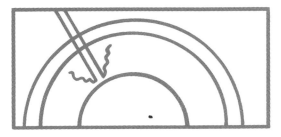

The thick atmosphere of carbon dioxide on Venus lets in radiation from the Sun, which turns to heat. When the heat hits the ground, it bounces back into the atmosphere, just as a hot street sends off heat on Earth. But the heat cannot escape. On Venus, the heavy atmosphere traps the heat. The heat stays on Venus, and temperatures reach 900°F.

The United States space probe Pioneer began orbiting Venus in 1978. It carried radar that could go through the clouds. Pioneer found craters on Venus, proving that volcanoes had erupted. Scientists are convinced that there are still active volcanoes.

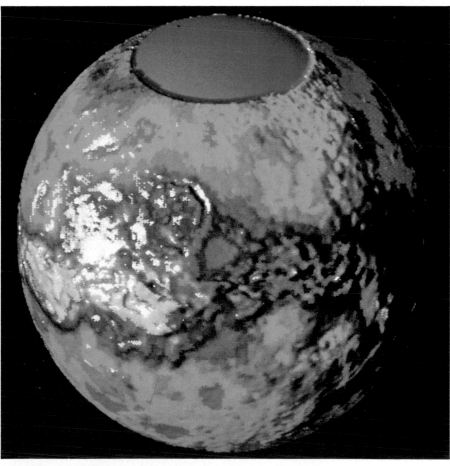

The Pioneer Orbiter took this picture of Venus. It used radar to strip the planet of its clouds so we could see the surface of the planet. Pioneer did not get information about the surface of the top of the planet.

Earth changes all the time. Scientists say that it is a "living" planet. Over time, rain and other weather wear away even mountains.

From space, Earth looks like a huge blue ball with white streaks across it. Earth gets its blue color from the oceans that cover much of its surface and from the air that surrounds it. The white streaks are clouds. Earth is the only planet in the solar system that we know has life on it.

Earth

Earth is the third planet from the Sun Like Mercury and Venus, it is a solid ball.

Earth's orbit is slightly oval. The planet rotates on its axis in 23.9 hours —our day. In that time, one side of the globe is in daylight, and one side is dark. Earth completes one revolution around the Sun every 365.25 days. Every leap year, we add a day in February to make up for that extra .25 day.

Earth is tilted on its axis. The Earth's tilt causes the seasons. When the top of the Earth—the North Pole —tilts toward the Sun, it is summer in the northern hemisphere. When the North Pole tilts away, it is winter. Winter in the northern hemisphere is summer in the southern hemisphere.

The atmosphere of Earth is made mostly of two gases—nitrogen and oxygen. These gases make it possible for life—humans breathe oxygen.

Earth's atmosphere lets heat in and out. Earth's atmosphere is layered. Most of our atmosphere, from the surface of the planet going up, is six miles thick. A very important layer of our atmosphere is the ozone layer. It shields us and filters out the Sun's harmful rays. Without the ozone layer, life on Earth would die. That is why scientists and other people are concerned that we don't put harmful chemicals in the air that might destroy the ozone layer.

Water is the key to life on Earth. Oceans cover nearly three quarters of the planet's surface.

The planet was named by the ancient Greeks for their goddess Gaea—Mother Earth. The symbol of Earth is the Greek symbol for sphere or ball.

Left: This ultraviolet photograph of Earth shows where the Sun's heat is hitting the planet. It is daytime in most of the red spots, and nighttime on the other side of the planet.

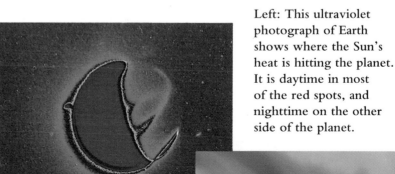

Right: Earth's weather keeps changing what our planet's surface looks like. Over time, rain and strong winds can wear away mountains.

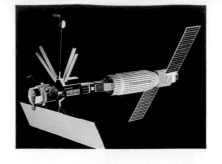

The spacecraft Seasat (right) allowed scientists to see what the ocean floor looks like (below).

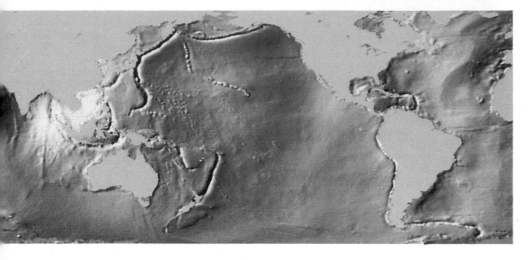

Some of the most exciting formations on Earth are hidden. They are on the ocean floor. Water covers the deepest canyons—called trenches—and some of the tallest mountains.

This is the beautiful view astronauts get of the Earth and the Moon from their spaceship window.

The oceans store heat and keep temperatures on Earth comfortable. Water evaporates from the surface of the oceans—the heat from the Sun turns water into a gas or vapor. The water vapor falls back to the Earth as rain. Earth is the only known planet with oceans of liquid water. Most living things on Earth—including you—are made mostly of water.

When Earth formed, it did not have oceans. More than four billion years ago, Earth was very hot. Gases erupted from volcanoes. Millions of years passed. The gas became clouds and turned to rain. Over time, that rain formed our oceans. Water made life on Earth possible.

Unlike Mercury, Earth looks very different from the way it used to. Volcanoes, like Kilauea on the island of Hawaii, erupt, building new land. Earthquakes shake the land.

The crust of Earth covers the planet, much as skin covers your body. The crust is a thin layer of rock with craters, mountains, and rivers. Below the crust is another layer of rock, called the mantle. The part of the mantle deep below the crust is melted—or molten—rock. The core is fluid rock around a solid center.

Much of the Earth is hidden. The Mariana Trench on the floor of the Pacific Ocean is 36,000 feet—more than seven miles—below the surface. Some ocean mountains are so high that they form islands. Iceland is the top of an underwater mountain!

The Moon

The Moon is Earth's satellite. It revolves around the Earth and is held in place by Earth's gravity. The Moon is about one quarter the diameter of Earth. It is about 240,000 miles away.

The Moon seems to change—sometimes we see only a sliver. Sometimes we see a great round yellow circle. That is because the Moon has days and nights, just as the Earth does. At times, shadows hide part of the Moon.

The Moon revolves around the Earth every 27.3 days. The Moon is frozen in its rotation—it completes one rotation in the same time as it completes one revolution. Because of this, we always see the same side.

In 1969, the first people landed on the Moon. Their spacecraft, the Apollo 11, was launched by NASA (National Aeronautics and Space Administration). Neil Armstrong was the first person to walk on the Moon! The Moon's gravity is much less than Earth's—so he bounced rather than walked.

The Moon has huge basins that were made when asteroids rammed it. Then, lava filled the basins. Astronomers call them maria—the Latin word for seas. One basin, called the Sea of Tranquillity, is 600 miles across. It is where Neil Armstrong landed, and his footprints are still there!

The Moon is a dry, dead place. There is no atmosphere and no water. It has not changed since shortly after the solar system formed.

The Moon was named Diana or Luna by the ancient Romans. Luna meant "shines." The symbol of the Moon is a crescent moon.

Neil Armstrong took this picture of fellow astronaut Buzz Aldrin on the Moon.

Mars

Mars was named after the Roman god of war.
The symbol of the planet stands for the god's shield and spear.

For hundreds of years, scientists have wondered about life on Mars, the fourth planet from the Sun. Stories and movies have been written about "martians"—aliens from Mars. The stories are fun, but scientists now know that there is no life on Mars.

The orbit of Mars is much larger and slower than Earth's. It takes Mars 687 Earth days to revolve around the Sun. And Mars's orbit is off-center. Sometimes the planet is much closer to the Sun than other times. Mars rotates on its axis every 24 hours and 37 minutes. So a day on Mars is just a little longer than a day on Earth.

Mariner 9 (left) sent back photographs of Olympus Mons (above)—the biggest volcano we know. It is 15 miles high, has a crater 45 miles wide, and is 355 miles wide at its base. Olympus Mons is 20 times bigger than the biggest volcano on Earth!

Mars   Earth

Like Earth, Mars has a rocky core. But the planet is only about half the diameter of Earth. Because it is much farther from the Sun than Earth, Mars gets half as much energy from the Sun as Earth does. Because Mars has a very thin atmosphere, much of the Sun's energy, which heats the surface, escapes back into space. It is very cold on Mars. On a hot summer day, temperatures might rise above freezing, but usually they are far below zero.

Mars is a frozen world that is covered with red dust.
The orange-red dust that covers the surface of the planet earned Mars its nickname—the Red Planet.

Two small moons revolve around Mars—probably pieces of asteroids. They are irregular-shaped blobs covered with craters. The moons are named Phobos and Deimos—Fear and Terror—after the two sons of Ares, the Greek god of war.

In 1965, the Mariner 4 space probe sailed past Mars and sent back pictures of its cratered surface. Mariner 9, launched by NASA in 1972, showed us that Mars has two very different landscapes. The northern part is largely worn looking and is covered with old lava flows from volcanoes. The south is covered with deep craters.

Mariner photographed a huge round basin on Mars. It is called Hellas. Scientists think the basin formed when a meteoroid smashed into the planet. Hellas is bigger than the whole state of Alaska. Dry channels on the surface of Mars look like old riverbeds. Perhaps the planet was not always so dry and cold.

In 1976, landers from the orbiting spacecraft Vikings 1 and 2 landed on Mars. Launched by NASA, the Viking landers looked for life on Mars. They had traveled through space for nearly a year to reach the planet. While preparing for the landings, scientists worried that they would not find safe places to land. The Viking 1 lander settled on a huge plain called Chryse Planitia—the Plain of Gold—on the northern hemisphere of Mars. Chryse Planitia looks very much like a rocky desert on Earth.

Left: Viking 1 and 2 were sent to Mars to further explore the "Red Planet." Below left: Both Viking 1 and 2 sent landers to land on Mars for a closer look. Below: The landers analyzed soil samples and radioed the information back to Earth.

Some scientists are trying to send astronauts to Mars to establish a space station there. They would like to do that within the next 30 years—in your lifetime!

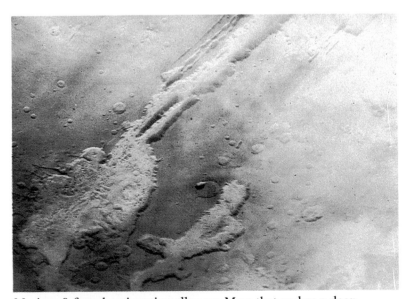

Mariner 9 found a gigantic valley on Mars that makes a deep scar across the middle of the planet. The valley was named after the Mariner spacecraft—Valles Marinaris. It is more than ten times as long as our Grand Canyon and three times as deep —more than three miles from the top to the bottom.

Jupiter

**Jupiter is two and a half times bigger than all the other planets combined.
It is as big as 1,300 Earths.**

Jupiter   Earth

2

Jupiter is named after the Roman king of the gods. Its symbol is the sign for the lightning bolt.

Jupiter's rings are beautiful when lit up by the Sun.

A voyage from Mars to the fifth planet from the Sun—Jupiter—could be very dangerous. Your spaceship would pass through the asteroid belt —millions of miles occupied by thousands of asteroids. The chances of being hit by an asteroid are small. But if one hit your spaceship, you and your spaceship would not survive.

Jupiter is five times farther from the Sun than Earth. Jupiter is the first of the outer planets—or gas giants. It is the biggest planet in the solar system. Unlike Earth and the other inner planets, Jupiter is made mostly of gases, but it probably has a molten rocky (liquid rock) core.

It takes Jupiter 11.8 Earth years to revolve around the Sun. But Jupiter has the shortest day in the solar system. It completes one rotation in only 9.9 hours. The planet's swift rotation makes the clouds swirl on the planet's surface.

Jupiter, like the Sun, is made almost entirely of hydrogen and helium gases. If the planet were very much bigger, it might have been a star. Because it is still cooling from the time of its formation, it gives off nearly twice as much heat as it receives from the Sun.

Spacecraft that flew by Jupiter sent scientists information they could not get from watching the planet through telescopes. Voyager 1 was launched in 1977 and approached Jupiter in 1979. It measured Jupiter's atmosphere and found that it is thousands of miles thick.

Jupiter has 16 moons. Four of those moons—the biggest ones—were discovered by a man named Galileo nearly 400 years ago. They were the first new objects in space discovered by looking through a telescope. Jupiter's four big moons are called the Galilean moons after the man who discovered them. They are Io, Europa, Ganymede, and Callisto.

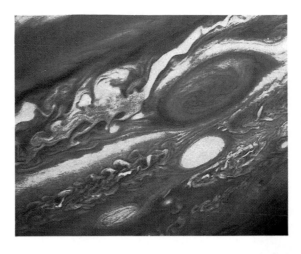

As scientists at the Jet Propulsion Laboratory in California studied Voyager pictures of Io, they got very excited. They found a volcano erupting on Io (see above). Until that moment, we thought only Earth had active volcanoes. Voyager showed us that Io, unlike most other objects in the universe, is very young. It is changing all the time.

Spacecraft, such as the Voyagers, have helped astronomers learn a lot about the planets. In 1989, NASA launched a spacecraft that will reach Jupiter in 1995. They named the spacecraft Galileo. Galileo will drop a probe into Jupiter's atmosphere of swirling clouds, and scientists will learn even more about the biggest planet in our solar system.

Jupiter is a world of swirling bands of colored clouds, which move at speeds up to 260 miles per hour. The atmosphere of Jupiter is like a bubbling pot of paints that swirl but don't mix. Near the cloud tops lightning is always flashing.

Left: Jupiter's Great Red Spot is a giant storm in its atmosphere. It is so big that three Earths could fit in it! Below: Jupiter, surrounded by four of its 16 moons.

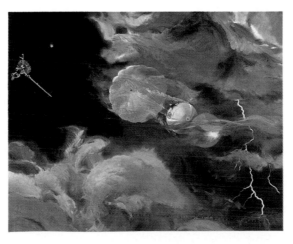

Left: This is an artist's drawing of the Galileo-Probe entering Jupiter's atmosphere.

Saturn

Saturn, the sixth planet from the Sun, is the second largest in the solar system. Saturn is the most distant planet you can see easily without a telescope. Until about 200 years ago, scientists thought Saturn was the last planet in our solar system.

Like Jupiter, Saturn is a gas giant. It is a cold world that receives only one hundredth of the heat and light from the Sun that Earth receives. Temperatures in Saturn's atmosphere drop to 290°F below zero.

It takes Saturn more than 29 years to revolve around the Sun. Imagine—you would have to wait 29 Earth years to have a birthday on Saturn. But Saturn spins rapidly. It rotates on its axis once every 10.7 hours. Saturn spins so fast that the big gas giant bulges in the middle.

Galileo discovered the rings around Saturn. To him they looked like ears, and for a long time Saturn was called "the eared planet." Scientists once thought Saturn had seven rings. Thanks to the Voyager spacecraft, we know much more now. We know that Saturn has hundreds of rings around it that extend for thousands of miles. The rings are probably pieces of ice that are from pebble-size to house-size. The rings are very thin—only about 40 feet thick.

Saturn looks like a huge round blob of butterscotch pudding. Haze and rings surround the planet. It is very beautiful.

The planet is named after the Roman god of the harvest. The symbol of the planet is a sickle, the curved blade on a pole people once used to cut down their crops.

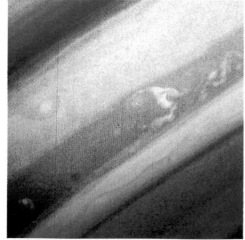

Saturn's atmosphere is mostly hydrogen and helium. It has belts and zones, like Jupiter's, and moves at speeds up to 1,100 miles per hour.

Enceladus

Tethys

Dione

Enceladus, a primary moon of Saturn, is made of ice. It reflects light like freshly fallen snow does. Tethys and Dione are also made of ice. The other four primary moons of Saturn are Mimas, Rhea, Iapetus, and Hyperion. Hyperion looks like a potato.

Saturn has more moons than any other planet—18! Most of them are balls of ice. Eight of Saturn's moons are middle-size to big. They are called primary moons. Titan, the largest, is the only satellite in the solar system that has an atmosphere similar to Earth's. Temperatures on Titan drop to almost 300°F below zero—much colder than any place on Earth.

Pioneer and Voyager spacecraft launched by NASA sent scientists a lot of information about Saturn. NASA is still studying the photographs. Until August of 1990, scientists knew only 17 moons orbiting Saturn. Scientists studying Voyager 2 photographs found the 18th moon. It is the smallest of Saturn's known moons, and its gravity keeps the ice particles on one of the planet's rings in place. When a moon does this, it is called a shepherding moon. The newest moon is named 1981 S13 for now. The man who found the moon would like its name to be Pan, after the Greek god who looked after sheep.

NASA plans to launch the spacecraft Cassini in 1995, which will reach the planet in 2004. They hope to discover more surprises about the butterscotch-colored planet with rings.

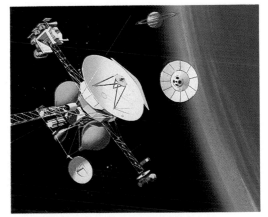
Scientists hope that the Cassini spacecraft will uncover new and interesting things about the butterscotch-colored planet.

Above: Seven of Saturn's rings are named. They are the A Ring, B Ring, and C, D, E, F, and G Rings. The A Ring is the outermost ring we can see from Earth. It is so big that it would take you 95 years to walk around it!

Uranus

Uranus, the seventh planet from the Sun, is only a faint gleam in the night sky. Uranus is more than one and a half billion miles from the Sun! Even with a telescope, it is very hard to see Uranus.

Uranus was named after the Roman god of the heavens. The symbol of the planet is the sign for the metal platinum.

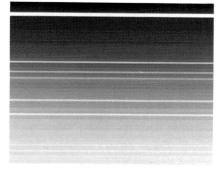

Scientists knew that Uranus had nine rings, but Voyager 2 discovered a tenth! The rings are only a few miles wide. They look like black hoops. Scientists think the rings are made of darkened methane ice.

It is very dark and cold on Uranus. The Sun is only a tiny circle of light, and temperatures in the atmosphere are about 350°F below zero. A music teacher who studied the sky for fun discovered Uranus in 1781, with a telescope he built himself.

Nearly every other planet in the solar system spins like a top. Uranus is tilted on its axis almost 98 degrees. It almost rolls around the Sun like a ball. Part of the time, one pole of the planet points almost straight at the Sun. Uranus rotates on its axis once every 17.2 hours. But a year on Uranus is very long. It takes Uranus 84 Earth years to revolve around the Sun.

Voyager 2 traveled nine years from Earth for a look at Uranus, which told scientists a lot. Until then, they did not know how long it took Uranus to complete one rotation. Uranus, like Jupiter and Saturn, is a gas giant. It is made mostly of gases and ice. But unlike Jupiter and Saturn, Uranus probably has no rocky core, but a molten mixture of rock and ice fills most of the planet.

The upper atmosphere of Uranus is made mainly of hydrogen and helium. Below that layer, clouds of the gas methane wrap the planet. Methane absorbs red light, so Uranus looks green and blue from space. Winds create barely visible bands of clouds.

The most exciting pictures that Voyager took were of Miranda, the smallest of the five major moons of Uranus. Miranda is a very strange moon. It has an icy surface marked with grooves, cliffs, and plains. Voyager sent back pictures of a canyon 10 times deeper than our Grand Canyon.

Astronomers are still studying the photographs Voyager sent back to Earth. They believe that during the formation of Uranus, many comets collided with and became a part of the planet. When Voyager flew by the planet in January of 1986, scientists were a little disappointed. The spacecraft could not see many individual clouds in the planet's atmosphere. Uranus still looked like a boring blue-green globe.

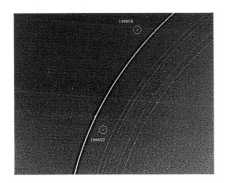

Shepherd moons

Until 1985, when Voyager began nearing Uranus, astronomers thought the planet had five moons. Voyager discovered 10 more! Scientists think that some of these natural satellites are shepherd moons that help keep the rings in place. Voyager also showed more about the five middle-sized moons that orbit Uranus. The two largest moons of Uranus are Titania and Oberon. They were named after characters in a play by Shakespeare. Oberon is much smaller than our Moon. Voyager sent back pictures that show Oberon is very cold and has a rough, rumpled surface.

In the last five years, we have learned more about Uranus than we have found out in the last 200 years. But we still don't know very much about this blue-green globe.

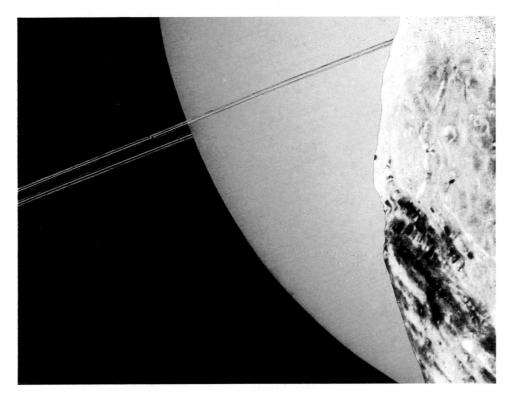

Above: Voyager 2 circles to see Uranus behind its small, strange moon Miranda. Left: This is an artist's drawing of what Voyager 2 looked like as it photographed Uranus.

Neptune

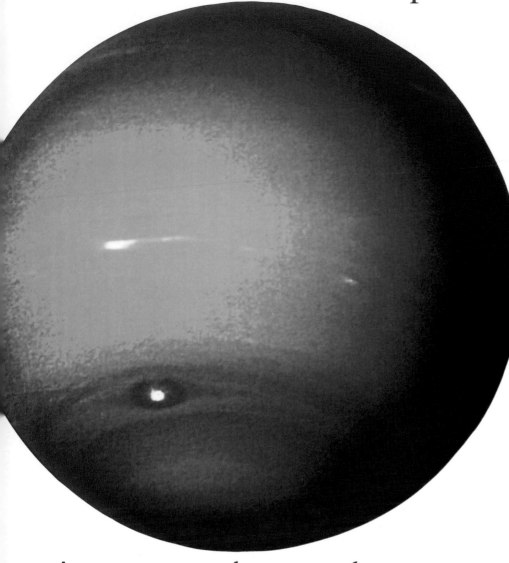

Neptune, the eighth planet from the Sun, looks a lot like Uranus. For years, scientists thought Neptune was the twin of Uranus. From Earth, Neptune is the same color and size as Uranus. Neptune looks like a blue-green ball. Neptune is the smallest and the last of the gas giants. Fifty-eight Earths would fit inside Neptune. Scientists think that the inside of Neptune, like Uranus, is probably a molten mixture of rock and ice.

Astronomers studying Uranus wondered why its orbit was funny. They began to think another planet was pulling Uranus away from the Sun—they were right. They found Neptune.

Neptune revolves around the Sun once every 165 Earth years. Neptune has not yet completed a full orbit since it was discovered. But a day on Neptune is 16.1 hours long. Through a telescope, scientists found that Neptune, like the other gas giants, has a deep atmosphere that is mostly hydrogen.

Astronomers need a strong telescope to see Neptune. Even with a telescope, the planet looks like a fuzzy pale blue circle. Neptune is 30 times farther from the Sun than Earth is.

Neptune was thought to have partial rings. Scientists knew it had moons—Triton and Nereid. Nereid is tiny and has the most elongated orbit of any moon in the solar system. Triton has always interested scientists. Triton orbits backward. It is the only large moon in the solar system that we know has a retrograde orbit.

Scientists knew that Neptune, like Uranus, has small amounts of methane gas in its atmosphere. It is the methane gas that gives Neptune its blue color.

Triton

Neptune is named after the old Roman god of the ocean—Neptune—because of its blue-green color. The symbol of the planet is the three-pointed spear—called a trident—that Neptune used.

In the summer of 1989, when Voyager 2 approached Neptune, scientists learned a lot more about the smallest gas giant. Pictures of Nereid were poor because of the moon's great distance. But Triton was spectacular. Its south pole is covered with nitrogen ice, and beneath the surface, water ice is rock hard. Temperatures on Triton drop to more than 390°F below zero. Its scarred surface shows signs of volcanic activity.

Studying the information and photographs from Voyager was special because it was a joint effort. Scientists from what was then the Soviet Union joined NASA scientists at the Jet Propulsion Laboratory, and they looked at the photographs together. Voyager showed the astronomers faint arcs, like dark rainbows, around the planet. Voyager proved these arcs were three rings around Neptune. Another planet with rings!

For years we thought Neptune had just two moons. Voyager found six more. Scientists are still learning about them.

Scientists all around the world watched as Voyager 2 sped past Neptune and traveled farther out into the solar system. They were happy because they had learned so much. But they were sad, too, because Voyager was finished with its studies of the planets and would fly far beyond their reach into outer space. Neptune was the last new world they would see close up.

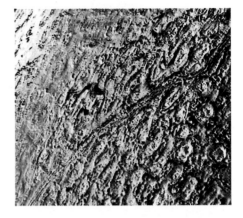

The volcanoes on the surface of Triton (right) are ice volcanoes. When the nitrogen and methane ices warm up, they turn to slush. Scientists think that the slush erupts much as lava erupts from volcanoes on Earth.

Neptune's rings

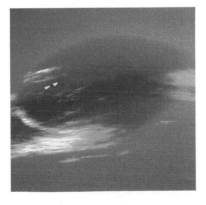

Another surprise Voyager discovered on Neptune is its violent weather. The planet is so far from the Sun that scientists did not expect much activity in the atmosphere. But Voyager 2 found winds swirling at speeds of 2,000 kilometers an hour. They named one storm system the "Great Dark Spot." It is a storm as big as Earth.

Pluto

This artist's picture of Pluto shows how close its moon, Charon, is. Also, it shows how far from the Sun it really is—the Sun looks more like a bright star than the center of our solar system.

Because of its elliptical orbit, sometimes Pluto is the eighth planet from the Sun! Most of the time, it is the farthest, or ninth, planet from the Sun.

P Pluto was named for the god who ruled the underworld in old Greek and Roman legends. The name of the god—Pluto—is the symbol of the planet.

Pluto, the ninth planet in our solar system, is an icy ball. Even with a powerful telescope, Pluto is only a fuzzy pinpoint of light. The planet is about one fifth the size of Earth—smaller than our Moon. Pluto is about 39 times farther from the Sun than Earth is. From Pluto, the Sun looks like a bright star that lights up Pluto's surface only a little better than a full moon lights up Earth.

Pluto is far from the Sun so its orbit is long. It takes the planet 248 Earth years to complete its revolution. And Pluto's orbit is strange. The path of its orbit is a stretched-out oval. If you hold a rubber band between the thumb and pointing finger of your hand and pull on the rubber band a little bit, it stretches out. That shape is similar to the shape of Pluto's orbit. It is the most oval, or elliptical, of any planet in the solar system. Sometimes Pluto is more than a billion miles closer to the Sun than other times. For 20 years out of every 248, Pluto moves closer to the Sun than Neptune. From 1979 to 1999, Pluto will be orbiting at its closest to the Sun. For that time, Neptune is the farthest planet. It takes Pluto 6.4 Earth days to complete one rotation.

Pluto is so small and so far from Earth that scientists did not discover it until about 60 years ago. In 1905, an American astronomer named Percival Lowell thought the gravity of a planet was pulling on Uranus and

Neptune, making their orbits oval. Lowell predicted where the planet would be, but he died before he found it. In 1930, Clyde Tombaugh discovered Pluto after searching the sky for many years.

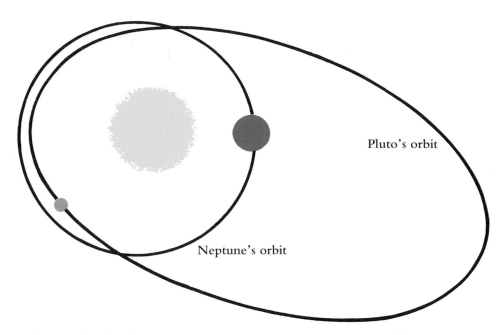

Pluto's orbit

Neptune's orbit

Pluto has one moon—Charon. Charon orbits so close to Pluto that scientists did not discover it until 1978. Astronomers found Charon because they noticed a bulge on one side of the planet in a photograph. That bulge was Charon. From Earth, the two objects look like they are touching. Charon is 20 times closer to Pluto than our Moon is to Earth. And Charon is about half the size of Pluto, making Pluto and Charon almost a double planet.

How the planet formed is still a mystery. It seems to be a snowball of methane gas, frozen water, and rock. Pluto probably has a surface of methane or nitrogen ice and a thin atmosphere of methane or nitrogen. It is tipped on its side like Uranus.

Someday we may find out more about the dark and distant world of Pluto. So far, no spacecraft has gotten near enough to the planet to answer our questions. But if you remember that we discovered Pluto so recently, you must admit we have learned a lot about it in a very short time.

Pluto is dark and cold—temperatures drop to more than 300 degrees below zero. Life is impossible on Pluto.

Pluto and Charon from Earth (left) taken from the Canada-France-Hawaii Telescope. The picture on the right was taken from the Hubble Telescope.

 Pluto

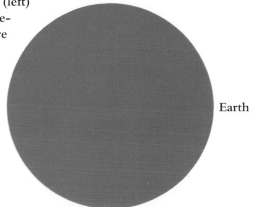 Earth

Pluto is about five times smaller than Earth, and is even smaller than our Moon.

Constellations

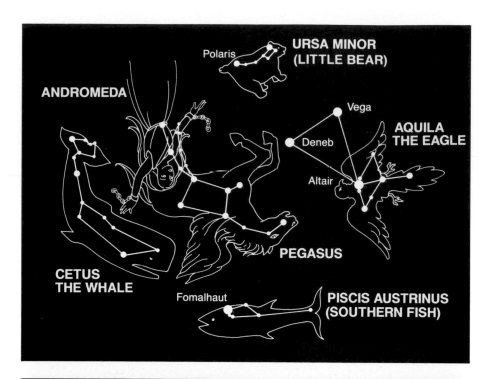

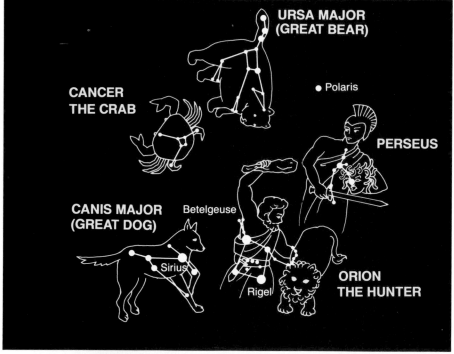

Top: This is an evening sky in late fall in the northern hemisphere. Center: Look at a late winter sky to see these northern hemisphere constellations.

For thousands of years, people have looked at the stars and seen imaginary shapes in the sky. These shapes formed by stars are called constellations. Because the Earth is round, you cannot see all the constellations unless you live at the middle of the Earth, the Equator. The area above the Equator is called the northern hemisphere. Below the Equator is the southern hemisphere.

One of the most famous constellations in the southern hemisphere is the Southern Cross. You can see it only in the southern hemisphere. The Crux, or Southern Cross, is made of four stars that look like a small cross.

In the northern hemisphere you can see the Northern Cross. It, too, looks like a big cross. It is part of a constellation called Cygnus the Swan.

One of the easiest shapes to see in the northern hemisphere is the Big Dipper. It looks like a big pot with a long handle. The Big Dipper is made of seven bright stars. Those stars are part of a constellation called Ursa Major, or the Great Bear.

Another constellation to look for in the northern hemisphere is Ursa Minor, or the Little Bear. Seven stars in Ursa Minor make the Little Dipper, another shape that is easy to find. Like the Big Dipper, the Little Dipper looks like a big pot. The star at the very tip of its handle is Polaris.

EARTH SCIENCES

Have you ever wondered how our planet works? The ground beneath your feet is made up of rocks and minerals produced deep within the Earth. The air that surrounds you is constantly being affected by winds, humidity, and changes in temperature. Movements in the Earth's crust cause earthquakes, volcanoes, and giant ocean waves. Events that are happening miles beneath the planet's surface and high up in the atmosphere affect us every day.

Our restless planet is a fascinating place. It is constantly changing, as the atmosphere, the surface, and the Earth's interior affect each other. The more you learn about how the Earth works, the more you'll understand about the hidden forces that touch your life in countless ways.

Earth's Layers

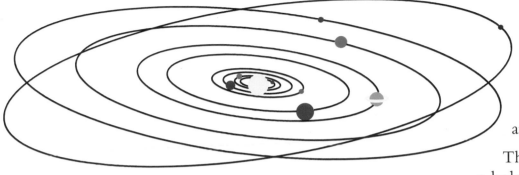

Earth is one of the planets of our solar system. The solar system is made up of the sun, nine planets, and all the moons that move around the planets. Our Earth is really an amazing planet.

The Earth is very big. If you dug a hole from the Earth's surface to its center, that hole would be 4,000 miles deep! That's just about the distance from San Francisco, California, to Washington, D.C.—and back again!

Our planet Earth is one of the nine planets in the solar system.

Planet Earth can be a very exciting place to live.

The Earth is also very, very old. Scientists think it is over four billion years old! Scientists have discovered other things about our planet. Among other things, they know the Earth has layers, just like a birthday cake.

Each layer is made up of different kinds of rocks that have different weights. Rocks in the earth's middle are heavier than rocks near its surface.

The picture we have developed of the Earth's inside structure is quite simple. Scientists believe our planet began as a cloud of hot gases mixed together. The cloud was part of the Solar Nebula (NEB-yuh-luh), a huge cloud of hot gas and dust. As the nebula cloud whirled around the sun, gases in the cloud began spinning off on their own. The gases cooled over time to become solid "balls," or planets.

The nebula from which our solar system formed might have looked very much like this.

As the Earth cooled, it separated into three main layers. The *core* is at the center of the Earth. The *crust* is the planet's outer skin. And the *mantle* is between the core and the crust.

The Core

The Earth's core is split into two parts—an inner and an outer core. Scientists have learned that the inner core is solid and that the outer core is liquid.

The Mantle

The mantle surrounds the core and takes up the most space inside our planet. It is completely solid. Even so, strong heat and pressure inside the Earth cause it to shift around, just like the liquid core. Later, we'll see how movements in the mantle can have a very noticeable effect on our lives. These movements miles beneath our feet bring about volcanoes and earthquakes.

The Crust

Rocks in the crust are cool. They are brittle. This means that they will break, like hard candy, when pressure is applied to them. The rocks may break and shatter to form long cracks called faults.

Sometimes faults extend all the way through the crust to the mantle. When this happens, the faults may form paths for gas, heat, and magma (MAG-muh) to escape to the surface through volcanoes. Magma is hot, molten rock from the mantle.

When magma works its way through the crust to the surface of the Earth, it erupts through volcanoes.

crust

mantle

outer core

inner core

By studying Earth's inner layers, scientists have learned more about how the planet works. They have also learned how volcanoes and earthquakes happen.

Magma is red-hot and liquid when it reaches the surface. Later, it will cool into solid rock.

Plate Tectonics

This photo shows the center of Australia. Millions of years ago, this island continent was joined to Antarctica and formed part of one giant continent.

If you look at a globe or map of the Earth you will see some familiar patterns. Imagine Earth as a giant puzzle.

Look at Europe and Africa. See how they may fit together with North and South America? You can also see how India, Australia, Antarctica, and east Africa may also fit together.

Scientists tell us these large pieces of land, called continents, once did fit together. Millions of years ago, they formed one giant continent. Pieces of this great continent have moved apart through the ages and are still moving today.

This movement is very, very slow. It takes thousands of years for a continent to move just a few feet. Still, a map made today will look much different from a map made in a million years.

What forces make the continents move around? Millions of years ago, the Earth's crust cracked into several pieces. As the mantle shifts around, it pushes and pulls the chunks of crust in different directions. The broken pieces of crust actually ride on broken pieces of the mantle's outer edge beneath them.

The chunks of crust, along with the pieces of mantle under them, are called *tectonic plates* (tek-TAHN-ik playts). "Tectonic" comes from a Greek word that means "builder." Tectonic plates build and rebuild the Earth's surface as they move over the shifting mantle. The study of moving plates is called *plate tectonics*.

This map shows the Earth as it looked millions of years ago when there was just one enormous continent. The outlines show today's continents and how they fitted together.

We know about seven major tectonic plates on the planet's surface. These are the North American, South American, Pacific, Australian, African, Eurasian, and Antarctic plates. Some plates include just landmasses. Others also include oceans. In addition to these, there are a few small plates.

The Australian plate contains Australia, India, and the northeastern Indian Ocean. The Eurasian plate contains Europe and most of Asia. It moves slowly to the east. Some eighty million years ago, India "crashed" into Eurasia. The crash squeezed up huge amounts of rock to form the Himalayan Mountains. Many mountain ranges were formed by ancient plates crashing together.

Antarctica sits on a plate that is actually growing.

The Appalacian Mountains were formed when two plates crashed together.

The African plate holds the continent of Africa and parts of the Atlantic and Indian Oceans. It is moving eastward and northward. The Antarctic plate is actually growing larger. The Pacific Ocean is surrounded by plates moving inward. It is probably shrinking.

Cracks in the Earth's crust, at the edges of plates, are called faults. When faults shift, they cause earthquakes.

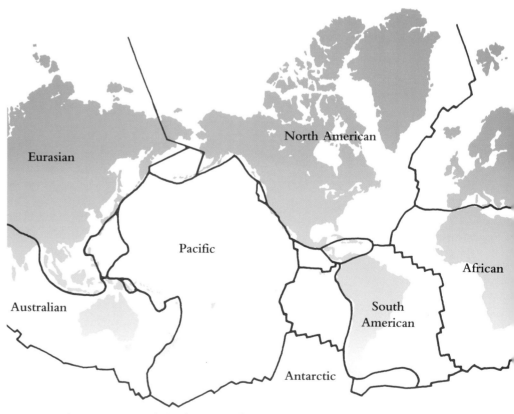
This map shows the boundaries between the major tectonic plates.

91

Plate Boundaries

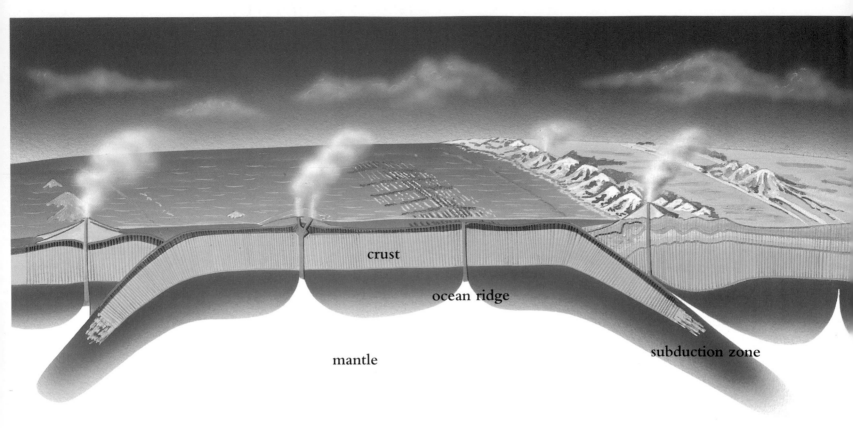

Tectonic plates move away from each other at ocean ridges. At subduction zones, plates collide and one dives under the other. This activity forms mountain ranges and volcanoes. It also causes earthquakes.

Ocean ridges stretch around the Earth and are often as high as mountains on land.

The places where tectonic plates touch each other are called *plate boundaries.* There are three types of plate boundaries.

Ocean Ridges

Just as the continents have mountain ranges, so do the oceans. They form along ocean floors, way down deep. Scientists have studied these from ships and submarines.

The underwater mountains rise up at places where plates are moving away from each other. This kind of plate boundary is called an *ocean ridge.* As the plates pull away from each other, magma squeezes up from the mantle to fill the space between the plates. The magma erupts through underwater volcanoes.

The magma forms a solid ridge when it reaches the ocean floor. In this way, ridges of ocean mountains separate some places. The plates pull away from the ocean ridges that form between them. This is known as *sea-floor spreading.* As the plates continue to move apart, cooled magma sticks to their edges. This is how new crust is formed.

Subduction Zones

A tectonic plate may travel for hundreds of millions of years. It may bump against another plate moving in the opposite direction. This other plate is moving away from an ocean ridge beyond it.

When plates collide, one of them gives way. Its edges sink beneath the other plate, back down into the mantle. This process is called *subduction* (suhb-DUHK-shuhn).

As subduction occurs, curved valleys several miles deep form in the ocean floor. Lines of volcanoes often erupt behind these valleys, which mark *subduction zones*. Some subduction zones occur in the Atlantic, Pacific, and Indian Oceans.

Subduction zone volcanoes are very explosive. They release steam, a fine-grained, dustlike material called *ash*, and many types of magma. Well-known volcanoes of this type occur in Japan (Mount Fuji), southeast Asia

(Krakatoa), western North America (Mount St. Helens), and the Mediterranean (Mount Vesuvius, Mount Etna, Santorini).

The volcano Arenal, in Costa Rica, is a subduction-zone volcano. It is near the place where the small Cocos plate collides with the North American plate.

Subduction-zone volcanoes are tall, smooth cones.

The Cascade Mountain Range in Oregon and Washington is really a line of ancient volcanoes formed at the subduction zone where the Pacific and North American plates meet.

Plate Boundaries

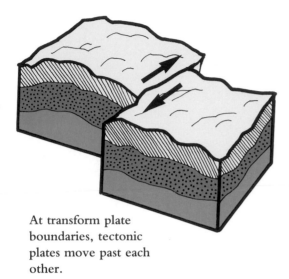

At transform plate boundaries, tectonic plates move past each other.

The San Andreas Fault, and the smaller faults that branch off from it, can be seen at the surface.

Transform Plate Boundaries

When scientists see ocean ridges, they know they are looking at places where two plates are moving apart. When they see subduction zones, they know they're looking at places where two plates push together.

Another type of plate boundary forms where two plates scrape sideways alongside each other at their edges instead of bumping together or pulling apart. This is called a *transform plate boundary.* Faults form along these boundaries.

One of the most famous examples of a transform plate boundary is the San Andreas Fault. It is in California. This fault has formed between the North American and Pacific plates. East of the fault is the North American plate. The Pacific plate lies west of the fault. These enormous plates are moving alongside each other in different directions.

Measurements taken during past earthquakes tell us this fault cuts right down to the mantle. The North American plate moves an average of about an inch and a half each year against the Pacific plate.

This does not happen all the time, though. And without movement, pressure may build for many years. Then the fault's boundaries may move many yards in a short time—and an earthquake occurs!

San Francisco is a big city. A strong earthquake could cause much damage here.

The San Andreas Fault runs through the whole state of California. It has caused earthquakes in Los Angeles, San Francisco, and many places between.

The San Andreas Fault is just one place where the North and South American plates move against the Pacific plate. The Mexico City earthquake of 1985 was caused by a movement along the boundaries of these plates.

Hot Spots

Some volcanoes are far from plate boundaries. They are not caused by plates moving apart or crashing into each other. These volcanoes often form ocean islands. Examples of volcanic ocean islands include Hawaii, Iceland, and the Galapagos Islands.

What produces these volcanoes? Scientists believe the island-forming volcanoes erupt when extra-hot spots in the mantle rise to the base of a plate. The hot spots cause magma to form and force its way to the surface through volcanoes. This type of activity is called *hot-spot volcanism*.

If you look at a map showing where earthquakes and volcanoes have occurred, you will see that most occur around the Pacific Ocean and throughout the Mediterranean Sea. Lines of earthquakes also run along ocean ridges and some other cracks in the Earth's crust. These places mark the main boundaries between plates.

This explains why a country like Japan has great earthquakes and explosive volcanoes. Japan is located where two plates come together. The same goes for Greece, Italy, and South America, all of which have volcanoes and earthquake activity.

Every year, visitors come to Hawaii to enjoy the ocean and the beautiful beaches. Many of them don't realize that they are sunbathing above a huge mantle hot spot.

The Hawaiian Island chain is far from any plate boundaries. It was formed by hot-spot volcanism.

Mount Fujiyama, in Japan, is not a hot-spot volcano. It is caused by a subduction zone nearby. This subduction zone also causes frequent earthquakes.

The Pacific Ring of Fire

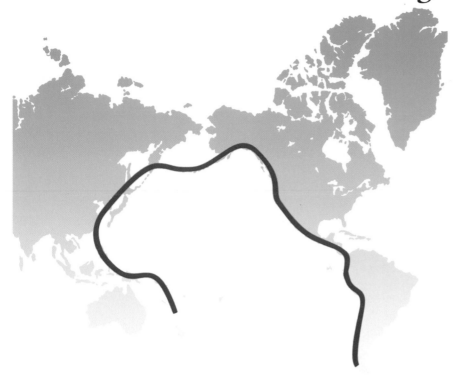

The Pacific Ocean is surrounded by explosive volcanoes. These volcanoes form what is called the Pacific Ring of Fire. What is the reason for this feature?

As plate tectonics tells us, North and South America are drifting away from Europe and toward Japan. In fact, all the plates around the Pacific Ocean are moving slowly toward the subduction zones that circle the ocean.

The Ring of Fire volcanoes lie close to these subduction zones. Mount St. Helens and other volcanoes in the northwestern United States lie on the subduction zone between the North American plate and the small Juan de Fuca plate.

The lines of these volcanoes form long, graceful curves, either along the edges of the continents or as chains of islands. Japan is a good example of a volcanic island chain. Japan is made up of about 50 volcanoes along four curved chains. The nearby subduction zone also causes earthquakes.

Millions of people live near the Ring of Fire. They are at risk from sudden eruptions. For their safety, it makes sense to study the way Ring of Fire volcanoes work and to understand them better.

Ring of Fire volcanoes occur over one hundred miles behind the deep valleys formed where plates crash together.

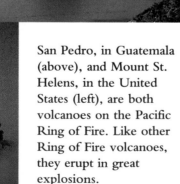

San Pedro, in Guatemala (above), and Mount St. Helens, in the United States (left), are both volcanoes on the Pacific Ring of Fire. Like other Ring of Fire volcanoes, they erupt in great explosions.

Famous Volcanic Eruptions

There have been many volcanic eruptions since people first appeared on Earth. The volcano Vesuvius (vuh-SOO-vee-uhs) erupted in the year 79. Vesuvius is in southern Italy, near the city of Naples. Two Roman towns, Pompeii (pahm-PAY) and Herculaneum (HUR-kyuh-LAY-nee-uhm), were built at the foot of Vesuvius.

Thousands of people were killed in this eruption. People running from Pompeii and Herculaneum were buried by falling ash. So were the surrounding farm fields.

Much more recently, a great eruption took place in the western United States. In 1980, Mount St. Helens, in the Cascades mountain chain, erupted. The eruption blew out the side of the volcano and sent rivers of mud and ash flowing out over the countryside. Vast areas of forest were destroyed.

A volcanic eruption can go on for years. The Hawaiian volcano Kilauea began an eruption in 1983 that is still going on. In 1983, *lava* began pouring from a crack in the volcano's side. Lava is magma that comes to the surface in the form of molten rock. It formed a four-mile river that cut through the tropical forest. It burned everything in its path. The lava is still erupting, sometimes in small amounts, sometimes in great rivers.

The eruption of Vesuvius was one of the biggest in history. In two days, Pompeii and Herculaneum were destroyed.

The eruption of Mount St. Helens had more force than any explosion created by humans. Huge amounts of ash were thrown into the sky and thousands of acres of forest were destroyed.

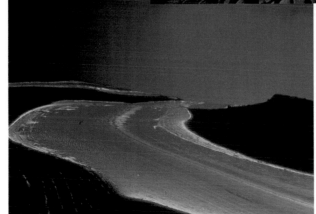

Unlike Mount St. Helens, Kilauea does not erupt with great explosions. Instead, the lava pours out onto the land in great rivers.

Structure of a Volcano

Some calderas fill with water between eruptions, forming beautiful mountain lakes. Crater Lake, in Oregon, is in a huge caldera.

Volcanoes are a special kind of mountain. Unlike other mountains, such as the Rockies, volcanoes can grow very quickly. In fact, they can grow as much as a thousand feet in just a few months!

Some volcanoes are perfect cones—such as Mount Fujiyama in Japan and Mayon in the Philippines. Others are like great bulging mounds or *shields*—such as the Hawaiian volcanoes and some of those on Iceland or the Galapagos Islands.

Craters are large openings at the tops of volcanoes. Gas, steam, ash, and lava escape through craters. A *caldera* (kawl-DAYR-uh) is a crater that forms when the top of a volcano caves in. Calderas can be many miles across.

Why do craters have many different sizes? A crater's size mainly depends on two things. The first is the type of *vent,* or opening, in earth's crust that allows the eruption to happen and the crater to form. The other is the type of magma that comes up through the crater.

Usually, the vent is a long crack in the rocks, like a fault. It is hundreds or thousands of feet deep and a few feet across. This crack allows magma to rise and pour out to the surface as lava.

How do volcanoes grow? What goes on inside while they are forming? Studying volcanoes from the outside helps scientists find answers to these questions.

Some volcanoes form wide floods of lava called *fields*—such as the Columbia River plateau of Oregon and Washington.

Sometimes, magma may come straight to the surface from the mantle. Other times, it gets trapped on the way up. Scientists know that deep inside many volcanoes magma is stored in large spaces called *magma chambers*.

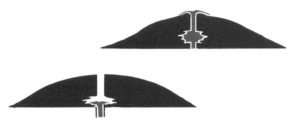

The Hawaiian volcano Kilauea has a magma chamber. This chamber is two to four miles below the volcano's summit, or peak. When Kilauea's chamber fills with molten magma rising from below, the volcano bulges outward. It bulges more and more until an eruption releases the pressure. The chamber empties. The volcano settles back down. Another batch of magma begins to collect in the chamber.

Some volcanoes have bigger magma chambers than Kilauea's. Magma may be trapped in a big chamber for a long time. If this happens, the magma may change. For example, magma may take up water as it cools. Also, crystals form and sink to the bottom of the chamber. This makes a volcano explosive.

Magma may pass quickly through a magma chamber on its way up, or it may sit and stew for a long time.

Magma does not stay in Kilauea's chamber for long. So, the material that erupts is basically the same as the material that flowed up from the mantle.

Devil's Tower, in Wyoming, was once hot magma in an ancient volcano's vent and magma chamber. When the volcano stopped erupting, the magma cooled. Over time, the outer parts of the volcano wore away, and the cooled magma is all that remains.

Types of Volcanic Eruptions

Fissure eruptions can occur on land. When they do, huge amounts of lava flow onto the Earth's surface. This creates *lava fields* that stretch hundreds of miles.

Fissure eruptions have formed huge lava fields in many parts of the world. These fields may be thousands of feet deep.

Eruptions can be divided into two basic groups: *fissure eruptions* (FISH-ur i-RUHP-shuhnz) and *central eruptions*. Fissure eruptions occur where the crust has pulled apart. The long cracks that form allow magma to rise to the surface. Fissure eruptions are common at ocean ridges and some hot spots, such as Hawaii and Iceland.

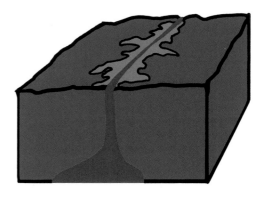

Floods of magma have poured through fissure eruptions in parts of the United States, India, Africa, and South America. The magma floods mark places where mantle hot spots split apart old continental plates.

In the Columbia Plateau in Oregon and Washington, lava poured out of fissures 20 million years ago. Nearby hills were buried by a layer of lava over four thousand feet high! The fissures that released the lava can still be seen.

Central eruptions are the best-known kind. Central volcanoes appear all over the world. They are found at ocean ridges, hot spots, and subduction zones. Central volcanoes also occur on land where continents are cracking along faults.

Central eruptions form tall cone-shaped volcanoes like this one.

100

Central eruptions occur in different ways.

Hawaiian eruptions are the most quiet. They are named after the kinds of eruptions seen at the Hawaiian volcanoes. Hawaiian eruptions are most common on hot-spot oceanic islands. The magmas do not contain much water, so they aren't explosive. These eruptions produce lavas that are hot and flow easily. These lavas are called *basaltic* (buh-SAWL-tik) lavas. They form large, smoothly sloping shield volcanoes.

Vulcanian (vuhl-KAY-nee-uhn) eruptions are another type of eruption. They are named after Vulcano, a famous Italian volcano. They can be quite violent. Huge chunks of rcd-hot lava and cold rock fly into the air. A cloud of gas and ash may rise several miles above the crater.

But *Peleean* (puh-LAY-uhn) eruptions are the most threatening of all. These are named after the 1902 eruption of Mount Pelée (puh-LAY) on the Caribbean island of Martinique.

During that eruption, several glowing gas clouds formed from a series of Vulcanian eruptions in Mount Pelée. Then, a plug of thick, sticky magma grew inside the volcano. It exploded with such force that a glowing white-hot gas cloud blew sideways through Mount Pelée.

The eruptions of Mount St. Helens in 1980 (above) and Mount Lassen in 1915 (right) were both *Vesuvian* (vuh-SOO-vee-uhn). A Vesuvian eruption is even more powerful than a Vulcanian eruption.

The lava and other materials that are put out by a central eruption build the volcano higher and higher around the vent.

Mount Etna, on the island of Sicily, is more explosive than a Hawaiian eruption, but less explosive than a Vesuvian eruption.

101

What Comes out of Volcanoes

In this picture, you can see two types of basaltic lava. *Aa* (AH-ah), at the top of the picture, forms a rough, blocky crust as it cools. *Pahoehoe* (puh-HO-ay-HO-ay), at the bottom of the picture, forms a smooth crust like the skin on a pudding.

Some volcanoes erupt only one kind of rock. Others may spit out many different types of rock in a short time.

These rocks are cooled andesite lava. Andesite is named after the Andes Mountains in South America.

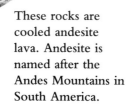

There are two main types of volcanic rocks. The first is lava, which is erupted magma. The second type, called *pyroclastic* (PY-ro-KLAS-tik) rocks, are broken bits of solid rock.

Basaltic lavas are runny and black. These lavas form shield volcanoes and flood eruptions because they can flow very far. When a basalt flow begins to cool, it forms a crust. The crust may be fairly smooth, like the skin that forms on pudding. Or, it may have a thick, rough surface containing loose blocks of solid lava.

When basaltic lava erupts on the sea floor, it forms small lumps. The lumps cool quickly, forming a glassy surface. These lumps are called "pillows" because they're about the same size and shape as pillows we sleep on.

Rhyolite (RY-uh-LYT) is the stickiest, thickest type of lava. It's usually white. This thick lava forms a rounded roof or a sticky plug over the vent. Rhyolite can sometimes explode if gas and water are trapped inside.

Andesite (AN-di-ZYT) is another type of lava. Its amount of stickiness falls between basaltic and rhyolite lavas. It is often greenish-grey in color. Andesite is the most common lava released from Ring of Fire volcanoes.

Pyroclastic Rocks and Pyroclastic Flows

Ash is the finest type of pyroclastic rock. It is released during most kinds of eruptions. Eruptions that are more explosive release more ash. Ash is made up of tiny particles thrown high into the air by a volcano. Falling ash can be like dust.

Blocks and *bombs* are larger pieces of pyroclastic rock. They are usually made of chunks of cooled lava. Blocks are already solid rock when they are erupted. Bombs are blobs of molten lava that cool as they fall to earth. Both can be thrown miles away from a volcano by the force of an eruption.

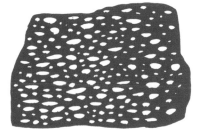

Pumice (PUHM-uhs) is a glassy rock that's very light because it has many holes. The holes are formed by popping gas bubbles. Pumice is so light that it can be blown high into the sky.

Pyroclastic rocks do not just get blown into the sky. Mud or ash may form *pyroclastic flows* during a violent eruption. Some volcanoes are famous for flows like these. Pyroclastic flows can move with great speed and cause much damage.

Volcanic blocks can weigh up to hundreds of pounds. Imagine the force needed to throw such a large object into the air!

After an eruption, chunks of pumice have been found floating in the ocean!

Right: Volcanic ash covers the ground in a thick layer. Below: Pyroclastic flows cover everything in their way.

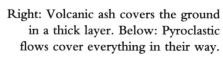

Faults

A normal fault has caused the rocks on the left side of the picture to drop down. If you look carefully, you can see the line of the fault in the rock layers.

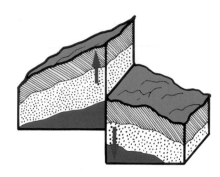

Some of the longest faults form where two plates come together. Faults can also be found within tectonic plates.

Imagine dropping a pebble into the water. The pebble causes a splash, then ripples fan out in all directions. The ripples are a sign that the pebble's splash created energy. The energy spreads through the water in waves.

Movements in the Earth's crust along faults also release energy. The energy spreads through the Earth in the form of an earthquake, just as the energy from dropping the pebble spreads through the water as ripples.

Scientists map faults through careful study of surface features and sudden changes in the rock. There are three types of faults: *normal faults, thrust faults,* and *strike-slip faults*. Let's look at each type.

Normal faults show up-and-down movements along the fault. The fault forms when the crust stretches until it breaks. Crust moves up on one side and down on the other side of the fault. As a result, one side of the fault is higher than the other. The steep edge of the higher side is called a *scarp*.

Sometimes two normal faults form a *rift valley*. Rift valleys are closed in by normal faults facing opposite directions. We see these at ocean ridges and within the continents.

Right: This cliff is a scarp at the edge of the East African Rift Valley, an ancient rift valley on the African continent. Below: In this photo, you can see how the Earth's surface drops down on one side of a normal fault when the crust is stretched.

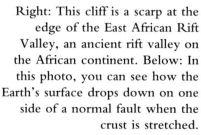

Thrust faults show up-and-down movement as normal faults do. But thrust faults form in a different way. They appear when the crust cracks from being squashed together under pressure, not from being stretched.

If rocks cannot fold under pressure, they will crack. Rocks on one side of the crack will be thrust, or pushed, over those on  the other side. This may sound familiar—remember how tectonic plates bump into each other at subduction zones? One plate is thrust over another. Subduction zones are simply large thrust faults!

Strike-slip faults are different from normal and thrust faults. There is no up-and-down movement of the sides of strike-slip faults. Instead, the fault's sides move sideways past one another. Strike-slip faults form transform plate boundaries. The San Andreas Fault is a good example. Strike-slip faults can also occur cutting across ocean ridges.

Some earthquakes happen in the middle of tectonic plates instead of at their edges. These earthquakes may mark hot spots deep in the mantle. Or, they could be caused by an ancient plate trying to crack apart.

Left: The city of Los Angeles is close to the San Andreas Fault, a strike-slip fault. Below: When rocks are pushed together, they break, just like this road. This is how thrust faults are formed.

A fault may be *active* or *inactive*. A fault is called active if it produces earthquakes. Inactive faults do not show any movement.

This strike-slip fault cuts right across a field. You can see how the sides of the fault have moved over time.

Measuring Earthquakes

The greater the intensity of an earthquake, the more it affects people's lives and their environment.

People in tall buildings will probably be the first to feel an earthquake's shaking.

Only sensitive instruments pick up earthquake waves that have an intensity of 1.

An earthquake with an intensity of 6 or 7 can shake the bricks off the outside of a building.

How strong is an earthquake? That's a question scientists are always interested in answering. The strength of an earthquake is called its *intensity.*

Scientists use the modified Mercalli scale to describe the intensity of an earthquake. The higher the number, the stronger the earthquake. On the modified Mercalli scale, "1" stands for the weakest earthquake and "12" stands for the strongest.

Let's take a closer look at what type of earthquake each number stands for.

1. This is the weakest measurable earthquake.

2. The earthquake is felt by a few people, mostly in the upper parts of buildings. Anything hanging will start to swing.

3. The earthquake is felt indoors and in parked cars, which may rock slightly.

4. The earthquake is felt by many people indoors, and by some outdoors. People may hear doors and windows rattle.

5. The earthquake is felt by most people. Dishes and windows may break. Objects may fall over.

6. The earthquake is felt by everyone. Heavy furniture may shift around. Plaster ceilings often fall.

108

7. Many ordinary buildings are damaged or destroyed.

8. The earthquake destroys ordinary buildings. Only well-made buildings escape damage.

9. The earthquake damages even sturdy buildings. Some will collapse.

10. The earthquake smashes most buildings. The ground cracks badly.

11. The earthquake leaves few buildings standing. Railroad tracks are bent and large cracks appear in the ground.

12. This is the strongest earthquake possible. It causes almost complete destruction.

The intensity of an earthquake and the amount of damage it causes depend on three things: the amount of energy released, the distance of a town from the epicenter, and the type of rock involved.

Scientists who study earthquakes also try to answer questions about their size, apart from the damage they cause. This earthquake measurement is called *magnitude* (MAG-nuh-TOOD).

The *Richter scale* is used to describe magnitude. A "0" on the Richter scale means that no earthquake waves are being measured. There is no maximum number on the scale.

Complete destruction like this is caused by earthquakes with intensities of 10 or more.

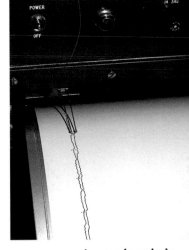

The greatest magnitude ever measured for an earthquake is 8.8. This magnitude seems to be about the highest possible.

An earthquake's magnitude depends on the size of the earthquake waves as measured by a seismometer.

Even when an earthquake does not cause total destruction, the damage can make it difficult for people to lead their daily lives.

Tsunamis

In the open ocean, people would not feel a tsunami passing beneath them. When the same wave hits the shore, it could be 90 feet high!

People living on the Pacific coast and around the Mediterranean Sea must watch constantly for tsunamis caused by distant earthquakes.

Sometimes, a large fault moves under the ocean floor. The movement causes an unusual water wave called a tsunami. Tsunamis cross the ocean at very high speeds. They sometimes rush along at hundreds of miles per hour. The most dangerous tsunamis are caused by large fault movements at subduction zones.

Tsunamis travel fast enough to cross whole oceans in a few hours! Tsunami waves are not very high in the open ocean, though. They only measure a few inches high or so.

As tsunamis approach land, the waves pack closer together. They rise even higher—even up to ninety feet! That's as tall as a nine-story building! When these waves hit the shore they can cause terrible damage.

One set of tsunamis hit Hawaii on April 1, 1946. These tsunami waves could hardly be seen at sea. They did not even affect ships in their path. Yet their speed was about five hundred miles an hour!

The 20-foot-high tsunamis reached the Hawaiian Islands in less than five hours. The waves arrived about twelve minutes apart. They swept over the land, destroying trees, houses, and crops in their path.

This ship was carried far from the place where it was anchored by the power of a tsunami.

110

Famous Earthquakes

Some of the best-known earthquakes of this century have happened in California. One of the most famous earthquakes occurred in 1906 in San Francisco. At that time, San Francisco was the state's biggest city.

What caused this earthquake? As you might have guessed, it was a sharp movement along the San Andreas Fault. The fault's sides moved as much as 18 feet in some places.

You may remember hearing about another earthquake that shook San Francisco in 1989. By this time, San Francisco was a far bigger city than it was in 1906. The nearby Bay Area was covered with houses, factories, freeways, and bridges.

Rush hour was just beginning at about 5 P.M. on October 17, 1989. Game Three of the World Series was about to begin in San Francisco's stadium. A few minutes after five o'clock, a sharp earthquake hit the Bay Area.

This was not as big an earthquake as in 1906. Still, it was a disaster for many people in San Francisco and nearby towns. Scientists say that California could be hit by another earthquake as strong as the 1906 earthquake, and that it could happen someday soon! The San Andreas Fault is a very active plate boundary carefully watched by scientists.

On October 17, 1989, one of the largest earthquakes since 1906 occurred in San Francisco.

Right: In 1906, San Francisco was almost completely destroyed by the earthquake. Below: The earthquake of 1989 did less damage, but the collapse of an important freeway caused many problems.

Predicting Earthquakes

Predicting earthquakes can't prevent damage to property. But, if people can be warned in time, a correct prediction could save thousands of lives.

Seismologists have tried different ways in the last 30 years to make useful predictions.

The San Andreas Fault is one of the most carefully watched faults in the world. Because so many people live nearby, it is important to try to predict when it will cause an earthquake.

Predicting earthquakes is harder than predicting volcanic eruptions. Earthquakes have been predicted by using many different methods. But no one method seems to work every time.

The most promising idea for predicting earthquakes has been *elastic rebound*. After an earthquake, the pressure starts building up again along a fault. Scientists try to measure this pressure and how fast it is building. They calculate how much pressure it takes to cause a major earthquake. They use this information to predict when the next major earthquake should happen.

Another sign of earthquake activity is the leaking of radon gas. Radon is a radioactive gas contained in the rocks in the crust of the Earth. Scientists are working on ways to use radon as a signal for predicting upcoming earthquakes.

One large earthquake, in northern China on February 4, 1975, was correctly predicted. Years before, the Chinese government had started a special program. People who lived near big faults were asked to watch for warning signs of earthquakes. For example, people watched for changes in the water level in wells. They also kept and eye on their farm animals. Many people think animals feel unusual ground movements before humans.

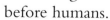

112

Predicting Eruptions

Volcanologists have two important goals. The first is to predict, or know ahead of time, the place and time of a future eruption. The second goal is to learn how explosive a volcano is. If scientists know a volcano's history, they have a much better chance of meeting their goals when studying that volcano. Still, the job of a volcanologist is not easy!

Mount Hood is considered dormant because it has not erupted for centuries. Still, it could suddenly begin to erupt, as Mount St. Helens did.

Volcanic eruptions seem to follow three main patterns. The first is random. This means the volcano seems to erupt without any pattern at all. This kind of eruption is the hardest to predict.

The second pattern is more regular. As time goes on, the volcano is more likely to erupt. In other words, once it starts erupting there is a strong chance it will continue with further eruptions.

Volcanoes that follow the third pattern erupt at regular periods. The period of time between eruptions may get longer as years go by. Once a team of volcanologists has decided which eruption pattern a volcano fits, they can try to figure out when the next eruption might start.

Right: Scientists do not yet know the pattern of Mount St. Helens' eruptions. The 1980 eruption was the first in centuries. Below: Mount Ngauruhoe, in New Zealand, erupts in a fairly regular pattern.

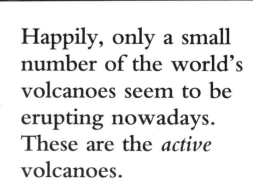

Happily, only a small number of the world's volcanoes seem to be erupting nowadays. These are the *active* volcanoes.

Mineral Properties

We use special words to describe minerals. These words, called properties, tell about the way minerals look and the way they stick together.

If iron gets into beryl, it will be yellow or blue. A bit of manganese makes it pink. Chromium turns beryl green. These colored crystals are pretty and beryl is often cut into gemstones.

Another optical property is fluorescence. Some minerals glow when they are put under black lights or ultraviolet lamps. Ultraviolet light also occurs naturally in sunlight. Mineral fluorescence is beautiful and ghostlike.

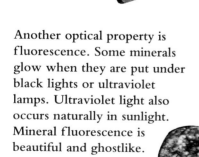

Optical Properties

Optical properties tell us what happens to light going through a mineral. One optical property is color. Minerals have some of the strongest and richest colors you will ever see. Vermeer, a famous painter, used a special blue paint that is named after him (Vermeer blue). His secret ingredient was lazurite. The color of some minerals is caused by the atoms that make them. Copper minerals are mostly blue and green. Manganese minerals are usually pink.

Some minerals have no color at all. Sometimes nearby atoms get inside the growing crystal. This can change colorless minerals into different colors. The atoms that do not belong are called impurities.

Luster is the optical property that explains the way a mineral reflects light. All minerals are either metallic (they look like metals) or non-metallic (they don't).

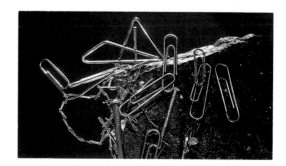

Bulk Properties

The most important bulk property is density. Density is how much a mineral weighs compared to water. Another bulk property is magnetism. Lodestone attracts small bits of iron, such as paper clips.

114

Mechanical Properties

The mechanical properties of crystals are caused by atoms sticking together in different ways. There are minerals that have different properties even though they are made of the same atoms.

Hardness is a very important mechanical property. The hardness of a mineral is determined by how easily it can be scratched if rubbed against another mineral.

A long time ago, a scientist named Friedrich Mohs put minerals in the order of which one would scratch the others. Mohs created a number scale, called the Mohs Hardness Scale, using ten common minerals. Number 10 is the hardest, and one is the softest.

On the Mohs Scale your fingernail is about a two and a copper penny is a three.

THE MOHS HARDNESS SCALE

1. Talc	6. Feldspar
2. Gypsum	7. Quartz
3. Calcite	8. Topaz
4. Fluorite	9. Corundum
5. Apatite	10. Diamond

Cleavage is the mechanical property of minerals that describes how it breaks. If a mineral breaks unevenly, the break is called fracture. But if a mineral breaks only in certain directions, it has cleavage.

Mineral properties happen because minerals are built of rows of atoms.

A good example of cleavage is the mineral mica. This mineral has a perfect cleavage. Mica can be split into paper-thin layers with a razor blade. The mineral above shows fracture.

115

How Crystals Grow

Crystals are made of layers of neatly stacked atoms. A crystal starts with a tiny "seed." The crystal gets bigger and bigger as the right atoms are added to the seed.

These crystals were grown in a solution.

Atoms must be able to move to just the right place in order to fit into a crystal. Atoms floating around in a liquid or a gas can move. They move over the surface of a growing crystal until they find the right place to stick. Once an atom is in place, it can vibrate a bit, but it can't move.

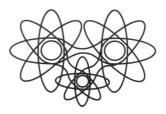

Mineral crystals sometimes grow in gases, like the ones found coming out of volcanoes. Most crystals grow in liquids. The liquid can be a solution, which is hot water that has atoms floating in it. The liquid can also be a melt, like the melted rock magma that is found deep within the Earth.

Minerals from a Melt

The inside of the Earth is very hot. Most rocks stay melted until they get near the surface. When melted rock (magma) cools, the atoms start to form crystals. A melted rock usually has many different kinds of atoms in it. These atoms can form many different kinds of crystals.

Magma reaching the surface and flowing out of a volcano is called lava, which forms rocks.

Minerals that grow in melted rock almost never become perfect crystals, because the crystals bump into each other. When the rock cools, different kinds of crystals are all jumbled together. This mixture is usually hard to see with just your eye.

Minerals Formed in Water

If magma gets close enough to the Earth's surface it may find a crack in the rock. The water inside the magma can then fill the crack. This water is very hot and can contain an amazing number of different kinds of atoms. As the water cools (it can take thousands of years), the atoms start to form mineral crystals. Water is much thinner than melted rock, so the atoms can move around easily. Also, the crack in the rock is usually big enough so that the crystals don't bump each other.

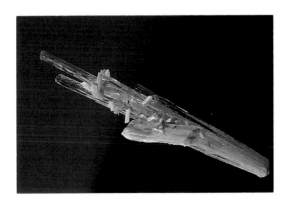

Mineral crystals that form this way are some of the most beautiful natural objects. These are the crystals that people travel miles to see in museums. Sometimes they look like flowers. The nicest of these crystals are sometimes clear enough for light to go through. These crystals may be cut as gemstones.

You can see the small crystals in a rock with a special kind of microscope. To do this you have to slice off a very thin piece of rock. Under the microscope you can see all the different crystals in the rock and how they grow together.

Sometimes crystals look like a bouquet of flowers.

117

Mineral Shapes

Atoms in crystals make special patterns. Each different mineral is made of different kinds of atoms.

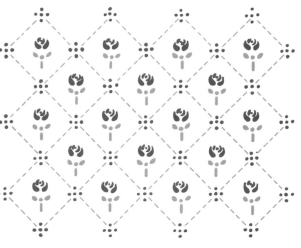

A good example of symmetry on a flat surface is wallpaper. Most wallpapers have repeating shapes that you see over and over as you look in different places.

The combination of a special pattern and special mixture of atoms is what makes each mineral different from every other mineral. Scientists have described more than 3,700 different minerals. The list grows every year as scientists find new ones.

The patterns in crystals are simple groups of shapes. These shapes are described by the way they look if you turn them around and around in different directions. The way a shape looks when you turn it all around is called symmetry.

A crystal doesn't have pictures on it, but it does have flat areas called crystal faces. Symmetry in a crystal means that if you turn the crystal around and around you see faces with the same shape over again. The symmetry in the crystal is described by the number of times the same face appears.

A cube (the shape of your first toy: the alphabet block!) has four-fold symmetry. All the faces on the cube are squares. If you hold the cube between your fingers and turn it completely around one time you see a square four times. Other shapes may have faces that appear twice (two-fold symmetry) or even six times (six-fold symmetry).

Along with being different colors, beryl often forms different crystal shapes.

118

Mineral shapes can be very complicated. Some crystals have more than 100 different faces! People who studied minerals in the last century spent most of their time describing crystals and drawing pictures of them.

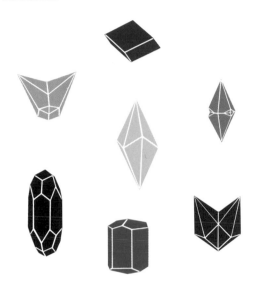

How Big Do Minerals Grow?

A mineral crystal will grow as long as there is space around it and atoms to attach to it. The crystals that grow in hot water inside cracks can be very large. You can see crystals in museums that are as tall as a person.

Crystals of the mineral spodumene from the Etta Mine in South Dakota were nearly 40 feet long. Giant crystals of quartz from Brazil weighed more than 10 tons (about the same as six cars). A crystal of feldspar discovered in Russia was reported to be as big as two railroad boxcars. But perhaps the largest of all is a crystal of beryl found in Madagascar in 1976. It was 59 feet long, almost 12 feet across, and weighed 187 tons!

Perhaps the most fascinating thing about minerals is that a single mineral can form a hundred different-shaped crystals! Calcite forms all the shapes on the left. On the right and below, topaz also forms many shapes.

Giant crystals of gypsum were found in Mexico. The crystals are so large that the place they came from is known as the Cave of Swords.

These large crystals are from a cave in Mexico.

Igneous Rocks

Igneous rocks are created when magma (melted rock within the earth) cools.

If lava cools inside the Earth, the igneous rock is called intrusive. If lava cools on the Earth's surface, the rock that forms is called extrusive. Extrusive rocks are the result of volcanic eruptions—when magma spills out of cracks or explodes into the air! Magma that reaches the surface in this way is called lava.

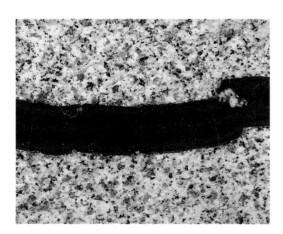

A dike is an intrusive formation that cuts across rock layers. Dikes are very easy to see because they are usually a different color from the rocks they cut across.

Intrusive Rocks

Intrusive rocks form large masses within the Earth. The largest of these is called a batholith, and some batholiths are as large as 100,000 square miles. A batholith usually increases in size going downward. The melted rock at the top of a batholith might push up to form a volcano.

A laccolith is an intrusive rock formation that forces its way between layers of rock and usually pushes them up into a dome shape. Sometimes the bottom and top of the laccolith are flat. This kind is known as a sill.

The Grand Tetons are made of batholithic rock.

An igneous rock called a pegmatite has a coarse texture, which means the crystals in the rock are large. Pegmatites usually form underground but close to the Earth's surface. Often they fill up large cracks so crystals may reach a very large size, sometimes many feet long. Pegmatites are usually made of three minerals: quartz, mica, and one of the members of the feldspar group.

Granite is made of the same minerals as pegmatite, but the crystals in the rock are smaller. Granites are the main rock of batholiths, and are found all over the world. There are many different kinds of granite, depending on what minerals are present along with quartz and feldspar. Syenite is a rock that is like granite, but has no quartz and the crystals in it are smaller.

There are also dark-colored intrusive rocks that usually form dikes and sills. Some of these rocks are called gabbro, diorite, monzonite, norite, and diabase. Finally, there is a group of intrusive rocks that are very dark colored and are made up mostly of the minerals olivine and pyroxene. This group includes peridotite, dunite, and kimberlite.

Pegmatites are also special rocks because they may contain rare minerals— sometimes even gem minerals.

Peridotite is made mostly of the minerals olivine and pyroxene.

Kimberlite is rare but important. It is the rock in which diamonds are found!

The Rock Cycle

Have you ever been to an ocean beach? Perhaps you have tried swimming in the surf and been knocked down by a big wave. Then you know about the power of water.

Rocks on Earth's surface are damaged by wind, rain, ice, and tiny animals and plants. Some of the gases in the air make an acid when they mix with rainwater. This acid can, over a long time, dissolve some kinds of rocks. Tiny plants called lichens also make acids that slowly wear away the rocks on which they live.

One interesting thing that results from the acid in falling rainwater is that some underground cracks in rocks are widened. The cracks become tunnels, and finally caverns.

Moving water can smash rocks hard enough to break them. After many years, the rocks are broken into sand. Look at beach sand with a magnifying glass. You will discover that it is a mixture of tiny bits of many different minerals. The name for the breaking up and wearing away of rocks at the Earth's surface is weathering.

At one time, all the rocks on the Earth's surface were igneous. The world was covered with volcanoes, and there were no oceans. But magma has water dissolved in it. After millions of years, the erupting volcanoes put enough water into the air to form clouds, and finally rain. Millions of years later enough rain had fallen to start making oceans.

Sometimes caves dry out. Water can drip from the ceiling and evaporate. This water has minerals in it, usually calcite. When the water disappears, it leaves interesting shapes. Long needles of rock may hang down from the ceiling—these are called stalactites. Needles that grow up from the floor are called stalagmites.

Without volcanic eruptions, Earth might not have its oceans.

Erosion is the name for all the ways that Earth materials are moved around on the surface by wind and water.

The oceans and the rain started to wear away the igneous rocks over the Earth's surface. Rain on the land turned into streams, and the streams into rivers. Moving water picked up the rock powder and dug into the land, carving holes and channels. In some places, the water filled up valleys and made lakes.

Every storm carried more rock pieces, large and small, into the waters. The layers got thicker and thicker. They got so thick that their weight squeezed all the water out of the sediments at the bottom of the pile. These sediments were pressed together so tightly that they became rocks. Rocks made in this way are called sedimentary rocks.

Movements of the Earth pushed some of these sedimentary rocks up to the Earth's surface. Water and wind treated these new rocks in the same way as the igneous rocks. The sedimentary rocks were torn apart and pushed into the streams, rivers, and oceans to make new sediments. Earth movements also pushed and squeezed both igneous and sedimentary rocks. The squeezing was so strong that the rocks were folded and bent. Sometimes this happened deep underground where it is very hot. Then the rocks were squeezed, folded, and also partly melted. Sometimes the minerals in the rocks were destroyed and new minerals were created.

The bits of rock, called sediments, carried by streams into lakes and oceans started to build up into thick layers.

Rocks formed by pressing, squeezing, and folding of other rocks are called metamorphic rocks.

Sedimentary Rocks

Most of the rocks we see at the Earth's surface are sedimentary.

What makes sedimentary rocks different from other rocks is that they are usually layered.

Mechanical Sedimentary Rocks

Mechanical sedimentary rocks are made by a lake, streambed, or ocean filling up with pieces of rocks that have been worn away by weathering.

Mechanical sedimentary rocks are usually cemented together. Nature's cement is the small amount of minerals dissolved in water. Imagine a thick pile of sand, pebbles, and clay buried deep underground. Water trickles through this pile and leaves tiny bits of minerals in the spaces between the sediments.

Another way of making a sedimentary rock is by squeezing. Clay pieces are small and flat. When these are piled in layers and squeezed, the water is squeezed out. The clay sheets stick together and form rock.

Rocks made of mineral bits that have been moved by water and settled into layers are called clastic rocks. Conglomerate is a cemented clastic rock made of large, rounded pieces.

The cement in a sandstone is often mixed with minerals that contain iron. These minerals are usually orange, red, yellow, or brown in color. The "painted deserts" in the western United States owe their bright colors to iron minerals.

Rocks made of clay are called shale and mudstone. The sediments in them are too small to see with a magnifying glass.

When smaller, sand-size grains are cemented together, the rock is called sandstone.

Arkose is an orangy-brown sandstone made of quartz and feldspar. Graywacke is a gray sandstone made of rock bits and clay.

Chemical Sedimentary Rocks

The most common minerals formed in sea water are calcite and dolomite. A rock made only of calcite is limestone.

The most common minerals formed in sea water are calcite and dolomite.

Some animals, such as clams, snails, and coral polyps, in the sea make shells out of minerals. These animals take carbon and oxygen out of sea water and make carbonate minerals in their bodies. Coquina is a limestone made of shells.

Coal is a sedimentary rock made of the remains of plants that lived in swamps millions of years ago. The plants died, fell into the swamp water, and were buried. The weight of the sediments pressed the ones at the bottom so tightly that they hardened into coal.

Evaporites are sedimentary rocks formed when surface water evaporates and minerals are left behind. The most important evaporite rocks are made of the minerals halite and gypsum.

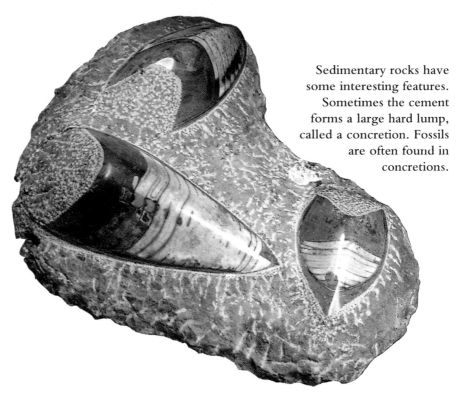

Sedimentary rocks have some interesting features. Sometimes the cement forms a large hard lump, called a concretion. Fossils are often found in concretions.

Sedimentary Features

Rounded lumps of mineral that are found inside other rocks are called nodules. Some nodules are made of very small crystals of quartz. The quartz can be stained by impurities. A nodule that forms with bands of color is agate. In jasper, the colors may form pictures.

Another sedimentary feature is bedding. You can see the different colors of rock and different grain sizes in those layers. This is what makes the Grand Canyon so amazing!

Metamorphic Rocks

At the contact, a whole group of new minerals may be created. Minerals already present in both the igneous rock and the limestone are broken apart and reassembled into new minerals. This new rock is called a skarn.

Metamorphism is like baking a cake. If you put flour, eggs, milk, and sugar into a bowl and stir, you have batter. But if you put this into a pan and bake it, you have cake.

Metamorphism means change of form. Metamorphic rocks are created by heat and pressure within the Earth. Older rocks may be melted and squeezed and take on new forms.

Metamorphic rocks have their own special appearance, or texture, as a result of squeezing. The most obvious one is layering, but not the same kind as we find in sediments. Metamorphic layering happens when the mineral crystals are squeezed until they are flattened. Sometimes the entire rock is folded and bent. Long, skinny mineral crystals may line up because of pressure.

Some metamorphic rocks are banded. The bands are caused by the minerals in the rock forming layers. Some metamorphic rocks also develop cleavage. This is not the same as the perfect cleavage in a mineral. Cleavage in a rock is a splitting in layers caused by the lining-up of flattened mineral crystals.

Regional metamorphism is a process that affects a large area, sometimes hundreds or thousands of square miles. Contact metamorphism happens when a hot igneous rock is forced into sedimentary rocks, such as limestone. The heat of the igneous rock causes many changes in the limestone. Most of these changes take place right where the igneous rock is touching the limestone (called the contact). The changes get less obvious farther inside the limestone.

Contact metamorphism is the effect of heat, pressure, and chemical changes in a small area.

We can list metamorphic rocks by describing the rocks they originally were. For example, if a shale is metamorphosed, it turns into the rock called slate.

Stronger metamorphism will turn the shale into a rock called phyllite. Phyllite has larger crystals than slate. These give the rock a shiny appearance.

Even stronger metamorphism will turn shales and other rocks into schist. Schist breaks with a kind of wavy surface. The rock looks twisted and bent because of the heat and pressure it has suffered. Different kinds of schist get their names from the kinds of minerals they contain.

Metamorphosed limestone is marble. Marble usually has a lovely pattern of dark swirls on a light gray or pink background. The dark pattern is made of minerals formed by heat and pressure from clays and other small mineral grains in the limestone. Marble is used all over the world for buildings, carvings, even furniture.

Igneous rocks can be metamorphosed also. Granite turns into a rock called gneiss (this word is pronounced "nice"). The minerals in a gneiss are the same as in granite, but the pressure of metamorphism has pushed them into layers.

This ruin marble is from Florence, Italy.

There are different kinds of gneiss. Like schist, gneiss is named by the minerals it contains.

127

Elements

About 20 elements are found in pure form as minerals— these are called native elements. They are divided into the metals and the nonmetals.

Sulfur is yellow and brittle, and it is one of the nonmetals. Large sulfur crystals are found in Sicily, near Italy. Sulfur also comes out of volcanoes in the form of bad-smelling gases.

Silver nuggets almost always have some copper mixed into them. Silver also forms other interesting shapes. Some look like old trees.

Pure carbon is found in nature as two minerals: graphite and diamond. Graphite is the "lead" in pencils, but has many other uses. Diamond is a very valuable gemstone. Carbon is a nonmetal.

Copper is a much more common metal than silver or gold. There are many copper minerals.

Gold nuggets may be very large and pure. Gold almost never forms compounds, but seems always to be found as native metal. Gold is also one of the heaviest metals.

Sulfides

Cinnabar is the only important ore of the element mercury. Mercury is an unusual metal. It is very heavy, and is a liquid at room temperature. Cinnabar crystals are bright red. The best ones come from a mine in China.

Sulfides are compounds that have atoms of sulfur and atoms of a metal. The sulfides are important because they provide important metals. Minerals that are mined for their metals are called ores.

Galena is the most important ore of the metal lead. Lead has been used for centuries to make tubing, fishing sinkers, and bullets. It is a heavy metal, heavier than silver. Galena forms bright, silvery crystals that are usually shaped like cubes. These crystals are found in many places in the world.

Sphalerite is the main ore of the element zinc, which is another useful metal. Zinc is used in dry-cell batteries, paint, and in the chemical industry. Sphalerite is usually orange, red, brown, yellow, or green. Crystals are common throughout the world.

Marcasite is iron sulfide. It is brassy yellow and very common in all parts of the world. Iron sulfide also forms crystals where the iron and sulfur atoms are arranged differently than in marcasite. This other arrangement produces the mineral called pyrite. Pyrite is the most common sulfide mineral on Earth and is found just about everywhere. Pyrite has many habits. Pyrite is brassy yellow and looks like gold. Pieces in streams have fooled miners, so it was nicknamed "fool's gold."

Sulfosalts/Halides

Halite is an evaporite mineral. It is found in thick layers that form when sea water evaporates. Sometimes it makes perfect cube-shaped crystals. These can be very large. Halite must be purified to make the table salt that we eat. But ground-up halite is put on roads to melt snow.

Pyrargyrite, like proustite, is a sulfide of arsenic and silver. It is also red but is darker than proustite. The crystals are not as clear.

Sulfosalts are minerals that have sulfur, a metal (either silver, copper, or lead), and a semimetal. The semimetals are bismuth, antimony, and arsenic.

Proustite is the sulfosalt best known to collectors. It is also one of the prettiest of all minerals. Proustite is bright red. It is sometimes called "ruby silver." Crystals are bright, shiny, and sometimes clear.

Fluorite is a compound of the metal calcium and the halogen gas fluorine. Fluorite makes cube-shaped crystals. These are found in many parts of the world, and can be many different colors. Fluorite is very beautiful, and mineral collectors always want it in their collections.

Oxides

Spinel is an oxide of magnesium and aluminum. It forms perfect crystals that can be many colors. Spinel is very hard and is often cut and polished as a gem. Other minerals that are similar to spinel are magnetite (an oxide of iron), and chromite (the oxide of the element chromium).

Bauxite is the only ore of the metal aluminum. Actually, bauxite should be called a rock because it is a mixture of several aluminum hydroxides.

The oxides are very important minerals. Oxygen is a part of the air we breathe.

Hematite is iron oxide. The mineral is dark red, but always looks black unless it is broken into very small pieces. Hematite is found in many different forms. Reniform hematite is a mass of kidney-shaped round balls. Specular hematite is made of tiny black flakes, like mica schist. Hematite is the mineral that makes rocks reddish. It is one of the most common minerals on Earth.

Rutile is the oxide of the metal titanium. Titanium, like molybdenum, is a metal used in making special kinds of very hard steel. Rutile is usually red, but the color is very dark and big crystals may look black. Sometimes rutile forms needles. These needles may be trapped inside other minerals. Rutile in quartz is usually a golden yellow color.

Carbonates

The carbonates are a group of beautiful and very common minerals. They all contain metal atoms and groups of three oxygen atoms that make a tiny triangle around an atom of carbon.

Aragonite, like calcite, is made of calcium carbonate. Aragonite crystals are different from calcite crystals and are not rhomb shaped. Aragonite is made from sea water by oysters to cover the inside of their shells. This is called mother-of-pearl. Oysters also make aragonite to cover bits of sand that get inside their shells. The layers of aragonite build up around the sand and are known as pearls.

Rhodochrosite is manganese carbonate. It is always a rose-red or pink color and often forms beautiful crystals. This is one of the most popular minerals among collectors.

Azurite and malachite are two of the most beautiful and desired carbonate minerals. Both are copper carbonates and are found almost everywhere copper is mined. Azurite is a lovely dark blue color, and malachite is green. Both minerals can form in layers like sedimentary rocks, or in nodules. Sometimes they are mixed together. Azurite may form large and perfect crystals, but malachite almost never forms crystals.

Calcite is the most common carbonate. It makes up the rock limestone. It is also the mineral produced from sea water by thousands of different marine animals to make shells. Calcite is found in hundreds of crystal shapes, or habits. There are some collectors who collect only different habits of calcite crystals. Calcite is found in many different colors also.

Nitrates/Borates

Nitrates have a nitrogen atom surrounded by three oxygen atoms. The only two important minerals in this group are niter, the nitrate of the metal potassium, and soda niter, the nitrate of sodium. Both minerals are found in dry, desert areas, because both minerals dissolve easily in water!

Colemanite is a calcium borate that forms perfect, colorless crystals. California is the most important place to find them.

There are more than 100 borate minerals, but only a few are commonly found. Almost all are colorless (or white), soft, and delicate.

Borax forms clear, perfect crystals that quickly turn white as they dry. Borax has been used for hundreds of years as a medicine and for cleaning. Borax is sold in stores, along with soap powders, for washing clothes. Borax usually forms when salt lakes dry up. Kernite is similar to borax but does not form good crystals. It is found only in the Mohave Desert in California, where there are millions of tons of kernite.

Ulexite is an unusual borate. It forms masses of long needles all packed tightly together. These have a "satiny" look when seen from the side. But if you grind and polish the ends of a mass of these fibers, you discover something amaz-ing. The stone appears to be as clear as glass when you look down the length of the fibers! Polished pieces of ulexite are sometimes called "TV stone" because looking at a polished end is like looking at a TV screen.

Sulfates & Chromates

Barite is the most common sulfate mineral. It is a sulfate of the element barium. The name barite comes from the Greek word "barys," which means "heavy." Barite is so heavy that if you make a fine powder out of it and mix it with water, rock chips will float in the "mud." This special mud is used in drilling oil wells. The mud is pumped down the drill pipe to wash up pieces of rock at the bottom. Barite forms in a wide variety of crystal shapes and colors. Some crystals are very large.

Crocoite is the only chromate mineral that is important to collectors. It is the chromate of lead. This is a wonderful, bright red mineral. It is very rare, and good specimens come only from one place—Dundas, Tasmania.

Minerals in these groups are brightly colored and form lovely crystals that are prized by collectors.

Celestite and anglesite are the sulfates of strontium and lead. Celestite is almost always white or pale blue in color. The Malagsy Republic has a spot where perfect, sometimes clear celestite crystals are found in geodes. Anglesite is usually found together with other lead minerals, such as galena. It comes from many places in the world.

Gypsum is probably the most common sulfate. It is often found in caves, where it can form huge crystals. Ground-up gypsum is used to make the building material called plaster of Paris. Gypsum has a Mohs hardness of two, and can be scratched with your fingernail. The variety called selenite is clear. Another variety is called satin spar. Alabaster is solid, massive gypsum. Thick beds of gypsum are formed by evaporation of sea water.

Phosphates, Arsenates & Vanadates

Apatite is calcium phosphate. It is one of the apatite group of phosphates, which contain four minerals (apatite, pyromorphite, mimetite, vanadinite). It is the most common phosphate mineral, and it is found all over the world. Collectors can often find large crystals. The colors are usually green, yellow, or brown, but can be dark pink or dark blue. Apatite is used as a fertilizer.

Turquoise, a copper phosphate, is always blue or green and has been used as a gemstone for thousands of years.

These minerals are secondary. This means they formed when other minerals were broken apart or were altered.

Mimetite is similar to pyromorphite. Mimetite is a lead arsenate.

Vanadinite, lead vanadate, is one of the most popular of all minerals. It forms bright red groups of crystals, and they cover rock surfaces.

Erythrite, a bright purple mineral known best from Morocco, is an arsenate of the metal cobalt.

Tungstates & Molybdates

Wolframite is iron tungstate, and forms black, shiny, and very perfect crystals. Tungsten, like molybdenum, is a very important metal that is used to make steel harder.

Scheelite is calcium tungstate, a lovely yellow or colorless mineral that forms crystals up to several inches across.

The best known mineral in this group is one of the minerals that every collector wants to own: wulfenite.

Wulfenite is lead molybdate, and forms perfect crystals that look like square wafers. These come in several colors: yellow, brown, orange, and red. Wulfenite crystals are very pretty and can be large. Wulfenite is also a common mineral in lead mines. The most famous source is the Red Cloud Mine in Arizona.

Silicates

Single Tetrahedra

Topaz is a popular mineral with collectors. It is found as perfect crystals in locations all over the world. The biggest crystals can weigh 100 pounds and still have perfect shapes. Topaz can be colorless, yellow, blue, pink, or orange.

Olivine is a group of minerals that melt at a very high temperature. These minerals are among the first to form crystals when magma starts to cool deep within the Earth. The gemstone cut from olivine is called peridot.

All silicates are made of metal elements and a silicon tetrahedron. This is an atom of the element silicon surrounded by four oxygen atoms. The oxygen atoms are arranged in a tetrahedron.

Garnets are found in many rocks in all parts of the world. The garnet family includes a dozen minerals. Six of them are well known: pyrope, almandine, spessartine, uvarovite, grossular, and andradite. All the garnets form beautiful crystals. Most garnets are either red, orange, or brown. Some come in many different colors, including shades of yellow, green, purple, and red. Garnets are important gemstones.

Two Tetrahedra

Epidote is a common mineral, usually brown or green. The epidote group also includes other minerals. One of them, zoisite, is found in Africa as large, clear blue crystals. These can be turned into an even darker blue by heating them. Cut gemstones made from these crystals are called tanzanite.

Silicates

Silicates make up half of the Earth's crust. About one quarter of all known minerals are silicates.

Rings of Tetrahedra

Beryl is one of the best known of all minerals. It is found all over the world, usually in pegmatites. It can form huge crystals, some of them weighing many tons. These giants are opaque—you cannot see into them. Beryl does form completely clear crystals in all colors, and some of these can still be large. Beryl is often cut and polished as a gemstone, and each color has a different gem name. The most popular beryl colors are blue, green, pink, and yellow.

Chains of Tetrahedra

Spodumene is a silicate of the element lithium. It is a member of the pyroxene family. It can form giant crystals 40 feet long, but these are very rare and are opaque. Clear crystals up to three feet long have been found in Brazil and Afghanistan. The color can be pink, green, or yellow. Spodumene is sometimes cut and polished as a gemstone.

Tourmaline is another ring silicate that is found in pegmatites all over the world. Tourmaline comes in many colors—probably more than any other mineral. Some tourmaline crystals can be several feet long. Many of these have two or more colors—they change color along their length. Watermelon tourmaline is pink on the inside and green on the outside. Tourmaline is a very popular gemstone.

Hornblende is one of the most common members of the amphibole family. Crystals are dark green or black. Tremolite is a white amphibole. It forms long, thin crystals that look like hairs. These can grow together to make a solid mass—it looks a little like the matted hair of a wet dog!

Sheets of Tetrahedra

Talc, a very soft mineral, almost never forms crystals. Talc is familiar to everyone—parents use talcum powder on babies to keep them dry!

Corner-Linked Tetrahedra

Feldspar is the name of a large group of minerals that are present in almost all igneous rocks. The feldspars are divided into two groups based on chemistry. These are called potassium feldspars and plagioclase feldspars. The important potassium feldspars are called orthoclase and microcline. A pretty blue type of microcline is known as amazonite. The plagioclase

group includes albite, oligoclase, andesine, labradorite, bytownite, and anorthite.

Most of the Earth's crust is made of corner-linked tetrahedra minerals.

Biotite is a member of the mica group, which is a family of related minerals that all have perfect cleavage. Sheets that have been split off these minerals can be bent quite a bit without breaking.

Quartz is one of the most common minerals on Earth. Quartz is found in many kinds of rocks. When these rocks are weathered, the quartz grains may wind up as desert, river, or beach sand. Quartz crystals come in different colors and can be cut as gemstones.

Precious Metals

Copper, silver, and gold (below) often form interesting shapes.

Most of the known minerals are chemical compounds. They contain different kinds of atoms arranged in regular patterns. But some minerals are elements. The metals that are found by themselves arc called native metals, and there are only a few.

Copper is an important metal, but it is not expensive. Other native metals are gold, silver, and platinum. These are very valuable. For centuries, gold and silver have been thought of as treasure. These metals have been symbols of wealth since the beginning of history.

Gold and silver form natural crystals that are very beautiful. Gold crystals are usually found in "veins," thin layers of white quartz that have filled in cracks in certain rocks. Platinum seldom forms crystals. But all three metals are found as lumps called "nuggets." Some of these nuggets are very large. The "Welcome Stranger" gold nugget, found in Australia in 1869, weighed more than 150 pounds. An even bigger silver nugget was found in Mexico around 1820.

Gems

Gems are valuable. Some gems, like pearls and amber, are made by living things. Most gems are minerals, but not all minerals are gems! Gems are usually (but not always) hard, rare, and pretty. Not everyone agrees about what "pretty" looks like. So people often have different ideas about what minerals should be called gems.

Minerals, as we have seen, come in many colors. A single mineral, like tourmaline, may be found in dozens of different colors. Different colors of a single mineral are called varieties.

Corundum, an oxide mineral, is found in dozens of colors. Gemstones cut out of all colors of corundum, except red, are called sapphire. Red corundum has its own special name: ruby.

Beryl is also found in many colors. Dark green beryl is called emerald. Pink beryl is morganite. The blue or blue-green variety of beryl is called aquamarine. Colorless (pure) beryl is called goshenite. Yellow beryl is called heliodor or golden beryl.

Garnets are used as gems, especially almandine, spessartine, rhodolite, and grossular. The color varieties of grossular are some of the loveliest of all.

Gemstones are made by grinding minerals to a certain shape and then polishing them. Faceted stones are polished with small flat surfaces called facets. These facets make the gemstone sparkle.

Diamond is one of the most valuable gemstones. Colorless diamonds are very rare.

A natural crystal looks much different when it is polished and cut.

It is truly amazing that the Earth can produce such beautiful and interesting objects as mineral crystals!

141

Our Weather

The density of the air near the ground is one of the things that makes the weather change so much. Conditions high in the atmosphere also affect the weather.

Climbers sometimes feel out of breath on top of very high mountains because there is less oxygen there.

This computer-generated model (above) shows areas of high pressure. The atmosphere above a high pressure system is much denser than the atmosphere above a low pressure system. This drawing (right) shows typical wind patterns across the globe. Winds move mainly because of differences in air pressure and temperature.

Weather is what the air around us is like at a certain time. This might mean the weather at two o'clock today or the weather predicted for tomorrow morning. When we think of the weather, we usually think of things like hot and cold, cloudy and sunny, or rain and snow. The air around us has many other qualities, too. The pressure of the air and the amount of gases and dust particles it holds can tell a lot about what the weather will be like. What happens in the air high above the ground also affects conditions near the ground.

Air surrounds Earth like a thick blanket. We call this blanket the *atmosphere*. We all live most of our lives at the bottom of this blanket of air, and the weight of all the air rests on us. The air near Earth's surface gets pressed down by the air above it. This is a lot like what happens to a sponge when you hold it in your hand and squeeze it. The sponge gets *denser* or more solid when you squeeze it and less dense when you let go of it. You always have the same amount of sponge, but it's packed tightly and fills less space when you squeeze it.

In the same way, the air near the surface is squeezed by the weight of all the air above it, so it is quite dense. The air becomes less dense as you move farther and farther away from the ground. When you get very high in the atmosphere, there is very little air left.

Earth's atmosphere contains many different kinds of gases and dust particles. Most of the air within 50 miles of the ground is a gas called nitrogen. Less than a quarter of the air is oxygen. The air also has argon, carbon dioxide, and many other gases. The atmosphere also contains many kinds of dust particles that are important to weather patterns.

Weather is what the air is like at a certain time, and it changes from day to day. But how can we describe changes in the weather that occur over a whole year, over a decade, or over your lifetime? *Climate* is the term that describes the weather during a long period of time.

The air has some qualities that are not obvious, but they are very important to understanding weather.

Studying climate is similar to looking at the grade you receive in a class over a whole year. You might have trouble with one homework assignment or one test, and that will affect your grade. If you do well on your other work, though, you'll still get the same kind of grade you usually do. In the same way, your area might have one really hot summer or one very rainy spring. That doesn't mean that your climate has changed. Conditions in the years before and after the unusual seasons will be normal, and your climate over all that time will be the same.

Tiny particles such as salt enter the air when water evaporates from rivers, lakes, and oceans. Pollution from factories and cars also adds particles to the air. Water droplets form around these particles. The droplets then group together to make clouds. Without these tiny particles, our skies would have almost no clouds.

143

Studying the Weather

Satellites are important tools for studying weather systems.

We use many different measurements to describe the weather. Each measurement requires a piece of special equipment. *Temperature* tells us how hot or cold it is. We measure temperature with *thermometers. Humidity* is the amount of moisture in the air, and we measure it with *hygrometers. Anemometers* measure the speed and direction of wind near the ground. *Atmospheric pressure*—the weight of the air in a certain area—is usually measured by *barometers.*

We take measurements like these at thousands of locations around the world every hour at ground level. Weather balloons carry equipment that measures temperature, humidity, and wind at different heights in the atmosphere.

All this information goes to major weather centers across the world for processing and storing. The centers use complex computer programs to help predict the weather. These programs use equations to describe rules about the way air

In the United States, the National Weather Service collects information from weather stations (left) all around the country.

The satellite photos you see on your local news programs probably come from the National Meteorological Center in Camp Springs, Maryland.

moves. With such programs, meteorologists can make very accurate forecasts of weather for the next few days for almost any area of the country or the world.

Some scientists have studied what Earth's climate was like in the past. The atmosphere came from inside Earth billions of years ago. Violent volcanoes, cracks, and fissures in the planet's crust shot gases from deep underground. Gravity kept the gases from escaping, and they eventually surrounded Earth.

Scientists have also studied how the atmosphere has changed since it first appeared. They've looked at weather as it is today, at rocks and fossils, at changes in the continents and oceans, and at air bubbles trapped by ice thousands of years ago.

Predicting what the climate will be like in the future is a very difficult but very important task. Generally, scientists believe that global temperatures will rise by the turn of the century. Pollution, deforestation, and other things that people have done will be the main cause. No one really knows when or how much the temperatures will change. Climate changes will probably mean that we will have to make changes in where and how we live.

Scientists have learned that Earth had no permanent ice at the poles for most of its history. Conditions everywhere were too warm for ice and snow to stay on the ground year round like they do today.

When the atmosphere first formed, it was quite different from the atmosphere we see today.

Trees help keep the balance of gases in the atmosphere, and they affect the natural water cycle. By studying weather, we learn how our actions today could affect our world in the future.

145

How Weather Works

The seasons are a result of Earth's tilt and its path around the sun.

Every day we see the sun rise and set, and it sends its heat to Earth. Of course, the sun doesn't really travel across our sky. Actually, it's Earth that moves. Our planet spins on an imaginary line called the axis that runs through the North and South Poles. This spinning makes it seem to us like the sun is moving overhead each day.

Earth's axis does not point straight up and down. Instead it is tilted a bit. The axis always tilts in the same direction, but Earth also travels around the sun. This means that sometimes the North Pole is tilted toward the sun and the South Pole tilts away from the sun. Other times it's just the opposite: The South Pole is tilted toward the sun and the North Pole is tilted away from it.

All this has a big effect on Earth's weather. When a part of the planet leans toward the sun, it gets more sunlight than it does at other times of the year. The ground absorbs the heat from this and passes it on to the air.

If that were the whole story, then places near the Equator would always be warmer than places away from the Equator. Also, the temperature would warm steadily as summer came and then cool steadily as winter came. Weather isn't that sim-

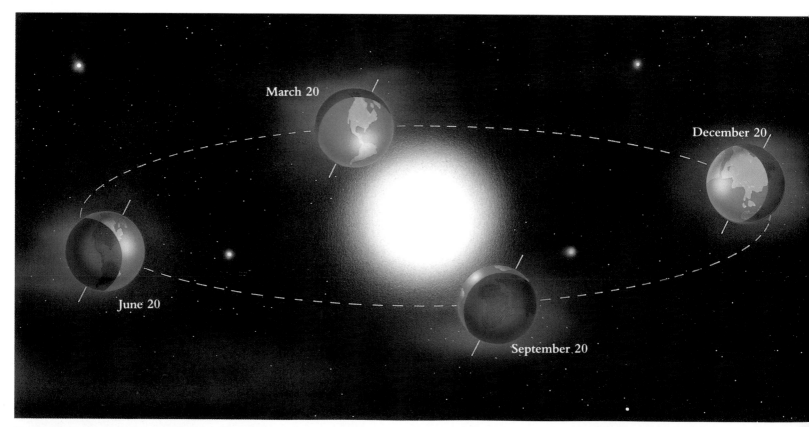

From about March 20 to September 20, the northern hemisphere leans toward the sun and has spring and summer. In the southern hemisphere, the seasons are reversed. The Equator gets direct sunlight year round, so its always warm there.

146

A cold front forms when a cold air mass pushes into a warm air mass and forces the warm air up. Both cold fronts and warm fronts often create stormy weather.

ple though, mainly for two reasons. Not all of Earth's surface gets warmed the same amount by the sun, and air doesn't stay in one place.

Several things can affect how much the sun warms a patch of ground. The number of clouds in the sky, how high up the ground is, the number of plants or the amount of cement on the ground, and other things can make a difference. The biggest difference is that some areas are land and others are water. Land areas warm up much faster than water areas.

When air stays over a cold place for a long time, it cools and forms a bubble or dome of cold air. We call this a *cold air mass*. When a warm dome of air forms over a warm area, we call it a *warm air mass*.

Earth's spin, differences in the air's temperature, and other things make air masses move, and that also affects weather. If a cold air mass moves over your area, the temperature will become cooler. If a warm air mass moves over where you live, the temperature will go up.

When a cold air mass and a warm air mass move close to each other, a wall called a front forms between them. When the cold air mass is advancing, we call the wall a *cold front*. When the warm air mass is advancing, we call the wall a *warm front*.

As you move away from the Equator and toward the poles, areas spend less of the year getting direct sunlight and average temperatures are lower. Temperatures also change as you go from the continents to the oceans. This satellite image shows that land areas tend to be warmer than water areas.

147

How Weather Works

Barometers can gauge the air pressure very precisely. They provide one of the most useful measurements for making weather forecasts.

Some people say that you can catch more fish when it is raining. If you like to go fishing, you might like low pressure systems better than high pressure systems.

Clouds like these often form along fronts because the air is rising. Large, bumpy clouds usually form when the air rises quickly. Wide, layered sheets of clouds cover the sky when the air rises slowly.

Air pressure has a lot to do with the way that fronts and air masses act. Put simply, air pressure is the amount of push you feel on your body from the weight of the air around you. If you dive into the water, your body feels like it's being squeezed a little. The squeezing is because of the water's pressure. Air presses against us the same way, but we are used to feeling the air's pressure so we don't notice it.

Warm and cold air masses usually have a lot of pressure, so we call them *high pressure systems*. In high pressure systems, the air is slowly moving downward from high in the atmosphere. Clouds usually form in air that is moving upward, so high pressure systems almost always have clear skies.

Fronts have less air pressure than the air masses that they separate. Once in a while, an area of much lower pressure, called a *low pressure system*, forms along a front. Low pressure systems are the centers of storms that can be hundreds of miles across. The air in low pressure systems is moving upward into the atmosphere, so there are usually clouds and rain or snow near them.

Measuring the air pressure can tell a lot about what kind of weather to expect. In general, clear weather usually occurs in high pressure systems and stormy weather usually occurs in low pressure systems.

Wind direction also affects what kind of weather is coming. Wind is simply what we call moving air. The most important thing that causes the air to start moving is pressure differences. Air tries to make the pressure equal everywhere by moving from high pressure systems toward low pressure systems.

The wind tries to move in a straight line from the high pressure system to the low pressure system. Instead, it curves away because Earth rotates underneath it. Imagine that you have a record turning on a record player and you have to draw a line from the center of the record to the edge. If you moved your hand straight from the edge to the center, the line would curve around the record. In the same way, Earth's spin causes the wind to curve.

If you looked at a high pressure system in the northern hemisphere from above, you'd see that the wind has a clockwise rotation. Around a low pressure system, you'd see the wind turning in the opposite direction that a clock's hands move. This wind has counterclockwise rotation. In the southern hemisphere, the wind directions are just the opposite. Wind in high pressure systems spins counterclockwise. Wind in low pressure systems has clockwise rotation.

Wind power is one way that people can harness weather's great energy.

Most of the time, Earth's spin turns the wind so much that the air simply circles around the high and low pressure systems.

The bigger the difference in pressure between the systems and the closer the systems are, the stronger the wind will be.

149

Water in the Atmosphere

The easiest way to understand what water molecules do in each state is to think about what you can do with water in each state. You can pass your hand easily through misty vapor, let water run through your fingers, or hold an ice cube.

The atmosphere has water in it, but water doesn't act like the other parts of the air at all. It's always changing and always moving. Water comes in three forms or *states*. When it is a gas, we call it *vapor*. When it is a liquid, we call it *liquid water* or just *water*. When it is a solid, we call it *ice*.

Like all things, water is made of tiny particles called *molecules*. The state that water is in depends on what these molecules are doing at the time.

The molecules in a piece of ice are very organized and closely attached to each other. They don't move around much, and it's easy for you to handle them.

In a liquid state, the molecules in water are not as well organized and only some of them are stuck to each other. The molecules are moving around more, and it's harder for you to handle them. Liquid water changes its shape easily and flows from one place to another. It will take the shape of whatever container it is in.

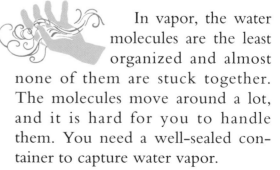
In vapor, the water molecules are the least organized and almost none of them are stuck together. The molecules move around a lot, and it is hard for you to handle them. You need a well-sealed container to capture water vapor.

The state that water is in depends mainly on temperature. When the temperature is below 32°F (Fahrenheit), water turns to ice. Water that is above 212°F turns to vapor. Between these temperatures, water takes the form of liquid. Other things can affect the state that water is in, too. For example, small amounts of water will turn to vapor even when its temperature is below 212°F. As a general rule, though, these temperatures are the changing points.

When the temperature of water goes up, the molecules have more energy, so they move around more and are less likely to stick together. As the temperature goes down, the molecules have less energy, they move around less, and they are more likely to stick together.

At any given time, nearly all Earth's water is in the liquid state. About 97 percent of it is in rivers, lakes, swamps, and oceans. Two percent of the water is ice frozen in snow, glaciers, and the ice caps at the North and South Poles. Only one percent is vapor, but this tiny amount is very important to the weather.

Water is always changing from one state to another. Ice from glaciers falls in the sea and turns into liquid water as it floats to warmer areas. Water from oceans and lakes evaporates in the heat of the sun and becomes vapor in the atmosphere. Vapor in the atmosphere cools into water and forms clouds, fog, rain, and snow.

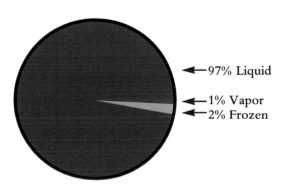

←— 97% Liquid

←— 1% Vapor
←— 2% Frozen

Temperature changes the state of water because it changes the way the molecules act. Temperature is a measure of heat, and heat is energy.

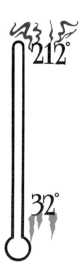

Water in the Atmosphere

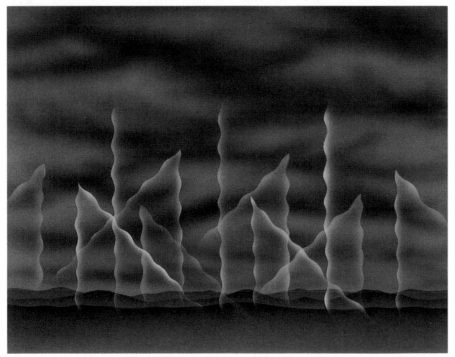

On clear nights (top), heat escapes from the ground easily. Clouds (above) can keep heat from escaping. On cloudy nights, it usually takes longer for the ground and the air above it to cool. Desert areas often get very cold at night because conditions there let heat escape easily. Deserts get a lot of heat during the day, but they are also very dry. No water means no clouds, and no clouds means all that heat escapes into space at night and leaves the area very cool.

Water vapor is always in the air, but the exact amount is always changing. The temperature of the air determines how much water vapor can be in the air. When it's warm, more vapor can stay in the air. When it's cold, there is less vapor. Think of the air as a bucket that changes size as it changes temperature, and think of water vapor as water in the bucket. When it's warm, the air is like a large bucket that can hold a lot of water. When its cold, the air is like a small bucket that can hold less water.

Relative humidity is the amount of vapor that *can be* in the air compared to the amount of vapor that *is* in the air. If the relative humidity is 50 percent, the air has half as much vapor as it can hold. If it's 100 percent, the air can't hold any more vapor. When the humidity is more than 100 percent, some vapor condenses into liquid water. Two things make this happen: Either more vapor enters the air, or the air cools down so it can hold less vapor.

Air near the ground gets colder if the ground beneath it gets colder. The most common way for the ground to cool is by radiating heat into space. During the day, the ground gathers heat from the sun. At night when the sun is gone, the heat escapes into space. First the ground loses its heat to space by radiation. Then the cold ground cools the air above it.

152

The other way for air to cool is by passing over ground that is already cold. This happens a lot in winter when winds in a warm air mass blow over an area that has snow on the ground. It also happens near large bodies of water because the water is usually colder than the nearby ground.

All of the threads in a spider's web can be seen when there is dew on it, as if nature decorated it with shining silvery beads.

If the air near the ground cools enough, some of the water vapor in the air will condense into liquid water. Tiny droplets of water form on almost anything on the ground. This is called *dew,* and it is the reason

grass is often wet in the morning even though it hasn't rained.

If the temperature is below 32°F, dew will freeze into tiny ice crystals called *frost.* A frost in the fall is often the first sign that winter is coming.

Sometimes, winds in an area mix up the air so that even the air hundreds of feet up is cooled by the ground. Vapor condenses around tiny particles in the air and forms a thick, swirling mist called *fog.* Sometimes a fog can blanket an area for many days.

Frost on a house's windows can add a pretty border to the view. Frost can also cover a car's windshield or cause damage to plants and farm crops.

Thick, heavy fogs often form over lakes and bays when the water is much cooler than the nearby land.

Clouds in the Sky

Temperatures are typically colder at higher elevations. When warm, moist air is forced up over a mountain range, water condenses and forms clouds. Mountains sometimes have clouds and rain or snow, even when it is sunny just a few miles away.

If you took one step for every droplet in a thunderstorm cloud, you'd be able to walk to the sun and back.

Clouds form in much the same way that dew and fog form. Air cools down and can't hold as much water vapor. The water vapor then condenses into tiny droplets of liquid water.

You can get some idea of how clouds form by watching them. Many clouds, such as the thunderstorm cloud, look like they are made of bubbles, each pushing to get out of the cloud.

Most clouds form in bubbles that are rising in the air. When cloud bubbles are able to rise easily, like a beach ball rising to the top of a swimming pool, the air is *unstable*. The air is *stable* when bubbles of air can't rise easily, more like rocks that would sit on the bottom of a swimming pool.

Air moves up through the atmosphere for different reasons. It will rise if it runs into a large obstacle on the ground such as a mountain. When the air hits the mountain, it has to go up.

The atmosphere has its own obstacles that can make the air rise. The atmosphere has large areas of warm or cold air called air masses. The borders between these air masses are called fronts. As the air masses move, air is forced up and over the fronts. This is probably how most clouds form.

When bubbles of air rise into the atmosphere, the air gets colder and colder. Because colder air can't hold as much water vapor, some of the vapor condenses on dust particles. Billions of these dust particles enter the air when winds blow dirt and sand, when ash and smoke from fires rise in the air, and when cars and factories release pollutants. The vapor builds up on the dust particles and makes tiny cloud droplets.

The cloud droplets are so small that you can't see them. You can see the clouds because each one has so many cloud droplets. If you could grab a bucketful of cloud, you'd be holding as many as a quarter of a million cloud droplets.

If the air gets cold enough as it rises, the cloud droplets may begin to freeze and form ice crystals. These ice crystals have many different shapes and sizes and they help rain to form in the cloud. You can tell the

difference between a cloud of water droplets and a cloud of ice crystals by looking at them. The water droplet clouds usually look like they have hard, clear edges. The ice crystal clouds usually have soft, fuzzy edges.

These computer-generated images show a typical thunderstorm cloud as it forms. In the real world, it would take about 60 minutes for the cloud to develop.

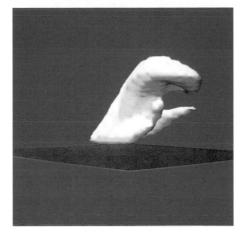

Types of Clouds

When you see stratus clouds getting thicker and covering more and more of the sky, you might be in for a long period of rain or snow.

You can sometimes tell what kind of weather is coming by looking at the clouds.

When cumulus clouds are getting taller and their bottoms are getting darker, you might be in for a short period of heavy rain, lightning, or even strong winds and hail.

Even though all clouds form in basically the same way, there are some differences between them. Conditions in the atmosphere can affect the way the air moves, and that can affect the way that clouds form. We can put most clouds into two groups. *Cumulus* clouds are bumpy and look like a pile of cotton balls. *Stratus* clouds are usually flat, they don't have many bumps, and they may cover a large portion of the sky.

These two kinds of clouds look very different because the air in them is moving in different ways. The air bubbles in cumulus clouds are rising very quickly, like bubbles in a pot of boiling water. The air moves up quickly and the clouds take on the shapes of the rising bubbles. This makes cumulus clouds look bumpy and bulgy. These types of clouds might form within a couple of hours during warm summer afternoons, when the air is unstable.

The air in stratus clouds is also rising into the atmosphere, but it is rising much more slowly. Because of this, the clouds tend to spread out horizontally, and they look flat. These kinds of clouds form when the air is more stable, and they may stay over your area for days. Stratus clouds form as the air rises over a warm front. They also form in low pressure systems, especially in fall and winter.

There are also different types of cumulus clouds and different types of stratus clouds. The names of different clouds in each group tell you a little more about the cloud. In the cumulus group, small clouds that are not very far from the ground and do not grow very deep into the atmosphere are just plain *cumulus* clouds. *Altocumulus* clouds are a little higher in the atmosphere, and they look a lot smaller to people on the ground. *Cirrocumulus* clouds are very high up in the atmosphere. In the same way, low clouds in the stratus group are called *stratus* clouds. When they are a little higher up, they are *altostratus,* and when they are very high, they are *cirrostratus.* If rain or snow is falling from cumulus clouds, they are

Cirrus clouds are a third group made mostly of ice crystals. These scattered, wispy clouds form at very high altitudes.

called *cumulonimbus.* Raining clouds in the stratus group are called *nimbostratus* clouds.

Of course, clouds aren't always this simple. You might see a cloud that looks flat and spread out like a stratus cloud, but it also has some places in it that bulge up into the sky like a cumulus cloud. A *stratocumulus* cloud is one cloud like this.

Some clouds don't really fit into any one cloud group.

Large stratus clouds that you might see in winter low pressure systems often have parts where the air suddenly rises very quickly. A few cumulus clouds might form here and there within a large area of stratus clouds.

Rain & Snow

After about a million cloud droplets join together, a raindrop might be big enough to fall all the way to the ground.

Clouds are actually made of tiny water droplets. These droplets are the water that helps make rain and snow.

The droplets in a cloud are very, very small. For water to fall to the ground, the clouds have to make drops that are big and heavy.

Clouds can make drops large enough to reach the ground in a few different ways. One way that raindrops form is when the cloud droplets run into each other and stick together. This process is called *coalescence*. Raindrops can also grow if water vapor continues to condense on them. As the vapor turns to water, it condenses on droplets in the cloud and the droplets can eventually become big enough to fall.

As raindrops fall through the air, the air pushes upward on the bottoms of the drops. This forces the water in the drops to spread out so that the drops look a lot like hamburger buns. Raindrops don't always stay in that shape, though. Very often, they actually change back and forth between shapes. One instant they look like a hamburger bun with the flat side down, and the next they look like a football that's standing on its end. Raindrops seem to sparkle as they pass by a street light because the light bounces off them in a different direction each time they change shape.

The dark streaks coming from the bottoms of these clouds are actually rain.

Snow grows almost in the same ways that raindrops grow. Sometimes cloud droplets will freeze into tiny ice crystals if the air is very cold. These tiny snowflakes grow very fast when there are also cloud droplets nearby. When this happens, the cloud droplets evaporate and become water vapor and this vapor condenses onto the snowflakes, making them larger.

As the snowflakes grow, they also begin to fall downward through the cloud. Just like raindrops, they might run into more vapor as they go down and grow larger. Snowflakes can also run into cloud droplets as they fall. The droplets freeze and stick to the snowflake, and the snowflake gets bigger. This process is called *riming*.

Snowflakes come in two basic shapes. The shape of the snowflake depends mainly on the temperature of the air when the snowflake grew.

Columnar flakes are long and thin. They look a lot like sewing needles. Flat flakes are *planar* flakes. Planar snowflakes usually have six arms, although once in a while they have 12 arms. If you see one that doesn't have six or 12 arms, some of them probably broke off as the flake was falling to the ground. Planar snowflakes actually come in a couple of different shapes.

Large snowstorms often form in the same way that large rainstorms do.

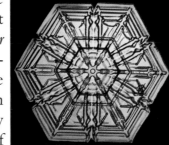

Flat plates (left) look like dinner plates, except that they're flat and have six sides. *Dendrites* (below) may be the most common type of flakes, and they're probably the most beautiful. Each of the six arms is shaped like a tiny Christmas tree.

Some people say that no two snowflakes are ever exactly the same. This may be true, but all snowflakes have some things in common about their shapes.

Thunderstorms

Thunderstorms occur at one time or another in almost every part of the world.

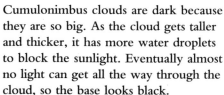

Cumulonimbus clouds are dark because they are so big. As the cloud gets taller and thicker, it has more water droplets to block the sunlight. Eventually almost no light can get all the way through the cloud, so the base looks black.

Even though we are all used to them, thunderstorms can be very severe. Most of the time they just pass by without causing any real problems. Once in a while, though, a thunderstorm can damage trees, buildings, and almost anything that happens to be in its path.

Thunderstorms form when air rises very quickly into the atmosphere. Air rises when it is heated by the ground, when a front is approaching, or when the air is forced to move over a mountain or a hill. Clouds form in the rising air. These clouds can climb very high into the atmosphere. Clouds that are high enough to cause thunderstorms are called cumulonimbus clouds. The bottoms of cumulonimbus clouds are often very close to the ground, but their tops can stretch up several miles.

Rain, snow, and hail often form in cumulonimbus clouds, even though they may not always reach the ground. They can evaporate as they fall. Hail probably forms in most thunderstorms, but it usually doesn't reach the ground. In some parts of the world, the air is so dry that people see thunderstorms with no rain at all.

Severe thunderstorms can be dangerous for several different reasons. Lightning is a surge of electricity moving within a cloud, from one cloud to another, or from a cloud to another object. It can strike with no warning, and it can be very dangerous if you are close by. Lightning can strike anywhere, but will usually hit tall objects, such as trees or towers.

Another danger in thunderstorms comes from the rain. Heavy rains can cause flooding. Normally, rainwater is absorbed by the soil, but sometimes it rains so hard that the soil can't absorb all the water. During very heavy rains, huge amounts of water can rush violently down the sides of large hills or mountains. The water can also run into nearby streams or rivers and cause them to overrun their banks.

Hail is not very common, but it can occur during thunderstorms. Usually hailstones are too small and too few to cause any serious widespread problems. Sometimes, though, they come down in great numbers or they grow to an inch or more in diameter. Then they can cause damage to plants and property. Thunderstorms also can have very strong winds. Thunderstorm winds can damage trees, plants, and buildings.

The great heat from a lightning flash causes thunder. The air around the lightning is heated so much that it expands very quickly. The movement of the air creates the crashing boom we call thunder.

Thunderstorms are one of the most common types of storm. At any one moment, hundreds of them are occurring over Earth.

Hail (left) and floodwater (right) cause millions of dollars of damage every year. Hail can severely damage farm crops. Floods can destroy property and even take lives.

161

Tornadoes

A tornado that forms over an ocean, lake, or other large body of water is called a waterspout. Waterspouts are usually not as strong as tornadoes, but they tend to last longer.

Tornadoes occur most often in places where very different air masses run into each other and cause strong, violent thunderstorms.

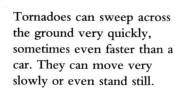

Tornadoes can sweep across the ground very quickly, sometimes even faster than a car. They can move very slowly or even stand still.

A special type of wind that happens in some thunderstorms is called a tornado. Tornadoes are tall columns of air that are spinning very fast, like a top. Tornadoes often are shaped like funnels, but sometimes they

aren't. At times, tornadoes can be over a mile wide. Other times, they can look like spinning ropes dangling out of the sides of the clouds. Tornadoes can even be invisible. When this happens, all you can see is the swirling of the bottoms of the clouds and dirt being blown around near the ground.

The winds in tornadoes are very strong. Sometimes they reach over 250 miles per hour. The winds near tornadoes can change directions so quickly that they seem to be coming from many different directions at once.

Strong winds in tornadoes can cause a lot of damage in a very short time. Pieces of straw or hay have been blown around hard enough to stick into the sides of trees. Cars and trucks have been tossed around like they were toys. Trash cans, boards, and other objects that are caught in the winds are very dangerous and can cause a lot of damage when they hit something else. When tornadoes blow them around, even dirt, sand, and rocks can peel the paint off of cars and houses.

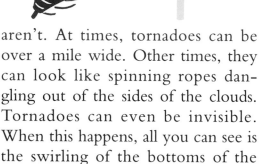

Tornadoes form in very strong thunderstorms. They can dip down out of the bottoms of thunderstorms with no warning. Many tornadoes form in thunderstorms that are spinning, although the storm clouds spin a lot slower than tornadoes do.

When the conditions in the atmosphere are just right for tornadoes to form, the National Weather Service issues a Tornado Watch. If there is a Tornado Watch where you are, you should keep a good lookout for any approaching thunderstorms. You might also want to stay close to a safe place where you can go if a thunderstorm or a tornado does develop.

When a tornado develops, the National Weather Service issues a Tornado Warning. This means that there is probably a tornado nearby. When a Tornado Warning is issued where you are, you should go to a safe place right away. The best place to go when this happens is somewhere low, preferably below ground.

A few places are particularly dangerous when there is a tornado nearby. Mobile homes, especially those that are not tied to the ground with special cables, are not safe in strong thunderstorms with high winds or in tornadoes. If you are in a car, you shouldn't try to outrun a tornado because it might be moving faster than you are. It is usually better to get out of the car and go to a building or other shelter.

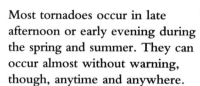

The Central and Southern United States probably have more tornadoes than any other place on Earth.

Most tornadoes occur in late afternoon or early evening during the spring and summer. They can occur almost without warning, though, anytime and anywhere.

Hurricanes

Before we had satellites that could track storms, it was difficult to know where a hurricane was or where it was going. Sometimes, the only information came from ships at sea. With satellites, though, meteorologists can track a hurricane's movements very carefully.

Like most other large, violent storms, hurricanes are low pressure systems.

Hurricanes are probably the most dangerous storms. They are almost always several hundred miles across. They last for many days, traveling from one area to another.

The best way to see what a hurricane looks like is by looking at it from above. In satellite photographs, hurricanes look like huge spirals of clouds that get deeper as you go toward the center of the spiral. Right in the middle of the hurricane, you can usually see the eye, a place that has no clouds in it.

Hurricane winds get stronger as you go from the outer edges of the spiral toward the center. They can reach speeds of over 150 miles per hour. In the eye, however, the winds are very light.

A lot of things go into making a hurricane, so it is difficult to say exactly how they form. Hurricanes develop at sea close to the Equator, mainly during the late summer. When a hurricane forms, the temperature of the water is almost always over 80°F. The storm does not start strong; at first it is a lot like a group of thunderstorms. When the group of thunderstorms rotates with winds over 35 miles per hour, it is called a tropical storm. If the winds reach 75 miles per hour, the storm is officially a hurricane.

Small islands can disappear under the water when hit with a hurricane's storm surge.

In the northern hemisphere, the usual path a hurricane takes starts near the Equator where it forms and then moves to the west. At some point, the hurricane usually turns to the northwest, then north, and finally to the northeast. This makes its path look like a huge hook. It will usually move faster once it turns toward the northeast.

Hurricanes need to be over warm waters to stay strong. When a hurricane moves very far to the north where the water's temperatures are cold, it begins to weaken and eventually dies out.

When hurricanes reach land, they often weaken very quickly. They can still cause a lot of damage to places near the shore before they disappear. Hurricane winds can blow around tree branches, boards, and other good-sized objects. Tornadoes sometimes occur when hurricanes first reach shore. The heavy rains in hurricanes can cause floods strong enough to wash away cars and even houses.

The biggest danger in hurricanes, though, is a storm surge. A storm surge happens when the hurricane actually lifts up part of the ocean. The pressure in a hurricane can get so low that it pulls ocean water upward. When the storm surge reaches the shore, the ocean sweeps across the land and carries buildings, cars, and anything else in its path with it.

Tropical storms gain energy as they take in warm, moist ocean air. This creates most of the power that drives hurricanes and makes them so dangerous.

Hurricanes leave great destruction behind them. They can even change the shape of a coastline.

Strange & Beautiful Sights

The sky is blue because of the way sunlight acts as it passes through the atmosphere.

A special device called a prism can separate a beam of light into all of its colors.

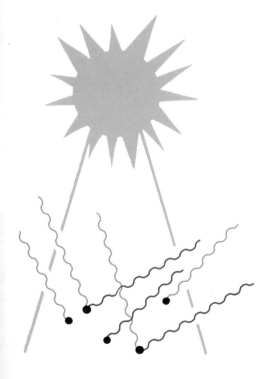

The atmosphere contains trillions and trillions of molecules of all different sizes, and the sunlight is constantly running into them.

Every day, light from the sun, called *solar radiation*, strikes the top of the atmosphere and travels all the way to the ground. This radiation causes most of the atmosphere's motion and it also creates colorful rainbows, sparkling snow, and blue skies.

The sun's light reaches the top of the atmosphere in a couple of ways. Most of it travels through millions of miles of space until it reaches Earth. Solar radiation also reaches the atmosphere at night when it hits the moon and bounces back toward Earth. That's what moonlight is, and it's the reason we are able to see the moon so clearly even though it doesn't create any light of its own.

The sun's light that makes it to Earth contains many different kinds of radiation, including all the colors of light that we can see. This visible light is violet, blue, green, yellow, orange, and red all combined together.

When sunlight goes through the atmosphere, it runs into whatever happens to be in its path. The way the light reacts depends mostly on the size of the thing it strikes. If the light hits very tiny things, like the gas molecules that make up the atmosphere, then some of the colors in the sunlight scatter in all directions. If the particles that the sunlight hits are a little bit larger, more of the colors in the sunlight scatter and bounce away.

Light travels in waves, just like waves of water in the ocean. The waves come in different sizes, or wavelengths. Each color of light has a different wavelength. Blue and violet have a shorter wavelength than red and orange do. Because of the shorter wavelength, blue and violet light are more likely to run into molecules and bounce off of them. The wave moves up and

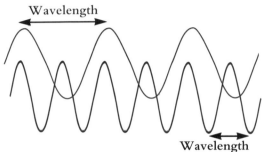

Wavelength

down more often over the same distance, so it is more likely to hit something. The atmosphere scatters more blue and violet light than any other type of light we can see. That is why the sky looks blue to us. We see the scattered light waves, and most of them are blue and violet.

At sunrise and sunset, the sky changes color. Parts of it actually become orange and red, the light with the longest wavelength. At these times of day, the sunlight has to go through more of the atmosphere before it gets to you than it does during the middle of the day. The light has to pass through more molecules so it is more likely that even the light with long wavelengths will run into something. More orange and red light is scattered, so the sky seems to be orange and red.

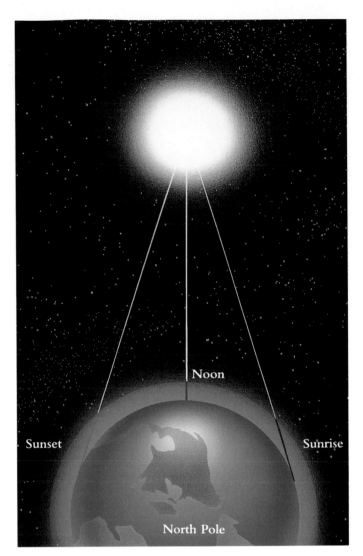

The farther a light wave travels through the atmosphere, the more likely it is that it will hit something and be reflected. The sunlight we see travels through more atmosphere at sunset and sunrise than at any other time of day.

Sunsets are usually more colorful and vibrant than sunrises. This is largely because the air contains more light-scattering particles—dust, salt, and so on—at the end of a busy day than at the end of a quiet night.

Light runs into many different things as it passes through the air, and these encounters have some beautiful results.

LIVING THINGS

Planet Earth is home to an astonishing number of living things. In the air, on the ground, in the water, and even in the soil, creatures of all kinds surround us. The smallest can only be seen through a microscope. The largest, like the giant sequoia trees and the blue whales, astound us with their great size. And millions of years ago, animals that no longer exist today walked through prehistoric forests.

But all living things, no matter their size, have some important things in common. All need food to survive. All are made up of basic building blocks called cells. And all living things, including humans, are parts of a food chain. When we study living things, we learn about the wonderful variety of life on Earth and the similarities that link us all together.

Life on Earth

How many different kinds of living things exist on Earth? No one knows for sure. Guesses range from 5 million to 100 million species. Only about 1.5 million of the plants, animals, and microorganisms that share our planet have been named.

Living things are alike in certain ways. For example, all contain molecules of DNA (deoxyribonucleic acid), a kind of genetic blueprint that determines what we and every other living thing look like.

Scientists organize living things into a series of related groups: species, genus (JEE-nus), family, order, class, subphylum (SUB-fie-lum), phylum (FIE-lum), and kingdom. Similar species go into the same genus, similar genera (JEN-er-uh), plural of genus, go into the same family, and so on.

For a long time, all living things were classified as belonging to either the plant or animal kingdom. But not everything fit. Today, biologists recognize at least five kingdoms: the Kingdom Monera (mo-NEAR-uh), which includes bacteria; the Kingdom Protista (pro-TIS-tuh), which contains more complex one-cell organisms; the Kingdom Fungi (FUN-jie), representing mushrooms, molds, yeasts, and similar organisms; the Kingdom Plantae (PLAN-tie), which contains all plants; and the Kingdom Animalia (on-i-MAH-lee-uh), representing all animals, including humans.

The earliest known fossils of living cells date back 3.6 billion years. Since then, many life forms—the dinosaurs among them—have come and gone.

Each year, biologists discover thousands of new life forms—mostly small plants, insects, and bacteria.

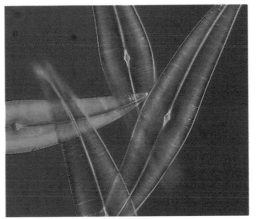

Microscopic view of diatoms, tiny plants that live in lakes, rivers, and oceans. There are thousands of different kinds of diatoms, providing food for a variety of insects and water creatures.

Human beings and animals both belong to the same scientific kingdom: Animalia.

169

Cells

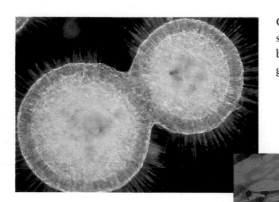

Once a cell reaches a certain size, it divides into two cells, both of which carry the same genetic information.

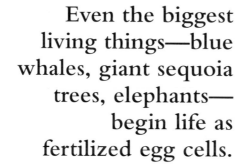

Human skin cells as seen through a powerful microscope.

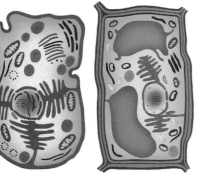

There are thousands of different kinds of cells, but they are surprisingly alike in many ways. Note the similarity between a typical animal cell (left) and plant cell (right).

Even the biggest living things—blue whales, giant sequoia trees, elephants— begin life as fertilized egg cells.

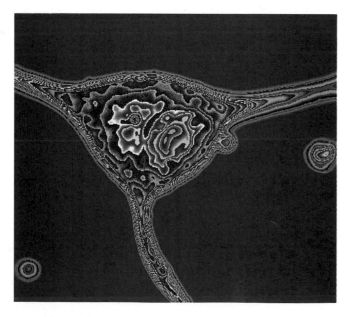

Magnified cross section of a nerve cell.

Cells are the building blocks of life. An organism can be made up of just one cell or, like you, it can be composed of billions of cells.

Most cells are so tiny you need to use a microscope to see them. But as small as they are, cells are powerful chemical factories.

Cells break down food molecules in order to release and use energy. They also use raw materials from outside to build proteins, fats and oils, carbohydrates, and other molecules that living things need to grow and to maintain themselves. Cells also break down other molecules to reuse raw materials and get rid of waste. All the building up and breaking down a cell does is called *metabolism* (me-TAB-oh-lizm).

Cells are either *prokaryote* (pro-KEAR-ee-oat) or *eukaryote* (yew-KEAR-ee-oat). The one-cell bacteria that make up the Kingdom Monera are prokaryotes. These simple-looking cells are like the cells found in the earliest fossils. Like all living things, prokaryotes use DNA to reproduce themselves, but they differ from eukaryotes in that they do not have visible nuclei. Protists, fungi, plants, and animals are eukaryotes.

There are thousands of different kinds of cells. Your body has about 100 special types. Blood, skin, nerve, and other cells all have their own jobs to do to keep your body functioning.

170

Bacteria

"There are more [things] living in the tooth scum in a man's mouth than there are men in a whole kingdom," wrote Anton van Leeuwenhoek, who in the late 1600s made the first microscope powerful enough to see them.

Bacteria are the oldest, smallest, most numerous, and perhaps most important organisms on Earth, considering the roles they play in the world's food chain.

Many are *decomposers* (de-kum-PO-zerz). They break down dead things and make their body materials available for recycling into new organisms. Others, like the *cyanobacteria* (SIE-uh-no-back-tear-ee-uh), otherwise known as blue-green algae, and sulfur bacteria, are *photosynthetic* (fo-to-sin-THET-ick). Like plants, they use the sun's energy to make their food.

Many cyanobacteria use nitrogen, the odorless gas that air is largely made of, in a process that helps maintain life on Earth. Called nitrogen fixers, the bacteria are able to take nitrogen gas from the air and turn it into a form that plants can use as a nutrient. Nitrogen-fixing cyanobacteria often live with plants and animals and help supply them with the nitrogen they need. They also live in the roots of beans, peas, clover, and other plants.

Some bacteria cause diseases. In humans, bacteria cause tuberculosis, diphtheria, strep throat, food poisoning, whooping cough, and other serious illnesses.

Algae that live in hot springs create unusual patterns when they bubble up to the surface. Shown above is Grand Prismatic Spring in Yellowstone National Park.

Bacteria exist everywhere—in the Antarctic, in boiling hot springs, and deep within ocean sediments.

A bacteria (*E. coli*) dividing.

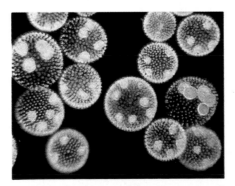

The slimy scum that you see on the surface of lakes and ponds is algae. Shown at left is a magnified view of *Volvox,* a green algae. Although the marine algae at right look like miniature plants, like all algae they are more closely related to bacteria.

Protists

Algae are found in all of Earth's waters. In tropical climates, they help build coral reefs.

The tiny organisms known as protists generally eat food—algae, bacteria, and other life forms—much as animals do. Some, like amoebas, seize prey with their armlike pseudopods (SOO-doh-pods), then engulf them.

One type of protist is the protozoan. Some protozoans live as parasites. They infect other organisms and take nutrients away. The malaria parasite is one that infects humans. This parasite lives part of its life in certain mosquitoes. When an infected mosquito bites a person, it injects the parasite into the person's bloodstream.

Although protozoans are mostly one-celled, many species clump together, forming simple colonies. The colony cells often react together to a light or electric shock applied to just one cell.

Most algae, which live off of sunlight, are protists. Like plants, they use the sun's energy to make food. The open sea is full of floating *plankton*, the microscopic algae and other animals that start the ocean's food chain.

Algae live in all of Earth's waters and in most of its other habitats. Those that have moved onto land make their homes in the soil, on tree trunks, and even in deserts and glaciers.

If you've ever slipped on seaweed at the beach, you have encountered a many-celled alga. One type of seaweed, known as kelp, grows to lengths of 125 feet or more.

Slime molds like this one creep along in streams, absorbing fungi, bacteria, and parts of dead plants.

The oddest-looking microorganisms are found among protists, a group that includes amoebas, most algae, and some fungi.

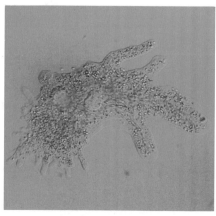
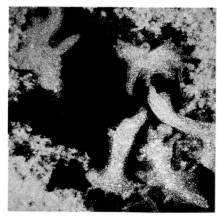

The amoeba (left) is a single-celled animal called a protozoan. Found in ponds and puddles, amoebas (right) feed on plant material and small prey like bacteria.

Fungi

People once thought mushroom circles were pathways for dancing fairies. In truth, each mushroom in what is known as a fairy ring is just one small bit of a big fungus organism growing underground.

Fairy rings may stretch 100 feet across, but they are not the biggest fungus organisms. Underground, fungus threads called *hyphae* (HIGH-fee) snake unseen for miles through soil and wood. Every tree in a forest may be connected to every other tree by the threads that make up the fungus. These *mycorrhizal* (my-kor-RIE-zul) fungi live in cooperation with the roots of the plants. They give the trees some of the nutrients they absorb from dead things in the soil. In return, the tree gives the fungi some of the food it makes using the sun's energy.

Many scientists think that the first plants to appear on land some 400 million years ago probably had root fungi to help them grow. Even today, organisms called *lichens* (LIE-kenz) are found in the harshest environments. Lichens are made up of algae and fungi. The food that the algae make and transfer to the fungi helps lichens survive in hot deserts, on windy mountain peaks, and even in the Antarctic.

Life on Earth could not exist without fungi. Like bacteria, many fungi work as decomposers.

Have you ever seen mushrooms pop up in the woods or on a lawn after a rain? Maybe they even formed a circle called a "fairy ring."

The facts about mushrooms and other fungi are even more amazing than the folktales that are told about them.

Often highly colored, cup fungi are so named because of their upturned caps.

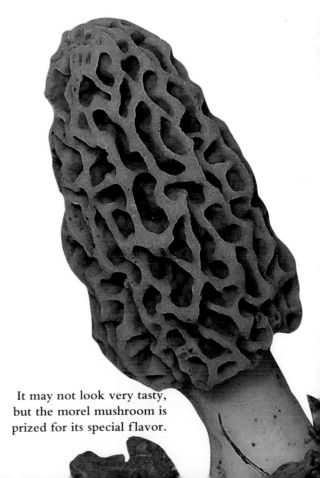

Many types of fungi, like this chicken of the woods, can be found in damp forests, especially during the fall.

It may not look very tasty, but the morel mushroom is prized for its special flavor.

173

Fungi

With each breath you take, you are breathing in tiny particles of fungi that float through the air like dust particles. They are everywhere!

The slightest breeze or smallest drop of rain may cause a ripened puffball to break open, releasing clouds of tiny spores.

Spores that land where they find the right amount of moisture, food, and temperature send out feeding threads. Molds on old bread, fruit, and vegetables are all fungi.

Bread doughs rise because of yeast, a one-celled fungus. The yeast feeds on sugar in the dough and gives off carbon dioxide gas, which causes the bread to rise.

Not all fungi get food from dead things. Some live as parasites. They take food from a living organism, weakening and sometimes killing it in the process. Still others attack and kill tiny soil creatures like amoebas. No matter what they eat, all fungi get food the same way. They send out proteins that dissolve the dead or living organism. Then the fungus absorbs it.

New fungi grow from spores, which are often produced by fruiting bodies such as mushrooms and puffballs. Much as an apple carries the seeds of a new apple tree, a fruiting body has spores that can grow into a new fungus.

We use fungi in many ways. Yeast is used to make bread, as well as wine and beer. Other fungi are used to make cheeses, soy sauce, soft drink ingredients, vitamins, and many other foods. People around the world eat mushrooms, truffles, and other fungi. In Mexico, corn smut, a fungus that grows on corn ears, is considered a special treat. The penicillin fungus is used to produce drugs that cure sicknesses and save many lives.

Fungi can also be very harmful. They cause diseases in plants, animals, and humans. Most plant diseases are caused by fungus parasites, as are ringworm, athlete's foot, and other human skin diseases. Fungi cause lumber to rot and food to spoil. In warm, moist places, they will attack almost anything—cloth, camera film, paint, leather, even jet fuel!

What Are Plants?

Photosynthesis, the process by which plants capture energy from the sun, doesn't just give us the food we eat, it also gives us the oxygen we breathe. The oxygen that we depend on has been released through photosynthesis over billions of years.

On land, plants feed most of the animals, including you. Plants use each of their parts to help in the food-making process. Plant roots dig through the soil, seeking moisture and nutrients. Tiny root hairs take in water from the soil, while tubes in the plant's roots and stem carry the water upward to the leaves, where photosynthesis mostly takes place.

Water and carbon dioxide are the plant's food ingredients. Now the plant needs energy from the sun to put the ingredients together. It traps light by using tiny green structures, called *chloroplasts* (KLOR-oh-plasts), inside each leaf cell. They are like miniature solar panels.

The energy-rich sugar a plant makes is its food. It uses it in the same ways that you use food—for energy, growing, making new cells, and staying healthy.

Some of the food you eat gets stored in fat and muscle tissue. Plants also store food—as starches, sugars, and oils—in their roots or stems. Some of their storehouses may even be among your favorite foods: potatoes, carrots, radishes, onions, beets, and celery, to name a few.

There are approximately 400,000 varieties of plants on Earth, from rare exotic flowers to common farm crops. All rely on the sun's light as an energy source.

Chlorophyll, the green substance that gives plants their color, captures light energy and uses it to make sugar.

Without the plants, algae, and bacteria that start life's energy chain, almost every living thing on our planet would die.

Plants need carbon dioxide gas from the air, as well as water from the soil, for photosynthesis. Plants take in air through tiny pores, called stomates (STOH-mayts), on the leaf surface. The stomates are like windows that the plant can open and shut. When they are open, they let air in and water out.

How many of the things you eat come from plants?

175

How Plants Grow

Sunflowers and many other plants turn their leaves to follow the sun as it moves across the sky.

Plants can't move around to find water and nutrients. Nor can they travel to sunnier spots where their leaves can make more food. So how do plants solve the problem of being stuck in one place? They keep growing at their shoot and root tips.

Plants also move their bodies to adjust to the world around them. These reactions are called *tropisms* (TRO-pizms) and are caused by cells growing at different rates. *Gravitropism* (gra-vi-TRO-pizm) is the response of plants to the force of gravity. Plant stems grow upward, and roots grow downward.

Plants adjust for changing light by stretching and moving their stems and young leaves to find the source—a process that we call *phototropism* (fo-to-TRO-pizm).

Some plants climb toward the light. Peas, cucumbers, and other climbing plants coil around objects they touch, while grapevines have sticky pads to grip objects. Bean plant stems spiral around their supports; other climbers put out anchor roots.

Most animals grow to a certain size and then stop, but many plants never lose their ability to form new leaves and other parts.

Carnivorous plants like sundews and Venus flytraps usually grow in marshy or boggy places where they cannot absorb all the nitrogen they need from the soil. To get proteins and minerals, they eat insects and other small creatures.

Trees and other woody plants grow outward even after parts of their bodies have stopped growing upward.

Even if you turn a potted plant on its side, its stem will gradually bend around so that it is growing upward again.

The hinged leaves of the Venus flytrap are coated with sweet nectar as bait. When an insect lands on the leaf and touches its sensitive hairs, the leaf springs shut like a mousetrap.

176

Using the story told by some very old tree rings, scientists figured out that when American Indians began to abandon their great cities and cliff dwellings in the Southwest in the late 1200s, a terrible drought lasting many years was in progress. Before, historians could only guess what caused them to abandon their homes.

Like you, plants need food, nutrients, and water to grow and develop. But they need a lot more water than you do, since they don't have a bloodstream to circulate liquids. Almost all the water that plants take up from the soil is lost to evaporation.

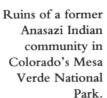 Plants take in water through tubes that stretch from the roots. The water travels up through the stem, into the leaves, and out through the stomates. You can trap this "plant sweat" yourself. Just fasten a clear plastic bag around some leaves on a plant, and check the bag the next day. Is there water in it?

Plants have a big problem with water loss. Remember how they make their food? One step is to take in carbon dioxide gas from the air through their stomates. But plants also lose water through their stomates, and if they lose too much they wilt. When that happens, they can't take in the carbon dioxide they need to make food. Their growth slows or stops. As you can see, plant survival is the result of a delicate natural balance.

Native to the Rocky Mountains, bristlecone pine trees have what is believed to be the longest life span of any conifer. A number of them have been dated at 3,000 years, and at least one tree in eastern Nevada is believed to be 4,900 years old.

Piecing together the climate story told by the growth rings of living and dead trees is like reading a region's history book.

Ruins of a former Anasazi Indian community in Colorado's Mesa Verde National Park.

177

Plant Inventions

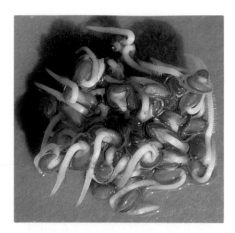

Like most other plants, cress seedlings need warmth, moisture, and air to germinate and grow properly.

Over time, plants developed roots to absorb water from the soil and leaves to make food from the sun's energy.

The whitish glaze on the outside of fresh blueberries and other fruits is the waxy, water-saving substance that the very first land plants relied on to help ensure their survival.

The first living things on our planet almost certainly lived in the waters that covered most of the world. Long, long ago—about 400 million years—plants, animals, fungi, algae, and other protists began to come ashore. Each came up with ways to *adapt,* or adjust, to the dryness of the land.

One way they did this was by covering their skin with fatty or waxy substances to keep from drying out.

The ancestors of the largest group of plants—the so-called *vascular* (VAS-kyew-ler) plants—developed tubes and similar structures to carry water from the ground through their stems.

One challenge for these early plants was to ensure the survival of the next generation. Some protected their spores—tiny bits of genetic material—with tough, watertight coatings. The wind blew these spores to new places, and if conditions were right, they would sprout.

By the time the first reptiles were appearing, the low, swampy landmasses were covered with forests of towering trees, giant horsetails, ferns that grew 25 feet high, and relatives of *conifers* (KA-ni-ferz)—the evergreen pine and fir tree.

Most of the plants that lived during this period died out as the land lifted, dried, and became cooler. But you still see and use the remains of these strange and wonderful plants every time you burn coal, oil, or natural gas.

178

Ferns, mosses, liverworts, and relatives of some of the other prehistoric plants were at a disadvantage as lands dried. Although their spores were protected with a tough coat, once they began to *germinate* (JER-mi-nayt), or develop, their sperm cells needed water to swim to and fertilize the egg cells.

One group of survivors solved this problem, and they are the dominant plants even today. These are the plants that produced seeds.

The seed plants protect their eggs with layers of tissue and food stores. Once pollen grains reach and fertilize the egg, the seed plants cover the *embryo* (EM-bree-oh) and its food supply with a tough seed coat. Now the plant can develop in safety. When the seeds are released, the seed coat prevents the plantlet from drying out.

Over the years, seeds have developed many ways to travel. Some have burrs or other sticky parts so they can hitchhike on a passing animal. Others are encased in fruits that animals eat and pass through their digestive systems, eventually eliminating them.

Most windblown pollen never reaches the egg cells of a plant it can fertilize. The most successful plants in today's world solved this problem by producing flowers. These plants use flowers to attract visitors that stop by and then carry their pollen to another plant for them.

The small, dry seeds of the dandelion have strands of down attached to them that help carry them away from their parent plant.

Plants use their colors, odors, and shapes to attract bees and other insects, as well as birds, bats, and other pollinators.

As a bee feeds on pollen, some of the yellow powder sticks to its legs and body and is carried to the next flower, where pollination may occur.

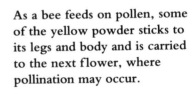

Maple tree seed pods have large wings that help whirl them to new locations.

179

Where Plants Live

Some plants rely on wildfires so their seeds can germinate.

Grasslands and savannahs go through periods of drought, when wildfires may sweep through them. Plants in these regions have adapted to the fires. Grasses have fast-growing networks of roots that, if laid end to end, would stretch hundreds of miles. The root hairs not only drink up every drop of available water, they also anchor the plant.

Early in the spring, wildflowers and other *herbaceous* (her–BAY–shus) plants carpet the forest floor. They have to bloom and release their seeds before the forest trees leaf out and cut off their sunlight.

In coastal areas, where the winters are mild and the summers are long, hot, and dry, the more widely spaced plants have tough leaves that can bear the summer's heat.

Far to the north or high in the mountains are the great conifer forests of spruce, fir, and hemlock that can bear the long, bitterly cold, snow-filled winters of these regions. Even farther north is the *tundra* (TUN–druh), where temperatures may be above freezing for less than two months each year. Low-growing grasses and herbs, as well as dwarf willows and birches, carry out their life processes in the short Arctic summers.

Different regions of the world have different kinds of plants. That's because plants developed many ways to survive in varied climates.

Wildebeests and zebras are a familiar sight on the savannahs of East Africa. These grassy plains cover almost a quarter of the continent.

Deciduous forests, the kind whose trees drop their leaves in the fall, usually have warm summers and cold winters.

180

Plants also have adaptations that enable them to survive in the rain forest. Pitcher plants are epiphytes (EP-uh-fyts). They grow on other trees but do not take nourishment from them. The pitcher plant has several containers at the end of long, thin stalks or tendrils that hang below the plant. These containers look like water pitchers, and they catch the falling rain. Insects are attracted to the pitchers because they contain sweet-smelling nectar. Once inside the lip of the pitcher, though, an insect is doomed. The inside has a waxy surface, and the insect slips to the bottom of the pitcher where the plant digests it.

Bromeliads are common plants in the rain forest. They are epiphytes, too. Some bromeliads collect water and plant debris that fall into a well in the center of the plant. The bromeliad draws food and water from these little pools. The pools actually become tiny habitats all of their own. Some species spend their entire lives inside a bromeliad pool. Others come just to visit.

Insects are common visitors to the bromeliad. Mosquitoes and giant dragonflies lay their eggs there. The dragonfly larvae feed on mosquito larvae and other small insects. Scorpions, crabs, and carnivorous beetles arrive to snatch up the resident insects. Sometimes a mammal, like the small mouse opossum, will stop by for a meal.

The pitcher plant gets its nourishment by catching insects— it is a carnivorous plant!

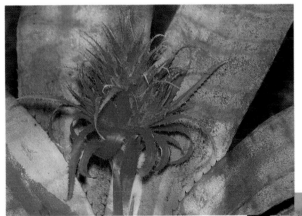

The bright red leaves of many bromeliad species attract hummingbirds, too.

Poison arrow frogs leave their tadpoles in bromeliads. The tadpoles stay there until they become adults.

181

Where Plants Live

Some desert landscapes lack any sign of plants. These dry lands are simply too harsh to support life.

All desert plants have tricks for dealing with great heat and long periods of dryness, or drought. Many small desert plants appear on the landscape only when heavy rains fall. These plants, which include grasses, shrubs, and flowering plants, "wait out" periods of drought underground. They exist for months or even years as seeds buried in the soil. When rains come, these seeds spring to life. The young

plants quickly grow into adult plants and, in turn, shed a new batch of seeds. Then they die. All this happens within a few weeks.

Other plants remain above ground to battle the desert's dryness head-on. These drought-fighting plants include trees, shrubs, and cacti (KAK-ty). The cacti are the best-known desert plants. Cacti are able  to store large amounts of water after a rainfall. They can survive months or even years without running out of water.

The biggest cacti are the cardón (kar-DON) and the saguaro (suh-WAHR-oh). Both are found only in the Sonoran Desert. They can weigh as much as ten tons! And most of this weight is water! Saguaros grow extra roots to suck up rain shortly after it falls.

The saguaro can grow up to 50 feet in height.

Insects

Crickets and Grasshoppers

On a summer night, you might hear the "chirp" of an American field cricket. It's a male, singing to attract a mate. Crickets and grasshoppers are well known for their "songs," which they make in several ways. Some species rub together special veins on their wings. Others rub a bumpy hind leg against their wings.

Crickets, grasshoppers, locusts, cicadas, and katydids (KAY-tee-didz) are all members of the same insect group. There are more than 20,000 different species, and they are found almost everywhere in the world, except for very cold places.

Crickets, grasshoppers, and locusts have evolved to live in numerous ways. Locusts live together in huge groups called "swarms." Desert locusts, for example, found in northern Africa and parts of Asia, swarm by the hundreds of millions. They migrate, or travel, across huge areas of land and eat millions of acres of crops in their path.

Other species live alone. To avoid predators, some of them have developed fascinating ways of hiding themselves from their enemies. The South American grasshopper looks exactly like a stick, blending well with its rain forest habitat. This makes it harder for predators to see them. A type of katydid that lives in Malaysia seems to disappear when it rests on the bark of a tree. This adaptation is known as *camouflage* (KAM-uh-flahj).

A cricket (left) has long feelers, or antennae, that wave continuously, picking up air currents. The antennae of a grasshopper (right) are much shorter.

Some katydids that live in the rain forest resemble bright green leaves.

These insects are known for their ability to jump long distances with their powerful hind legs.

Larger than the average grasshopper, the migratory locust travels in huge swarms that destroy farm crops and, in many countries, contribute to famine.

Insects

Among the better known beetles, ladybugs are beneficial to humans because they eat aphids (AY-fids), tiny bugs that destroy crops.

Beetles

Beetles come in all shapes and sizes, but they all have one thing in common. What looks like a front pair of wings are not really wings at all. They are *elytra* (EL-uh-truh), tight-fitting sheaths that cover and protect the hind wings used for flying.

There is a wide variety of feeding habits among beetles. Some of them are predators and feed on other insects. Other beetles, like leaf beetles, eat plants.

Beetles have a great many adaptations to suit different needs, such as finding a mate or escaping enemies. Fireflies, which are beetles in spite of their name, have certain chemicals on the tips of their abdomens that glow at night. Male and female fireflies use these "lights" to communicate with each other. Many beetles taste bad or are poisonous, and they advertise this fact with bright, distinctive color patterns. If touched, the South African blister beetle will release a chemical that can burn the skin. Its bold black-and-white body warns predators to stay away. When disturbed, the click beetle makes loud clicking sounds to frighten off enemies.

There are more kinds of beetles than any other type of insect— at least 300,000 species!

The dung beetle gets its nourishment from animal droppings, which it shapes into a ball and rolls into its burrow.

The word "scarab" is sometimes used to describe a stone or gem cut in the shape of the scarab beetle. Ancient Egyptians considered these insects a sign of good luck.

Flies

Blackflies, gnats, mosquitoes, and tsetse flies all belong to the same group of insects that are sometimes called two-winged flies. These insects are probably the most hated because of the terrible diseases they can spread to humans and livestock. Malaria, sleeping sickness, and other diseases are spread by these blood-sucking insects.

Unlike most other insects, two-winged flies have just one pair of short, strong wings. These wings allow them to fly very fast and even backward, to hover like a helicopter, and to land almost anywhere. Some species, like the common housefly, can land and even walk on ceilings!

Some flies are actually beneficial to humans. Certain species, like hover flies, are important pollinators of plants. Frequent visitors to our gardens, they move from flower to flower, accidentally spreading pollen as they feed.

Other species of flies are beneficial because they feed on dead animals or on animal droppings. This may sound disgusting, but it is an important service. Coffin flies and blowflies, for example, feed on dead animals. The waste material is digested by the fly and broken down into useful nutrients that are returned to the soil. These nutrients are then absorbed by plants through their roots.

The mouthparts of flies and mosquitoes are specially adapted for piercing through skin.

Most of us have been bitten by a housefly or a mosquito, but not all flies are pests.

Four wings allow the dragonfly to twist and turn with great speed as it hunts for flying insects.

Excellent mimics of bees, hover flies help keep predatory birds away!

Despite their unpopularity with humans, flies play a vital role in nature, pollinating flowers and recycling nutrients as they scavenge for food.

Insects

Like termites, ants are highly social insects that live together in nests called colonies. Within the colonies, the worker ants maintain the nest, protect it from invaders, and provide food for the queen and the young ants, called *larvae* (LAR-vee).

There are at least 14,000 different kinds of ants, considered by many who study them to be among the most fascinating animals on Earth.

Ants

Ants display an incredible variety of habits and ways of living. All ants live in groups called colonies, but these may be located underground, in wood, or in tall mounds. Unlike other ant species, army ants have no permanent nest. Instead, they are always on the move in search of food, "marching"

forward like soldiers in columns that can be yards long. The colony moves slowly—about one foot per minute.

Army ants feed mostly on other insects but they will attack any slow-moving animal in their path. Army ants usually pose no threat to humans because most people can get out of their way.

Some ants have developed unique relationships with plants or other insect species. The black garden ant lives with aphids and protects them from predators. In exchange, the aphids provide the ants with a special food called "honeydew." Honeydew is a sweet, sugary liquid that the aphids secrete after feeding on plants.

In Southeast Asia, certain plants provide a home for ants in exchange for food. These plants have hollow stems that make ideal nest sites for ants. The ants use some of the space as a "dump" where they store insect remains and other waste products. The plant will absorb the nutrients from this.

The carpenter ant is so named because of its preference for dead or decayed wood as a food source.

Leaf-cutting ants carry pieces of leaves to their underground nests, where they chew them up to make a kind of compost to fertilize the fungus they grow for food.

Most ant species are not as aggressive as army ants, which will attack any animal that happens to get in their way.

Bees and Wasps

Bees and wasps are related to ants, but not all species are social. Certain kinds of hunting wasps are solitary predators. They seek other insects for food and kill them with a powerful stinger. Paper wasps, however, are highly social, living in an intricate nest made from wood fibers and saliva.

Bees are strict vegetarians. They collect pollen and nectar from flowers and are among the world's most important plant pollinators. Many bees rely on one plant species for food.

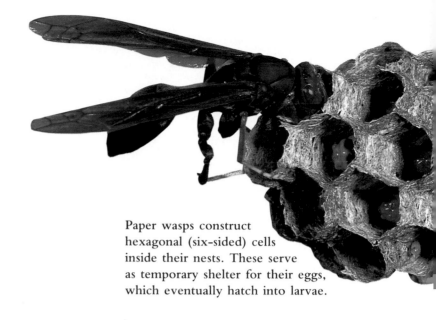

Paper wasps construct hexagonal (six-sided) cells inside their nests. These serve as temporary shelter for their eggs, which eventually hatch into larvae.

There are three kinds of honeybees. Each colony has one large queen bee, a number of slightly smaller males known as drones, and lots of much smaller worker bees, all of which are female. A big colony may have as many as 60,000 bees.

A colony can have only one queen. When an old queen sees worker bees building special cells that will produce new queens, she leaves the colony with as many bees as will follow her to start a new colony somewhere else.

If their hive is threatened by a predator, honeybees produce a chemical that signals all of the bees to attack. Honeybees have barbed stingers that usually remain in their victims. Most of the time, the bees die trying to free themselves.

A honeybee that has found food uses figure eights, circles, body-wagging, and loud buzzing to communicate the food's exact location to the other bees in the nest.

Not all bees have stingers, but even stingless bees inflict nasty bites. Some species can also release a stinging chemical.

Swarming occurs when a honeybee queen leads a large group of bees to start a new colony in another location.

Arachnids

When a tarantula catches a victim, it poisons its prey. A tarantula's bite isn't dangerous to humans. It's like a bad bee sting.

Spiders and Scorpions

Like many people, you might think that spiders are insects. But spiders are really *arachnids* (uh-RAK-nidz). Arachnids are related to insects, but they are not the same. Insects and arachnids have different types of bodies. Also, insects have six legs, while arachnids have eight.

There are many kinds of spiders all over the world. They range in size from about 3.5 inches to tiny spiders you can hardly see with the naked eye. You've probably seen many silky spiderwebs outside, or even in your house.

The world's largest spider is the tarantula. Tarantulas often live in deserts, where the daytime temperature can be extremely high. When the weather is very hot, tarantula spiders move only at night. They are covered with hairs that help them "feel" their surroundings.

Many tarantulas live in underground homes, or burrows. They spend most of their time there. The burrows are cool and moist. Even when the tarantula comes out to hunt, it stays close to its home.

Scorpions are also arachnids that are active at night. Scorpions are found in deserts worldwide. The scorpion has a poisonous stinger at the end of its abdomen.

When the scorpion finds an insect, it grabs it in its claws, or pincers, and stings it. When a scorpion has babies, she carries them on her back as they grow.

Unlike tarantulas, some species of scorpions can be dangerous to humans.

Butterflies

Butterflies and Moths

Unlike spiders, butterflies and moths are true insects. You can tell a butterfly from a moth in a number of ways. First, butterflies are usually more colorful than moths. Butterflies may be patterned in many beautiful colors. Moths are usually plain gray or brown. Secondly, butterflies hold their wings straight up when resting. Moths fold their wings flat over their backs. Thirdly, butterfly antennae are skinny with little knobs at the tips. Moth  antennae are either feathery or skinny without any knobs. And last, butterflies are active during the day, while moths are more active at night.

Skippers are a small group of unusual butterflies with large bodies like those of moths. Some skippers are brightly colored, but most are brown or gray, with white or silver spots on their wings. Skippers are active during the day, visiting flowers like other butterflies. But when it comes to flying, they are the fastest butterflies in the air! They also have knobbed antennae, but the knobs have little hooks at the tips.

Most of the butterflies and moths in your neighborhood can be told apart by their colors and by the time of day—or night—they are active. There are some day-flying moths and some plainly colored butterflies, though. You might be fooled once in a while! But don't let it bother you. Even a well-trained butterfly watcher may be taught a lesson by these unusual butterflies and moths.

This lawn skipper may be confused with a moth. Its body is large and hairy like a moth's, and it folds its wings like a moth when it rests. Its antennae are more like a butterfly's, though; they are not feathered like a moth's antennae.

The day-flying Uranus moth (right) looks like a swallowtail butterfly. Thousands of these moths (above) are swarming about flowering trees in Costa Rica.

Butterflies and moths form the second largest group of insects. Only beetles form a larger group.

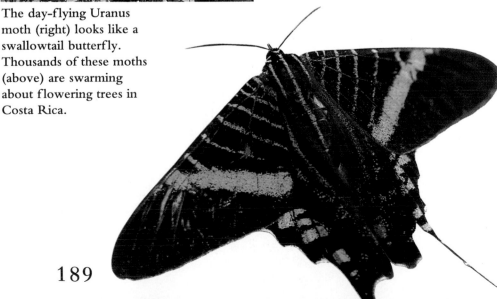

Butterflies

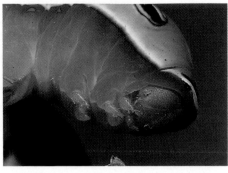

The caterpillar on the left is shedding its skin. Its tail end is not yet free of the old skin. The close-up on the right shows the head of a swallowtail caterpillar. You may be able to see its eyes and mouthparts as well as its six legs, which are attached to its thorax. The markings on top of its body are "false eyes" that help to scare enemies.

In a butterfly's first life stage, it may not even be recognized as a butterfly.

This is a close-up look at the breathing holes on a caterpillar's abdomen. These holes are known as "spiracles."

Birds, mice, spiders, and some insects eat caterpillars. Canned caterpillars are even sold in Mexico as human food!

A Butterfly's Life

A butterfly starts life as an egg that was laid by an adult female butterfly. In its second stage, a tiny caterpillar hatches from the egg and it begins to eat as well as grow. A caterpillar grows by shedding its outside skeleton and making a new, larger one. The old skeleton splits down the back and the caterpillar wriggles its way out. There is a very thin skin under the skeleton that keeps the caterpillar from "falling apart." This skin also makes a liquid "cement" that coats the caterpillar's body. This cement will form the new outer skeleton. But before the cement has hardened, the caterpillar fills itself with air and stretches the new skeleton. It grows to fit the larger size.

After shedding its skeleton about six times, the caterpillar turns into a chrysalis. Inside the chrysalis, the caterpillar is changing shape. When the change is complete, the butterfly will push its way out of the chrysalis and crawl free. A butterfly does not shed its skeleton, so once a caterpillar becomes a butterfly it will not grow any bigger.

Although they grow to be butterflies, caterpillars do not look much like butterflies. Caterpillars do have a head, thorax, and abdomen like all insects. But there are no compound eyes on the caterpillar's head. Instead, there are six single eyeballs on each side of the caterpillar's head. These eyes cannot see colors, but they can see some movement and shapes. Caterpillars also have two antennae. The caterpillar's mouthparts are found on the lower front part of the head, but instead of the coiled proboscis, there are two strong jaws. These jaws are perfect for chewing the leaves and other plant parts that are the caterpillar's food. A coiled proboscis would be of no use to a caterpillar!

The caterpillar's thorax has six legs attached to it, just like the thorax of all other insects. Each leg is jointed, and is divided into five sections. There is a claw at the end of each leg. The caterpillar uses its legs for crawling and for holding pieces of plant while eating. A caterpillar, of course, does not have wings on its thorax.

The abdomen is the longest part of a caterpillar's body. It is divided into ten sections. This makes it easier for the caterpillar to wriggle and move. Inside the abdomen are muscles, a heart, and a stomach. The abdomen—and the rest of the body—is filled with insect blood, just like butterflies. On each side of the abdomen there are about eight breathing holes.

There are several pairs of "false legs" on the underside of a caterpillar's abdomen. These legs are fatter than the real legs. The false legs have rows of tiny hooks on them. They are useful for crawling and clinging to branches or leaves.

If caterpillars do not have wings to fly away, how do they protect themselves? Some caterpillars are disguised to look like twigs, bark, or bird droppings—things that are not good to eat. There are even some caterpillars that eat poisonous plants, like milkweed, so that they taste bad.

The female butterfly lays her eggs on the right kind of plant so the just-hatched caterpillars will have food right away. Most caterpillars can eat only one or two kinds of plants.

Butterfly eggs are quite small. Some are only a little larger than the head of a pin. (These are magnified many times.) Butterfly eggs may be round, domed, egg-shaped, or sausage-shaped.

With any luck, this caterpillar's enemies will not be able to tell it apart from the twig on which it rests. Can you tell the twig and caterpillar apart?

191

Fish

The stingray is so named because of the spines that grow from its tail. The poison in them can be painful but will rarely kill a human.

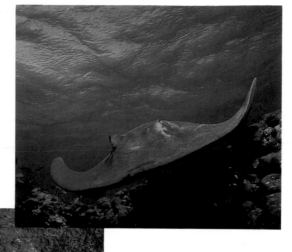

Cartilaginous Fish

Sharks, rays, and skates are all cartilaginous (kar-ti-LAJ-in-us) fish, which means their skeletons are mostly or entirely made of cartilage, not bone.

Sharks are carnivorous (kar-NI-vor-us), feeding on other sea animals. The great white shark, tiger shark, blue shark, lemon shark, and large hammerhead shark are considered the most dangerous to humans.

Hammerhead sharks are perhaps the most unusual-looking of all sharks. There are 12 species of hammerheads, so named because their heads have hammerlike extensions on each side.

Resembling sharks, sawfish are actually elongated rays. The largest can attain lengths of 23 feet or more.

Skates and rays are flat, with winglike fins that make them look as though they are flying through the water like butterflies. Most species live on the bottom of the ocean, where they feed on oysters, snails, lobsters, crabs, and shrimp. Skates and rays usually live in cool ocean waters, but several species of South American stingrays live in fresh water.

Sharks are probably the most feared of all fish, but only a few of the 225 shark species truly pose a threat to humans.

Sawfish are also members of the cartilaginous group. Sawfish have a long, armored snout with sharp teeth on each side. The "saw" is used as a weapon. The sawfish will swim into a school of fish and slash its saw back and forth, killing or wounding as many fish as it can before settling down for a meal.

The great white shark is the largest predatory fish. It can weigh as much as three tons, reaching lengths of 27 feet.

Salmon, Trout, and Pike

Salmon belong to a group of fish that includes trout, pike, and pickerels. These fish are among the most important food fish in the world.

The fish spends the first few years of its life in fresh water, then travels out to sea. After several years in the Atlantic, it returns, swimming upstream, to the same river in which it was hatched. Salmon seem to stop at nothing to reach their destination, making tremendous leaps to clear obstacles in their way. Once they have reached their birth river, the salmon will lay eggs, or spawn.

Scientists believe that salmon can find their way back to these rivers by using memory and a sense of smell. Salmon remember the smell of the water, rocks, and vegetation of their birth river.

Trout are also very tasty, and certain species are popular game fish. Trout can be found both in the ocean and in fresh water, but most species prefer cold, fresh water. The rainbow trout is so named because of the colorful stripe on its flank. The brook trout is a popular sport fish because it puts up a good fight when hooked.

Pike and pickerels are solitary, aggressive fish that are found mostly in fresh water. These fish have large, pointed teeth and are efficient predators. Pike and pickerels are long, slender fish that have alligatorlike snouts.

The Atlantic salmon performs what is perhaps the most amazing migration in the animal world.

Salmon are powerful swimmers, but are hardly a match for hungry bears that gather along the rivers where the fish come to breed.

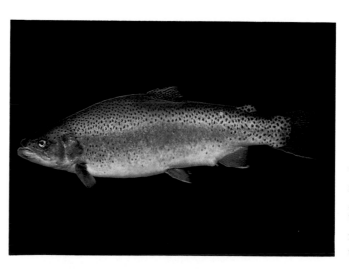

The rainbow trout is native to North America, but it has been introduced to many other parts of the world.

Fish

Catfish vary in size from the small varieties that are kept in aquariums to huge specimens that can weigh more than 250 pounds!

Most catfish are scavengers, feeding on animal and vegetable matter.

Catfish

Most of the more than 2,000 species of catfish live in freshwater, with just two families found in ocean waters.

Some species of catfish are quite unusual. Electric catfish can produce a strong electrical discharge with a force of up to 450 volts. These shocks are enough to kill small fish, which the catfish will eat, but it also uses these shocks as a powerful defensive weapon.

The upside-down catfish of Africa actually swims on its back with its belly up! This allows the fish to grab food that is floating on the water's surface.

The African polka-dot catfish is about seven inches long and is very popular with fish hobbyists. Also popular is the glass catfish of Southeast Asia. This fish is almost completely transparent, and you can often see its internal organs! This is a special type of camouflage that enables the fish to almost completely disappear in the reflection of the water.

All catfish have at least one pair of whiskerlike extensions, called barbels, on the upper jaw. Some may also have a pair on the snout and additional pairs on the chin.

Because of its highly transparent body, the glass catfish is a popular aquarium fish.

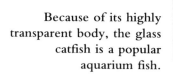

Cichlids

There are at least 600 species of cichlids (SICK-lids), most of them found in Central and South America, Africa, Madagascar, and parts of Asia. Nearly half of all cichlids are found in Africa, and most species live in freshwater streams and lakes.

Some cichlids are mouthbrooders. Either the male or the female holds the eggs in its mouth until they hatch. The young fish swim close to their parents' mouths and will often return there when danger threatens.

Cichlids have only one nostril on each side of the head, and many have two lines on each side of the body.

Body shapes vary. Some are long and slim, while others are slightly round. Certain African species can weigh as much as 20 pounds. These larger species are important food fish. Some smaller varieties are very colorful and are kept in aquariums.

Some species of cichlids are vegetarians, while others are meat-eaters. As a result, cichlid mouths are quite varied.

Some species have blunt, chisellike teeth for cutting plants or scraping algae off rocks. Others have strong, pointed teeth for seizing and tearing prey. Still others have very small teeth, which they use to take the eggs or tiny newborn right out of parents' mouths!

Cichlids come in a great variety of colors and patterns.

Popular with hobbyists, the fish of this group tend to be aggressive, actively defending their territory.

As a group, cichlids eat almost every kind of food: water plants, plankton, small water creatures such as snails, and even other fish.

During breeding time, rival males challenge each other in their efforts to attract a mate.

197

Amphibians & Reptiles

Unlike reptiles, salamanders generally have moist skin. Like this barred tiger salamander, they are often boldly patterned.

Caecilians and Salamanders

Caecilians are long, limbless amphibians that look very much like earthworms. There are 163 species, found in Southeast Asia, Africa, and Latin America. Scientists know little about these secretive creatures, which spend most their time burrowing beneath soil.

Caecilians are very diverse in size—ranging from the *Idiocranium* of West Africa, which measures about two and a half inches long, to the *Caecilia thompsoni* of Colombia, which is more than four feet long. Caecilians eat a wide variety of prey, from worms and termites to small lizards. Because most species are almost blind, scientists think they find food with a strong sense of smell.

Many people mistake salamanders for lizards. Salamanders live in cool, shady habitats in mild climate zones. They are usually active at night and, unlike their noisy relatives, frogs and toads, are usually very quiet. During the day, salamanders rest under layers of dead leaves or under rocks in creeks to avoid the heat of the sun. At night, they hunt for worms, insects, and other prey.

Salamanders have a variety of lifestyles. Some, like the cave salamander, live entirely on land. Others, like the so-called water dog (also known as a mudpuppy), live in rivers or streams. Most newts, on the other hand, divide their time between land and water.

Salamanders have slender bodies, long tails, and two pairs of legs that are about the same size.

Courtship behavior among salamanders takes many forms. Some species breed in water, others breed on land.

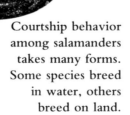

The bright color of this newt, a type of salamander, tells predators that it would not make a good meal.

198

Frogs and Toads

Many people wonder what the difference is between frogs and toads. Toads usually have short legs, plump bodies, and rough or warty skin. They generally live on land and cannot jump as well as frogs. Frogs have more slender bodies, with long limbs and smooth skin, and they usually live near water.

At certain times of the year, you can hear the chorus of frogs calling to each other at night. They do this by inflating one or more of the vocal sacs in their throats with air. Some of the species that you may have heard are the leopard frog, green frog, American toad, and American bullfrog.

During mating season, male frogs (left) call attention to themselves by making loud croaking sounds. With a body that is almost transparent, the glass frog (below) of Central America is an expert at going unnoticed.

All frogs and toads have at least a trace of poison that is produced in special glands in their skin. Most of the time this poison is not very strong. But the tiny poison-arrow frogs of Central and South America produce one of the strongest poisons in nature. Just the tiniest amount can kill a human! Many rain forest Indians put the poison from these frogs on the tips of their arrows.

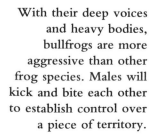

Frogs and toads are the most numerous of all amphibians. There are at least 2,600 species, found throughout the world.

With their deep voices and heavy bodies, bullfrogs are more aggressive than other frog species. Males will kick and bite each other to establish control over a piece of territory.

Amphibians & Reptiles

Turtles may be slow on land, but some are pretty good travelers. The green sea turtle, for example, has been known to swim 300 miles in 10 days.

Turtles first appeared on Earth about 200 million years ago, long before the dinosaurs. They have changed very little over the years.

Turtles can live very long lives. American box turtles have been known to reach ages of up to 120 years.

A protected species, the Galapagos tortoise has suffered from rats, dogs, and other "foreign" animals that people introduced to its island home.

Turtles

Today there are about 240 species of turtles and tortoises. These reptiles are found in tropical and temperate regions on every continent except Antarctica.

Some turtles, like sea turtles and softshell turtles, spend almost all of their lives in oceans, lakes, or rivers. Bog turtles and wood turtles live in wetland habitats. Tortoises, a term used to refer to a specific group of turtles, live only on land. But wherever they live, all turtles lay their eggs on land.

A turtle's most unique feature is its protective shell. A turtle shell has about 60 bones and is made up of two parts—the *carapace* (KAR-uh-pace), which covers the turtle's back, and the *plastron* (PLAS-trun), which covers its belly. Most species can pull their legs and heads inside their shells when a predator appears.

There are six species of sea turtles, but all are very rare because people have killed too many of them. Hawksbill sea turtles, for example, were hunted for their beautiful shells. These were made into jewelry, souvenirs, and eyeglass frames. Others, like the green sea turtle, were killed for their meat and skin. Today, all sea turtles are protected by law.

Turtles do not have teeth. They use their beaklike snouts to rip and cut their food. As a group, turtles eat an amazing variety of foods—from insects and fruit to jellyfish and worms.

Lizards

Lizard movement is fascinating to observe, as many species have adapted unique ways to get around. Geckos (GE-koze), for instance, have many ridges on the bottoms of their feet, which make them great climbers.

Chameleons (kuh-MEE-lee-uns) also are excellent climbers, moving slowly through trees in search of insect prey. These lizards have *zygodactyl* (zy-guh-DAK-tul) feet. This means that some toes face forward and some face backward.

Some lizards are excellent swimmers. The Bornean earless lizard uses snakelike movements to propel its body on both water and land.

Lizards have adapted a wide range of defenses. The horned toads of North America have sharp spines on their heads and bodies, and most predators avoid them. Chisel-teeth lizards and chameleons use camouflage to avoid being seen. Some lizards play dead when attacked. Predators that are stimulated by movement will lose interest in prey that seems lifeless.

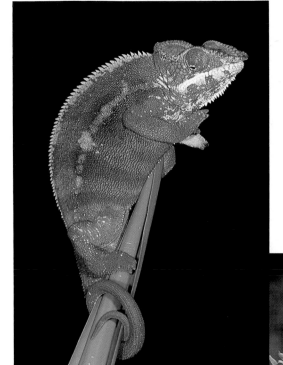

Chameleons have *prehensile* (pre-HEN-sil) tails, meaning that their movement can be controlled, allowing the animals to wrap them around tree limbs for extra stability.

The komodo dragon, the largest of all monitor lizards, can reach a length of 10 feet and weigh more than 350 pounds.

Numbering some 3,000 species, lizards are probably the most diverse of all reptiles.

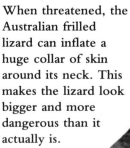

When threatened, the Australian frilled lizard can inflate a huge collar of skin around its neck. This makes the lizard look bigger and more dangerous than it actually is.

Amphibians & Reptiles

With a jaw that can "unhinge," many snakes can eat prey that is much larger than their own heads.

The body of a snake is covered with a scaly skin, which helps it move along the ground. Snakes shed their skins several times a year.

Snakes can detect prey with their eyes and noses, but also by using their tongues. When snakes flick their forked tongues in and out of their mouths, they pick up chemical signals.

Harmless to humans, the common garter snake may be found in grassy fields and along streams throughout southern Canada and the United States.

Snakes

There are at least 2,500 varieties of snakes in the world. Despite the fact that these reptiles have no legs, many species, like the American racer, are extremely swift. Most snakes move by flexing their bodies in a series of S-shaped curves, using plants, rocks, or rough ground as push-off points.

This same movement is used by water snakes and garter snakes, which spend most of their time in water, to swim. Snakes that live in trees, like American tree boas, vary this S-shaped movement. These snakes slither through the trees with accordion-type maneuvers, using their prehensile tails for a better grip.

Snakes are carnivores, feeding on insects, birds, worms, mammals, fish, lizards, and even other snakes. Food is swallowed whole, because snake teeth are designed for catching and holding prey, not for chewing.

Some snakes, such as pit vipers, have heat sensors on their faces that help locate the direction and distance of prey, even in complete darkness.

Some species, like boas, pythons, and rat snakes, dispatch their prey by *constriction* (kun-STRIK-shun), which means they wrap themselves around their victim and squeeze until it suffocates.

Others, like rattlesnakes and coral snakes, are poisonous, killing victims with venom. Poison enters a victim's body through the snakes' fangs.

202

Crocodilians

There are 22 species of crocodilians, a type of reptile. The list includes alligators and crocodiles. These fascinating reptiles have changed little in the last 65 million years.

All crocodilians live near water in warm regions around the world. They have adapted special features that suit their watery lifestyles: webbed feet that help them swim and also walk on mud or sand; eyes and nostrils set high on their heads so they can see and breathe while almost completely submerged; a third eyelid that protects their eyes underwater; and a strong tail that propels them through the water.

Crocodilians are powerful meat-eaters and will devour any animal they can catch. Strong, tooth-filled jaws tear and rip apart prey.

The gavial, also known as gharial (GER-ee-ul), is native to India. It gets its name from the potlike shape at the end of the male's snout. *Ghara* is the Hindi word for "pot."

Today, many crocodilians are rare because too many were killed for their beautiful skins. Crocodile and alligator hides have long been used to make shoes, purses, and other leather goods. Laws now protect most crocodilians. As a result, many species, including the American alligator, are making a comeback.

The American alligator belongs to the same family as the crocodile, but is typically heavier and less active. Alligators also have rounded snouts. Crocodile snouts are pointed and narrow.

A gavial (right) can grow to a length of 20 feet. Its main food is fish, but it will also eat frogs, birds, and other small animals.

Crocodilians spend most of their day basking in the sun, but become active at night in their search for a meal.

Alligators may attack deer and other large animals that come near the water.

Birds

The dull color of the female cardinal helps hide her as she sits on her eggs.

When building the nest, the female often stops to sit in it and shape it to her body.

Cardinals

The male cardinal is the only crested red bird in North America. It is red all over except for its black face and throat. The female cardinal has her matc's shape, including the crest that she can raise or lower as her mood changes. Her colors are much softer, though—brownish pink, with red on her crest, wings, and tail.

The cardinal's favorite food is black-oil sunflower seeds. When eating a sunflower seed, the cardinal uses its tongue to position the seed sideways in its bill. The cardinal cracks the seed open, spits out the hull, and swallows the nut meat. Cardinals also like to eat insects, pumpkin seeds, grains, and fruit.

In the days of the settlers, cardinals lived only in the southeastern states. Over the last 200 years, as forests have been cleared to make room for towns and farms, the habitat for cardinals has improved. Cardinals are now found in the northern states and in southern Canada.

Cardinals do not like deep wooded places. They prefer the forest's edge, suburban gardens, groves, and parks. Above the chatter of squirrels and scolding of jays, you may hear the cardinal's *who-it, who-it, who-it, cheer cheer cheer!*

The cardinal's heavy beak is especially suited for cracking hard seeds.

American Robins

The red breast of the robin not only makes it easy for people to identify, it is also the way other robins recognize each other. The male's breast is brighter than the female's; their young have speckled breasts.

Robins build their nest of twigs, grass, and mud. The nest is plastered to a tree branch, deep in a bush, or on a windowsill or another flat place.

from here to here in summer

from here to here in winter

Migratory Map

In winter, most robins migrate in flocks to the warm south-central states. Some robins will stay north, though, so you may see robins in your snowy yard. When their inner clocks tell them winter is over, the migrating males will flock back to their nesting grounds first. The females and yearlings will follow in the next few weeks.

Robins eat whatever is plentiful during the season. In winter, they will eat mostly vegetables, fruits, and berries. In summer, they eat mostly insects.

One of the first signs of spring is the red-breasted robin singing outside!

Can a robin hear a worm wiggling through soil? Ornithologists don't think so. Because its eyes are on the sides of its head, a robin must cock its head sideways to see its food.

Birds

Herons are long-legged, long-billed birds that spend all of their time near the water, even though they never swim.

Like some species of heron, the common egret was almost wiped out by feather hunters in the early 1900s. Today, it is found worldwide.

The tricolored heron is found in the marshes, lakes, and lagoons of the southeastern United States.

Herons

Herons (HEER-unz) and their relatives, bitterns (BI-ternz) and egrets (EE-grets), are found all over the world, primarily in wetland habitats.

Different species have different methods of locating prey—usually fish, insects, frogs, or worms. The black heron wades into shallow water and opens its wings, creating a shadow. It is not clear whether the fish mistake the shadow for shelter and swim toward it, or whether the shadow simply helps the heron see the fish better, but the system works.

The purple heron rarely wades into the water. It prefers to perch on reeds or low branches, waiting quietly for prey to appear.

Other species, like the great blue heron, wade deep into the water, using their feet to stir up fish and other creatures hiding in the mud. Once the prey has been located, the heron will use its long bill to stab it with deadly accuracy.

Herons have beautiful feathers in shades of smoky white, light gray, and blue. Early this century, millions of herons were killed for their feathers, used to decorate women's hats. Large numbers of herons were wiped out, and many species became rare. Today, laws protect herons and their relatives from this senseless slaughter.

The great blue heron stands four feet tall and has a wingspan of around six feet.

Vultures and Condors

With their bald heads and the slightly rumpled feathers that are common to some species, vultures are not as beautiful as their relatives, eagles and hawks. But vultures are important because they feed on dead animals, helping to keep habitats clean.

In Africa, the Griffon vulture and the Cape vulture follow the migration of large animals like the wildebeest (WIL-de-beest) and zebra. With their long, broad wings, these birds can soar in the sky for hours.

The king vulture (left), found in Central and South America, is the most colorful of all vultures.

With a wingspan of nine feet, the California condor is North America's greatest soaring bird. Unfortunately, few survive in the wild.

Another type of vulture, the Andean condor of South America, is also a *scavenger* (SKA-ven-jer). With a wingspan of up to ten feet, it is one of the world's largest birds.

Almost as large is the California condor. Overhunting and pesticide poisoning nearly wiped out this species. Today, there are only about 75 California condors in existence—the majority of them in captivity.

Vultures belong to a group of birds known as birds of prey, or *raptors*.

Vultures generally have keen eyesight, powerful beaks for tearing flesh, and bald heads that can be thrust into an animal's body without fouling any feathers.

207

Birds

Some domestic turkeys have white feathers, but most are black and bronze.

Smaller than the common turkey, this Central American species has never been domesticated.

Turkeys

When you hear the word "turkey," you probably think of the chubby gobbler that graces your holiday dinner table. This domestic turkey is a descendant of the common turkey, which is native to North and Central America. Domestic turkeys can be more than three times heavier than their wild relatives, sometimes weighing in at 60 pounds or more! The domestic turkey is raised on turkey farms and cannot survive in the wild.

The common turkey is a much more streamlined bird. It lives in open woodland and forest clearings, where it feeds on seeds, berries, and small reptiles such as salamanders and lizards. Turkeys have bare heads and necks, as well as large throat patches called *wattles* (WA-tulz). Males also have sharp horns on each leg called *spurs*. When a male is seeking a mate, he puts on a fancy courtship display. Strutting back and forth, he rattles his wing feathers, swells his wattle, opens his tail feathers, and gobbles loudly.

Female turkeys build nests by themselves, laying 8 to 15 eggs. Sometimes female turkeys will share a nest, so they can better protect their eggs.

Turkeys are game birds and are popular targets for hunters. Not good fliers, they prefer walking instead of taking to the air.

Europeans had never seen turkeys until Spanish explorers brought them home from Mexico during the 16th century.

Wild turkeys prefer wooded areas near water. Their diet consists of seeds, berries, nuts, insects, and an occasional frog or lizard.

Cockatoos

Found mainly in Australia and New Guinea, cockatoos are members of the parrot family.

Cockatoos have sharp, sawlike beaks that are used to open seeds and fruits. In fact, the name "cockatoo" is derived from the Malayan word *kakatua*, which means "pincers." Like other parrots, cockatoos can use their hooked bills as a third foot to climb trees or to grasp food. Some varieties have cheek patches that change color—to red or blue, depending on the species—when they are alarmed.

Cockatoos have large crests on the tops of their heads. These normally lay flat, but are raised when the bird is excited. The sulfur-crested cockatoo's bright yellow crest stands out nicely against its white body. Not all cockatoos are white, however. The great black cockatoo has grayish-black feathers and crimson cheek patches, while the gang-gang cockatoo is usually a grayish color.

Cockatoos spend most of their lives in trees, occasionally coming to the ground to feed. Like most perching birds, their claws are structured to give them a strong grip on tree branches. Cockatoos have a most unusual way of keeping clean. They bathe themselves by flying among wet leaves or by hanging upside down during rain showers.

Like most cockatoo species, the Moluccan cockatoo is mostly white in color.

Cockatoos are popular as pets, but too many have been taken from the wild. Today, many varieties are rare.

The sulfur-crested cockatoo has a tuft of yellow feathers atop its head that the bird can fan open at will.

The palm cockatoo is the largest of the 17 species in this group.

Different species of sandpipers will flock together in huge numbers of up to 100,000 birds.

Sandpipers

Sandpipers are found throughout the northern parts of both Europe and North America. Most species breed in wetlands or grasslands and winter along coastal areas.

Most sandpipers prefer open country near water, where they feed on snails, clams, lobsters, shrimp, aquatic worms and flies, and sometimes, plants. At low tide they feed together in the shallow mud and sand.

When the tide comes in, these wading birds retreat to high salt marshes or nearby farmland. In the morning, when the tide goes back down, the birds return to the shore to feed once again.

Most sandpipers are a spotted brown or gray, with pale or white feathers on their underparts. The feathers of some species change color with the seasons. All species have long wings and short tails, though many have pointed, falconlike wings that enable them to fly very fast.

Across the species, sandpipers have a variety of bill types because of the different ways they gather food. The curlew sandpiper, for example, has a large curved bill that it uses to probe for snails, clams, and other sea creatures, while the broad-billed sandpiper has a heavy bill that allows it to feed on larger prey.

Numbering 81 different species, sandpipers are the most common shorebirds in the world.

Sandpipers gather at sea beaches and inland mud flats to search for food.

During the winter, the western sandpiper looks almost identical to the semipalmated sandpiper.

Puffins

Short-winged birds with heavy bodies, puffins are found in the northern extremes of North America, Europe, and Asia. They are part of a group of some 22 species of seabirds known as auks.

Sometimes called sea parrots, puffins have large parrotlike bills that are brightly colored in shades of orange, yellow, and blue. This gives puffins an almost comical appearance, particularly during the summer breeding season when their bills become larger and brighter. When the season is over, the outer layers of the bills are shed—not unlike a deer shedding its antlers— and they return to their original size.

In one respect, at least, puffins are unlike parrots. They are silent birds, although they can make a deep growl.

Puffins can fly, but they are somewhat awkward in the air. Puffins are at their best in the water, where they use their wings as flippers to dive and swim in search of fish.

The birds live in large groups called colonies during the summer months. When fall arrives, they leave their breeding grounds to spend the next nine months at sea.

Puffins raise just one chick each year. Every day for the first six weeks after a chick hatches, one of its parents flies out to sea, returning to the nest with a bill full of small fish.

Puffins are similar to penguins in many ways, but the two species aren't even distantly related.

The Atlantic puffin (above) can carry as many as ten fish at a time, holding them crosswise in its beak. The tufted puffin (right) grows yellow plumes along the sides of its head during the summer breeding season.

The horned puffin is a Pacific relative of the common (or Atlantic) puffin.

211

Hummingbirds

Hummingbirds have long, needle-like bills, which they use to sip nectar from flowers. Their feet are small and weak. They can barely walk, and barely ever do.

The acrobatics of hummingbirds help them to defend their territories, attract mates, and scare other birds.

Hummingbirds have extremely powerful flight muscles. In most birds, only the muscles that control the downstroke of wing motion are enlarged. In the hummingbird, both the muscles that control the upstroke as well as those that control the downstroke are powerful. In flight, a hummingbird beats its wings 55 to 75 times a second!

Hummingbirds are the smallest birds in the world. This black-chinned hummingbird measures 3 to 4 inches from bill to tail.

Since the hummingbird is the smallest bird in the world, it naturally builds the smallest nest.

Hummingbirds can fly in every direction, including upside down! While they hover, their wings rotate at the shoulder; their tips trace a figure-8 pattern. Darting and dipping at a high speed is their best survival technique. Nothing can catch them!

Most North American species of hummingbirds produce two broods per season. Egg color varies according to the species, but many eggs look pinkish to white. The eggs are oval, and are less than one-half inch long. The female incubates the eggs from 11 to 19 days. The ruby-throated hummingbird egg hatches in 11 to 14 days.

The hummingbird's favorite color is red. Scientists believe that hummingbirds are not born with this preference, but learn it through trial and error. Hummingbirds discover that red flowers provide a source of nectar with the amount of sugar they prefer. To invite hummingbirds to your yard, hang a special red feeder that holds a sugar-water syrup made of one part table sugar and four parts water. Do not use honey and water. It spoils quickly and can poison the little birds.

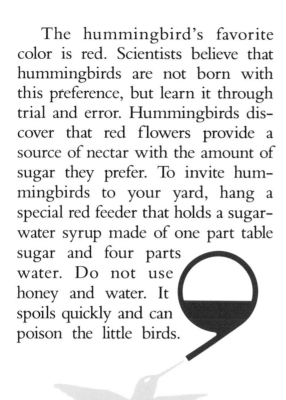

When hummingbirds sip nectar from flowers, they become dusted with pollen. Just as bees do, hummingbirds help to cross-pollinate flowers. In fact, some flowers rely on hummingbirds rather than bees for pollination.

Hummingbirds must eat enormous amounts of food to fuel themselves. Nectar is an easily digested source of quick energy. It is thought that a hummingbird eats half its weight in sugar each day. It collects the nectar by drawing its tongue in and out of the flower about 13 times a second.

Many species of hummingbirds have a narrow crop below the throat. The crop is a place to store food that is gathered but cannot be swallowed and digested at the moment.

The nest of a ruby-throated hummingbird is only as big around as a half-dollar; the eggs are smaller than a dime! The nest stretches as the babies inside it grow. Some hummingbirds use the same nest year after year.

213

Mammals

Like most lemurs, the mongoose lemur has large eyes and a somewhat doglike face.

Primates range in size from the tiny mouse lemur, which weighs only 2 ounces, to the gorilla, which can weigh 600 pounds.

The pygmy marmoset (right) is only about six inches long, but it is an excellent tree climber. The long, white "moustache" of the Emperor tamarin (below) gives it a comical look.

Primates

What do you have in common with a chimpanzee, a mountain gorilla, and a spider monkey? You are all closely related mammals—you are primates (PRY-mayts).

There is a wide diversity among primates, but there are some traits that all share. Most primates have "opposable thumbs," which means that their thumbs can rotate to touch the fingertips on the same hand. This helps primates climb trees and grasp food. Also, primates can see in color, and their brains are generally larger than those of other mammals.

The more primitive primates, called *prosimians* (pro-SIM-ee-unz), include the strange aye-aye, lemurs (LEE-merz), and the sifakas (si-FAH-kuz). These tree-dwelling primates live on the island of Madagascar. Galagos (guh-LAY-goze), lorises (LOR-i-sez), pottos (PAH-toze), and tarsiers (TAR-see-erz) are also prosimians. Scientists believe that the earliest primates that appeared on Earth some 70 million years ago were similar to some of the mammals in this group.

The "higher" primates include marmosets (MAR-moh-sets), tamarins (TAM-uh-rinz), monkeys, apes, and humans. Found only in South America, marmosets and tamarins are squirrel-sized primates that are some of nature's most spectacular mammals.

Marmosets and tamarins eat fruit, flowers, nectar, insects, frogs, and spiders. They live in close family groups of between four and 15 individuals. All members of the group help raise the young—sharing food and even carrying them from time to time. It's possible that these "babysitters" are learning how to care for the offspring that they will have one day.

Most primates do not exhibit this kind of family cooperation, but some do live in smaller family groups made up of a male and female and their immature offspring. Gibbons and their cousins, the siamang (SEE-uh-mang) monkeys, live in groups such as this. In titi (ti-TEE) monkey family groups, the male takes the lead role in caring for the young. He is the one who is in charge of feeding, protecting, and carrying the infant until it is about four or five months old and mature enough to keep up with its family.

The great apes—chimpanzees, orangutans, and gorillas—are human beings' closest relatives. These amazing animals have many behaviors and physical characteristics that are just like ours. Apes have no tails, and they have long arms and highly developed brains. Gorillas are usually described as being of either the lowland or mountain variety. The mountain gorilla is an endangered species. Only a few hundred remain in the mountains of East Africa.

The orangutan (left) is among the apes most clearly related to human beings. Despite its ferocious reputation, the gorilla (below) is for the most part a peaceful animal.

Scientists have been able to teach chimpanzees and gorillas words by using sign language.

Intelligent, sociable animals, chimpanzees communicate with each other using a variety of sounds and facial expressions.

215

Mammals

Raccoons make their homes in the hollows of large trees. There are only two species: the common raccoon shown here and the larger, crab-eating raccoon of South America.

Carnivores

There are about 230 species of carnivores. Cats, dogs, bears, raccoons, weasels, and hyenas are all carnivores, or meat-eaters. Most mammals in this group are well equipped for their meaty diets. They have long, pointed canine teeth and powerful jaws for holding and chewing meat.

Carnivores have different ways of hunting. Some, like wolves and hyenas, hunt in groups called packs. Tigers, jaguars, and other cat species usually hunt alone. Once caught, prey is usually killed with a bite to the neck. Mongooses and weasels bite the backs of their victims' heads, and African wild dogs will aim for their prey's soft underparts.

Meat-eaters are at the top of the food chain and help keep nature's balance. Predators help keep the populations of their prey from growing too large. When hunting, predators often seek the weakest, oldest, or slowest victim, because these are usually the easiest to catch. In this way, carnivores help "weed out" unhealthy individuals.

Some carnivores have a mixed diet. The giant panda, an endangered species found only in China, feeds mainly on bamboo, but it will also eat bulbs, insects, and rodents. Raccoons, found throughout North and South America, will eat almost anything—from frogs to fruit. Many live near urban areas, and their nighttime raids on garbage cans can become terribly annoying.

Although some people think that carnivores are cruel killers, they play an important role in the balance of nature.

Wolves will eat most small animals and birds, but their main prey is deer, including moose and caribou.

When angered, the giant panda (above) will hiss and spit. The lion (right) can produce amazingly powerful roars.

Hoofed Mammals

Sheep, zebras, camels, and deer all belong to a group of mammals called *ungulates* (UN-gyoo-layts)— mammals with hooves. There are about 200 species of ungulates. Classified as even-toed ungulates are pigs and peccaries (PE-kuh-reez), giraffes, antelopes, and hippopotamuses. Odd-toed ungulates include rhinoceroses, horses, and tapirs (TAY-pirz).

Ungulates are usually *herbivores* (ER-bi-vorz), feeding on leaves, flowers, fruits, and grasses. Many species of ungulates live in large groups called herds. Most ungulates have an excellent sense of smell and large eyes on the sides of their heads.

Elephants, known as "primitive ungulates," are related to this large group of mammals. There are two species—the Asian elephant and the African elephant.

Unfortunately, both elephant species have suffered great losses over the years. Although they are protected by law, both species are losing their habitats to a growing human population.

Elephants live in close family groups that are led by the oldest females. All members of the herd help raise the young elephants, which rely on adult care until they are 12 to 13 years old. When male elephants reach this age, they leave the group.

Elephants are the largest land animals in the world, and many people consider them the most magnificent. Unfortunately, many have been killed for their ivory tusks.

There are some 200 species of hoofed animals. The list includes pigs, horses, antelopes, elephants, giraffes, and hippopotamuses.

Even when they are only a few days old, young sheep, called kids, can go almost anywhere their mothers lead them.

Giraffes may look awkward, but when frightened or attacked, they can run faster than any horse.

217

Mammals

Related to the guinea pig, capybaras (left) are found in the swamps and riverside forests of eastern and northern South America.

Rabbits are cute, but they can be pests. They breed quickly, and they will eat almost any growing plant.

Rodents and Rabbits

Rodents are best known for the long, chisellike front teeth that stick out of their upper jaws. These teeth never stop growing. They must be ground down every day with a good chewing on a piece of wood.

Rodents range in size from the tiny harvest mouse to the capybara (ka-pee-BAR-uh)—an aquatic rodent that looks like a guinea pig but can weigh more than 100 pounds! Scientists classify rodents into three main groups, based on the structure of their jaw muscles. One group includes chipmunks, squirrels, and beavers. Rats and micelike rodents make up the second group. The third group includes porcupines and guinea pigs.

Although they look like rodents, scientists have grouped rabbits and hares separately because of differences in their teeth and skeletons. There are about 60 species of rabbits and hares. All have long ears and hind legs, furry bodies, and fluffy, upturned tails. Hunted by many animals, rabbits and hares can run very fast when threatened.

Pikas (PIE-kuz) are closely related to rabbits and hares. Fourteen species of pikas live in North America, Eastern Europe, and Asia. These lively creatures spend most of their summer and fall days collecting grasses and drying them in the sun. Later, they will store this hay and use it as winter food.

There are about 1,700 species of rodents in the world. Nearly 40 percent of all mammals belong to this group.

Squirrels are found all over the world, except Australia and the polar regions.

Bats

Bats range in size from the tiny Kitti's hog-nosed bat, with a wingspan of just six inches, to the huge Samoan flying fox, which has a wingspan of almost six feet! They live on every continent except Antarctica, feeding on everything from fruit and insects to nectar and, in some cases, blood. They make the most of their habitats.

Bats are not blind. In fact, some have excellent vision. More than 700 species of bats depend on a unique system, called *echolocation* (e-koh-loh-KAY-shun), to navigate around obstacles, locate safe places to land, and find food in the dark. Echolocation works something like a submarine's sonar. Bats make high-pitched clicking sounds that bounce off nearby objects and are returned to the bats' ears as echoes. The echoes help the bats determine the location of prey and also help them avoid flying into branches or wires.

Bats are not the evil monsters that some people think they are. Many bats, especially those that live in the tropics, spread seeds and pollinate plants. Bats also eat mosquitoes and other insect pests. Some bats may snatch as many as 600 insects out of the air in just one hour!

Bats are the only mammals that have wings and can truly fly. With almost 1,000 different species, they comprise nearly one quarter of all existing mammals.

Bats usually rest during the day, hanging upside down by their toes in a cave or other dark place.

Fruit-eating bats (left) are found only in warm regions, where fruit is available year-round. There are only three species of vampire bats (below), but none are found in the United States.

Mammals

The killer whale is the only member of the whale family that eats warm-blooded animals, particularly penguins and seals.

Mistakenly thought of as fish, cetaceans are actually mammals that have adapted to life in the water.

Because of its friendliness and apparent intelligence, the dolphin has fascinated humans since ancient times.

Unusual-looking beluga whales, also known as white whales, are found in the Arctic region and adjacent seas.

Whales and Dolphins

Some mammals have adapted completely to life in water. These mammals are called *cetaceans* (se-TAY-shuns). This group includes whales, dolphins, and porpoises. There are 76 species of cetaceans swimming in the oceans throughout the world.

The largest animal ever to live on Earth—the blue whale—still exists  today. Not even the biggest dinosaur that ever lived grew as large as this gentle giant, which can measure 80 feet or more in length and weigh as much as 150 tons! To help stay warm in chilly seas, cetaceans have a layer of fat, called blubber, just beneath their skin.

Cetaceans are highly intelligent mammals, and many species have evolved complex ways to communicate with each other. Scientists are still trying to determine the meaning of the high-pitched squeaks of the humpback whale.

Like other mammals, cetaceans breathe air and must come to the water's surface to do so. They take in and release air through one or two blowholes on the tops of their heads. Some species, like the sperm whale, can go for long periods of time without taking a breath. Sperm whales have been clocked underwater for over an hour without coming up for air!

Dinosaur Beginnings

Dinosaur History

Dinosaurs have amazed people for thousands of years. A Chinese book written between 265 and 317 A.D. mentions "dragon bones." These bones may have been dinosaur bones. Many dinosaur bones have been found in the same area that the "dragon bones" were found.

In England, Robert Plot found a thigh bone of what was probably *Megalosaurus* in 1677, but at first he thought it was a giant human thigh bone. Later, in 1824, William Buckland wrote about a tooth-filled lower jaw of *Megalosaurus*. It was the first scientific dinosaur write-up.

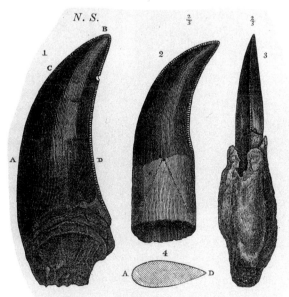

Teeth of Megalosaurus from Stonesfield, Oxon.

Dinosaur Beginnings

Riojasaurus was a Late Triassic prosauropod.

The Jurassic sauropods, including *Brachiosaurus,* were enormous. Some may have been as long as 100 feet!

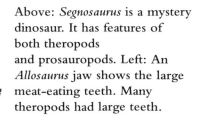

Above: *Segnosaurus* is a mystery dinosaur. It has features of both theropods and prosauropods. Left: An *Allosaurus* jaw shows the large meat-eating teeth. Many theropods had large teeth.

The prosauropods appeared in the Late Triassic and lived until the Early Jurassic. This group of dinosaurs was related to the sauropods, which appeared later. The prosauropods were large, some more than 20 feet or more. The most famous of this group is *Plateosaurus.* All prosauropods ate plants.

The sauropods were giant, four-legged plant-eaters with long necks and tails. They lived in the Jurassic, and survived into the Cretaceous. The vertebrae (bones of the spine) of these huge animals had deep hollows to make them lighter. These are some of the most famous dinosaurs, including *Apatosaurus, Brachiosaurus, Diplodocus,* and *Camarasaurus.*

The theropods are a large group of meat-eaters. All the predatory (meat-eaters that hunt for food) dinosaurs, except the most primitive, belong to this group. Theropods had advanced feet and ankles, and their feet had claws. All walked on two feet. Birds seem to be closely related to these dinosaurs. The size ranged from small, such as *Coelophysis,* to quite large, such as *Tyrannosaurus.*

The segnosaurs are an unusual group of recently discovered dinosaurs that are still a bit of a mystery. They were found in China and Mongolia. At first, scientists thought they were meat-eaters, but now they are thought to be plant-eaters. This group has features in common with both the meat-eating theropods and the plant-eating prosauropods. Paleontologists believe they are more closely related to prosauropods.

All ornithischian dinosaurs were plant-eaters. Later ornithischians split into five different groups of plant-eaters. Three groups walked on all fours, two groups walked on two legs.

The stegosaurs were the dinosaurs with the large plates on their backs that lived in the

Jurassic. They also lived in the Cretaceous. *Stegosaurus* is the best-known stegosaur. China has the most kinds of stegosaurs.

The ankylosaurs replaced stegosaurs in the Late Cretaceous. Ankylosaurs, or armored dinosaurs, had flexible body armor rather than a double row of tall plates. Where stegosaurs have spikes on their tails, some ankylosaurs had a bony club. *Ankylosaurus* is the best-known ankylosaur.

The ceratopsians (ser-a-TOP-see-inz) were the horned dinosaurs and their relatives. These animals had a special bone, called the *rostral*, which formed a parrotlike beak at the front of their mouths. The best-known ceratopsian is *Triceratops*. Many advanced ceratopsians had large, spectacular frills. A frill was a bony shelf that covered the back of their necks.

All ornithopods were two-legged plant-eaters that lived during the entire age of dinosaurs. The Late Cretaceous duckbills were the most advanced, with hundreds of teeth in their mouths for chewing. Some duckbills had a crest, which was a hollow or solid structure on top of their heads. Animals with hollow crests may have used them to "trumpet" to other members of their group. Some famous ornithopods were *Camptosaurus*, *Iguanodon*, *Maiasaura*, and *Corythosaurus*.

The pachycephalosaurs (PAK-ee-CEF-a-lo-SAHRS) (or bone-headed dinosaurs) were an unusual bunch of dinosaurs. They had thick skulls that they probably used in head-butting contests. They may have done this to compete for mates.

Though they ruled the world, dinosaurs died out at the end of the Cretaceous Period. They were amazing creatures—and we continue to study them millions of years after they lived.

Huayangosaurus was a Middle Jurassic stegosaur.

Stegosaur **plates may have fooled predators. They may have disguised which end was which— tail or head!**

Above: *Triceratops* was a large ceratopsian. Left: *Edmontonia* was a relative of *Ankylosaurus*.

This skull shows how thick the head of a pachycephalosaur was. This head belonged to *Prenocephale*.

Coelophysis

Although many later theropods were giants, *Coelophysis* was about eight or nine feet long, weighing about 100 pounds.

Coelophysis is the first known member of a group called theropods. Theropods were meat-eaters of all sizes that walked on long hind legs and had short front legs, big heads, and sharp teeth.

relative size

A later relative of *Coelophysis* was *Syntarsus* (sin-TAR-sus), which was more advanced. It had fewer teeth, a bigger head, and weaker hands.

The head of *Coelophysis* had big eyes and a pointed snout. Dozens of knife-edged teeth lined its jaws. Its tail was long and slender and, like other dinosaurs, held off the ground. The front legs were small and (as in other theropods) not used for walking. The hind legs were long and strong. Its bones were hollow (the name *Coelophysis* means "hollow limb shaft"). Like birds' legs, those of *Coelophysis* were lightly built but strong. The feet had three long toes and one very short toe.

The hind limbs of *Coelophysis* were made for fast movement. *Coelophysis* had to be quick on its feet to escape some of the larger meat-eating animals of its day. These bigger hunters were not dinosaurs, but huge four-footed reptiles such as the crocodilelike phytosaurs and rauisuchids.

When hunting for food, *Coelophysis* probably went after insects, lizardlike reptiles, and even other dinosaurs. This animal lived along streams, and it is possible that *Coelophysis* ate fish. Its pointed snout would have made fishing easier.

Coelophysis is one of the best known dinosaurs. This is because many *Coelophysis* skeletons were discovered in the Ghost Ranch quarry in northern New Mexico. The tangled remains of hundreds of animals ended up in a single grave.

248	TRIASSIC	**213**	JURASSIC	**144**	CRETACEOUS	**65**

MILLION YEARS AGO

Herrerasaurus

This early meat-eater probably looked like the later theropod (or meat-eating) dinosaurs. Like them, it walked on its hind legs with its tail held out and off the ground. Like them, it had small forelimbs, a rather short neck, a big head, and a large mouth with sharp teeth.

But there were also differences. *Herrerasaurus* had four toes (a primitive feature). Theropods had three toes. The pelvis and some of the backbones of *Herrerasaurus* look like those in much later theropods. The pubis (one of the bones of the pelvis) resembles the pubis bone of some later ornithischian dinosaurs.

Herrerasaurus cannot be classified with either the Saurischia or Ornithischia (the main dinosaur groups). In fact, this dinosaur lived earlier than even the earliest members of either group.

Herrerasaurus probably lived in a cool, moist world, among groves of ferns and tall conifer trees. Perhaps this dinosaur hunted by springing out from hiding and surprising its prey. When it attacked, it used both its sharp-clawed fingers and cutting teeth.

Herrerasaurus may have been primitive. And yet, it already had qualities needed to survive in a world still ruled by animals other than dinosaurs.

relative size

Herrerasaurus is one of the oldest dinosaurs we know. It lived about 225 million years ago in what is now Argentina, South America.

In life, *Herrerasaurus* stood about four feet high at the shoulders and weighed several hundred pounds.

| 248 | TRIASSIC | 213 | JURASSIC | 144 | CRETACEOUS | 65 |

MILLION YEARS AGO

Allosaurus

Allosaurus is the best known of all the Late Jurassic theropods. The name of this giant meat-eater means "other reptile."

Allosaurus is mostly known from fossils found in North America. Some remains found in Australia have also been called *Allosaurus*.

With its large skull, powerful neck, massive jaws, daggerlike teeth, powerful limbs, and three-clawed hands, *Allosaurus* and its relatives were the most dangerous meat-eaters of their day. Its large, strong back legs made *Allosaurus* a fast runner. It probably caught prey using its sharp teeth and claws. The curved, pointed finger claws could have held down a victim while *Allosaurus* ate. The dinosaur could not chew, so it probably gulped down meat in chunks.

What did a hunting animal like *Allosaurus* eat? Probably its victims were creatures its size or smaller. An *Allosaurus* menu might include baby or young sauropods, stegosaurs, or ornithopods of any age. Like the lion and other modern-day hunting animals, *Allosaurus* probably also scavenged. This means that if an *Allosaurus* found the body of an animal that died, it probably ate it.

Did *Allosaurus* attack the big sauropods? Probably not, unless the sauropod was sick, very old, or very young. Besides having their size to protect them, sauropods could put up a good fight.

The *Allosaurus* remains found at the Cleveland-Lloyd Quarry show all ages and many sizes. The smallest are little more than three feet long. The average size for adults is about 35 feet. But *Allosaurus* could get much bigger. At least one *Allosaurus* was over 40 feet long—making it as large as the later giant *Tyrannosaurus*.

relative size

| **248** | TRIASSIC | **213** | JURASSIC | **144** | CRETACEOUS | **65** |

MILLION YEARS AGO

Diplodocus

All sauropod dinosaurs were long. *Diplodocus* is one of the longest dinosaurs known from complete skeletons. The average length of an adult *Diplodocus* was close to 90 feet. Much of that was its very long neck and tail. This tail ended in a "whiplash" that might have been used as a weapon against theropods.

The name *Diplodocus* means "double beam." This refers to a small piece of bone called a "chevron." Chevrons can be found under each vertebra (the bone of the spine) of the tail. In *Diplodocus*, these chevrons ran forward and backward (like a double beam).

Diplodocus had a small, lightly built head. The nostrils were set on top of the head. All its teeth were at the front of the mouth. These teeth were long, slender, and shaped like pencils. The jaw bones were small and the jaw muscles weak. This tells us that *Diplodocus* probably ate soft plants. With such a long and flexible neck, *Diplodocus* could have eaten ferns that grew on the ground, as well as tall vegetation.

Shiny "gizzard" stones (called gastroliths) have been found in the stomach of some *Diplodocus* skeletons. These stones were swallowed to grind up food.

relative size

Diplodocus has become a fairly common sauropod. Its skeletons are on display at more museums the world over than any other sauropod.

Unlike many other Late Jurassic sauropods, *Diplodocus* was slender. It weighed only about ten tons. This is about half the weight of its more massive relatives. Maybe being slender helped *Diplodocus* move faster to avoid meat-eaters.

248	TRIASSIC	**213**	JURASSIC	**144**	CRETACEOUS	**65**

MILLION YEARS AGO

Heterodontosaurus

Heterodontosaurus was one of the earliest ornithopod dinosaurs. It lived in South Africa during the Early Jurassic.

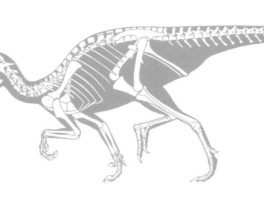

relative size

Heterodontosaurus was a fast runner— it needed to get quickly away from large meat-eating dinosaurs!

Heterodontosaurus was a small dinosaur. It was just three feet long.

Heterodontosaurus had short, strong front legs. The hands were probably able to grab food. The hind legs were long, with the thigh shorter than either the lower leg or foot. A shorter thigh is a sign that an animal could run fast.

The name *Heterodontosaurus* means "different-toothed reptile." Most dinosaurs had just one kind of tooth. *Heterodontosaurus* had three. The teeth at the front of the mouth were small. They were set on the sides of beaks on both upper and lower jaws. The teeth in the back of the mouth were tall and squared. They were angled so that the upper and lower jaws could meet and grind food. These "cheek teeth" were protected by enamel. This hard material kept the teeth from becoming blunt and dull. It also had two large tusk-like teeth, in both upper and lower jaws. These teeth were set in front of the cheek teeth.

The front teeth were probably used for chopping leaves and stems. The cheek teeth then ground the food. *Heterodontosaurus* probably also had fleshy cheeks to keep the food from falling out of its mouth. The tusks may also have been used in eating. Maybe only a male had these tusks to attract females.

248	TRIASSIC	**213**	JURASSIC	**144**	CRETACEOUS	**65**

230

MILLION YEARS AGO

Lufengosaurus

Many specimens of *Lufengosaurus* have been found in the People's Republic of China. *Lufengosaurus* was related to *Plateosaurus*, the biggest prosauropod of the Late Triassic.

Lufengosaurus had a small head. Its skull was long and flat. It had a small bony bump on its snout, just above the nostril. The teeth had wide spaces between them. They looked something like blades. The tooth crowns (the part that shows above the gum) were wider at the bottom. Though we believe that it ate plants, the teeth of *Lufengosaurus* were sharp.

Lufengosaurus had strong back legs. Just like its prosauropod relatives, its front legs were shorter than the hind legs. The animal probably walked on all fours. It could rise up on two legs to get at tall plants.

The hands of *Lufengosaurus* had a large thumb with a claw. This was common for prosauropods. Maybe this claw was used as a weapon against other animals, maybe even other *Lufengosaurus* individuals. The claw might also have let this dinosaur spear its food.

Lufengosaurus shared its Early Jurassic world with other animals. The bones of therapsids, early crocodiles, and even mammals have also been found along with it.

Lufengosaurus lived during the Early Jurassic. This dinosaur was named for the Lufeng Basin of Yunnan Province in southwestern China.

relative size

Like *Plateosaurus* (PLAT-ee-o-SAHR-uhs), *Lufengosaurus* was quite large. It was about 20 feet long. This animal had a very long neck.

There were other prosauropods, too, including one bigger than Lufengosaurus. It was named *Yunnanosaurus* (YOO-nan-o-SAHR-uhs), after the Yunnan Province in China.

| 248 | TRIASSIC | 213 | JURASSIC | 144 | CRETACEOUS | 65 MILLION YEARS AGO |

Mamenchisaurus

If *Mamenchisaurus* were alive today, this giant could look into a fourth story window!

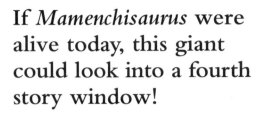

relative size

Mamenchisaurus is the largest sauropod known from China. Its weight may have been 10 to 20 tons. *Mamenchisaurus* seems to have been rather slender compared to other sauropods. Maybe it was graceful when it walked.

One of the most spectacular looking sauropods was *Mamenchisaurus.* Try to imagine an animal whose neck was almost as long as its entire body! *Mamenchisaurus* was a Late Jurassic sauropod that was about 72 feet long. Its neck was about 33 feet long.

This long neck can be explained by two things. The vertebrae (or bones in the spine) were longer than usual, and *Mamenchisaurus* had more vertebrae. If we add the length of the shoulders, we can picture the neck of *Mamenchisaurus* raising its head some 44 feet off the ground.

Mamenchisaurus remains have been found in the People's Republic of China. It was named after Mamenchi, the place of its discovery. ("Chi" means "brook," and "Mamen" was the name of the brook.)

Fossil bones believed to be dragons were collected at this site. These so-called "dragon bones" were ground into powder and sold as medicine. It was believed that "dragon bones" could cure sicknesses. Fortunately, *Mamenchisaurus* did not end up on medicine shelves.

Similarities can be seen between *Mamenchisaurus* and *Diplodocus.* Because of those resemblances, scientists can see a relationship between sauropods of China and of North America and Europe. This tells us that a piece of land may have connected these areas during the Late Jurassic.

248	TRIASSIC	**213**	JURASSIC	**144**	CRETACEOUS	**65**

MILLION YEARS AGO

Scelidosaurus

Scelidosaurus was one of the oldest ornithischians of the Early Jurassic. It was first found in southern England and described in 1860. It was a very complete skeleton with the bones still connected (or articulated).

Scelidosaurus was one of the earliest members of the group called the Thyreophora. Its later relatives included the plated stegosaurs and armored ankylosaurs.

Scelidosaurus was a heavily built animal. Its head was large. The teeth were simple and leaf-shaped. *Scelidosaurus* probably ate the leaves of shrubs and branches that grew near the ground.

The most unusual thing about *Scelidosaurus* was its armor. In life, the skin had many small bony plates in it. These plates could be found on the animal's back, sides, and tail. They probably protected the animal from meat–eaters.

Recently, new specimens of *Scelidosaurus* have been found. These specimens also show fossil skin impressions. From these impressions we know that the skin of this dinosaur had small, rounded scales. These are important in understanding how a dinosaur may have looked.

The name *Scelidosaurus* means "limb reptile." The dinosaur was named that because of its large legs. It walked on all four legs, and each foot had four toes.

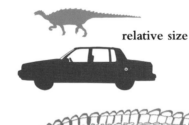

relative size

The tail of *Scelidosaurus* was longer than most other ornithischian dinosaur tails.

248	TRIASSIC	213	JURASSIC	144	CRETACEOUS	65

MILLION YEARS AGO

Shunosaurus

Shunosaurus had features similar to other sauropods. The head was small, it had a long neck, and its body was large. The whole animal measured about 40 feet long and weighed five tons.

In paleontology, some of the most exciting discoveries are completely surprising. One such discovery was made with *Shunosaurus*, a Middle Jurassic sauropod.

relative size

Future dinosaur discoveries will tell us whether *Omeisaurus* (O-mee-SAHR-uhs) also had a tail club like *Shunosaurus*.

The name *Shunosaurus* comes from "Shuo," the Chinese word for "Sichuan." So far, more than 20 almost complete skeletons of this dinosaur have been collected in the Lower Shaximiao Formation of Sichuan Province in the People's Republic of China. Five good skulls were also found, which are rare.

The skull of *Shunosaurus* was rather short (something like that of the North American *Camarasaurus*). *Shunosaurus* had many slender teeth.

But skeletons of *Shunosaurus* revealed something new and unexpected. Of the many *Shunosaurus* skeletons collected, some had a most unusual feature. The tail ended in a large club of bone. Jutting out from this club, there may have been two pairs of short spikes.

What was this tail club used for? Perhaps, like the tail clubs of the armored ankylosaurs, it was used as a weapon. The long tail of *Shunosaurus* could be swung with great force. The club could have hurt meat-eating dinosaurs that lived in the same time and place.

Was *Shunosaurus* the only sauropod to have a bony club on its tail? Might other sauropods also have had such clubs? Another Chinese sauropod, the very long-necked *Omeisaurus*, may have carried a tail club.

Stegosaurus

Stegosaurus is the largest of the stegosaurs. It is also one of the most famous of all dinosaurs. This dinosaur is well known for the triangular plates on its back and the spikes on its tail. Some of these plates were quite large. *Stegosaurus* means "roofed reptile."

This animal walked on all four legs. Because its head was held low, *Stegosaurus* probably ate what grew on the ground. The highest point of the dinosaur's body was at its hips. There the animal was about ten feet tall. The largest of its back plates was located above the hips. This plate added height to the dinosaur.

Its small head had weak jaws. There were no teeth in the front of the jaws, but there was a beak for chopping vegetation. The teeth on the sides of the jaws were leaf-shaped. These teeth had grooves for crushing food.

A tail specimen with the spikes in place shows that these were paired. The spikes must have made a deadly weapon when the tail was swung at meat-eaters like *Allosaurus*.

The brain of *Stegosaurus* may have been small, but so was its head. Compared to body size, the brain of this dinosaur is bigger than that of the sauropods.

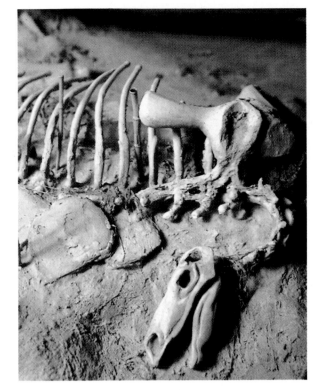

The plates on the back were set in two rows. There has been much debate about the arrangement of the plates. Were they set in pairs, one alongside the other? Most paleontologists think they alternated. No two plates were the same size, so they cannot be arranged in pairs. One *Stegosaurus* skeleton was found with the plates still in place. These plates were in an alternating position.

Stegosaurus was discovered in 1877 in Colorado. It was one of the first dinosaurs known from almost complete skeletons.

relative size

Stegosaurus was about 20 to 24 feet long. It weighed at least two tons.

| 248 | TRIASSIC | 213 | JURASSIC | 144 | CRETACEOUS | 65 |

MILLION YEARS AGO

Abelisaurus

Although *Abelisaurus* was probably from 25 to 30 feet long, we can only guess at the animal's true length. All that has been found so far is the dinosaur's skull.

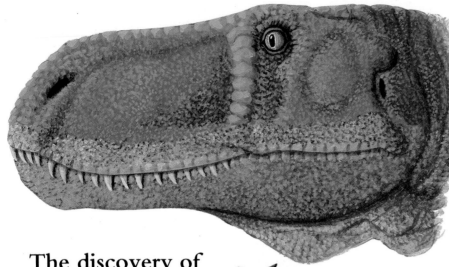

Abelisaurus (named after a scientist named Abel) was a large theropod dinosaur that lived in what is now Patagonia, Argentina, South America, during the Late Cretaceous.

The skull of *Abelisaurus* is about three feet long. The skull at first looks like the much bigger skull of *Tyrannosaurus*. On closer look, we can see that the *Abelisaurus* skull is quite different. One difference is the much larger openings in front of the eye openings (or orbits).

Abelisaurus is so different from other theropods that it has been placed in its own family. Another member of its family is the strange *Carnotaurus* (CAR-no-TAHR-uhs), a theropod dinosaur known from a very complete skeleton.

The discovery of *Abelisaurus* and *Carnotaurus* have given paleontologists a better understanding of South American theropods.

Carnotaurus (whose name means "meat-eating bull") had two bull-like horns on its head and very tiny front limbs. Like *Abelisaurus, Carnotaurus* was found in South America. *Abelisaurus* may actually be a descendant of *Carnotaurus*.

relative size

In the Cretaceous, dinosaurs that lived in southern parts of the world were very different from their relatives in the north. During the earlier Jurassic period, the northern and southern land masses separated. This separation resulted in some changes. Dinosaurs like *Abelisaurus* and *Carnotaurus* were cut off from the northern theropods. Left on their own, these animals evolved in their own ways, adapting to the conditions of their southern world.

248	TRIASSIC	**213**	JURASSIC	**144**	CRETACEOUS	**65**

MILLION
YEARS AGO

Deinonychus

Remains of *Deinonychus* were discovered in southern Montana in 1964. Dr. John H. Ostrom, the Yale University paleontologist who studied and named this theropod, saw that it was different. *Deinonychus* proved to be so different that it changed how we thought about dinosaurs.

The head of *Deinonychus* was quite large compared to its body, as were the heads of most meat-eating dinosaurs. Its brain was very large compared to its body. The small sharp teeth were pointed back and were designed for holding and biting prey. The arms were fairly long. The hands had three fingers, each finger ending in a large claw. The fingers were able to move so that the animal could use them during an attack. The tail was stiffened by long, thin bony rods. These rods helped the tail balance the body.

The most amazing thing about *Deinonychus* was the hind foot. The claw on the inner toes was very large. It was also sharply pointed and very curved.

With an understanding of *Deinonychus*, scientists began to look at dinosaurs in a new way. The image of dinosaurs being stupid and slow was reconsidered. Today we view dinosaurs as quick and intelligent.

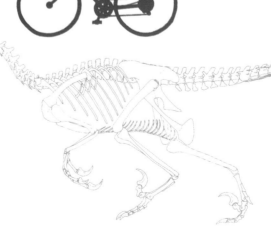

relative size

The sickle claw of *Deinonychus* was a deadly weapon, ready to go into action.

Deinonychus may have been rather small. This dinosaur was just eight to ten feet long and three feet high at the hips. Still, this theropod was a terror in the Early Cretaceous.

248   TRIASSIC   **213**   JURASSIC   **144**   CRETACEOUS   **65** MILLION YEARS AGO

Euoplocephalus

Ankylosaurs were the "armored tanks" of dinosaurs. They all had wide bodies, wide heads with small brains, small simple teeth and beaks, short necks and legs, and armor made of bony plates, spines, and spikes.

Euoplocephalus had a heavily armored body and was about 20 feet long. It ate plants growing close to the ground.

Closely related to Euoplocephalus were the Asian *Saichania* (sy-CHAYN-ee-uh) at right and the North American *Ankylosaurus* (an-KEE-lo-SAHR-uhs) below.

No specimen of *Euoplocephalus* has yet been found with its armor in place. However, we do know that it had a lot of armor on the head and body. Even the eyelids were protected by bone. Its name means "well-armored head."

Euoplocephalus also had a weapon. The tail of this dinosaur was long and probably was carried straight out and off the ground. At the end of the tail was the heavy, bony club. This club made a dangerous weapon.

Paleontologists think that *Euoplocephalus* may have had a good sense of smell. The air passages inside this dinosaur's nostrils were looped. This tells us that many nerves for smell were probably there. Another idea about these looped passages is that they were used to make a noise like a bugle to communicate with others of its kind.

Ankylosaurs were among the last of the dinosaurs—some kinds lived until the very end of the Cretaceous Period.

relative size

248	TRIASSIC	213	JURASSIC	144	CRETACEOUS	65

MILLION YEARS AGO

Iguanodon

Groups of almost complete *Iguanodon* skeletons were found in both Belgium and Germany. These skeletons were different ages and sizes.

Iguanodon walked on heavy back legs. The body was balanced by a tail stiffened by bony tendons. If it wanted to, the animal could come down on all fours and use its strong arms for walking. The head had a blunt snout covered by horn, perfect for cropping leaves, small branches, and shoots. This food would then be torn apart by the many cheek teeth in the back of the jaws.

The hands of *Iguanodon* are interesting. They had blunt hooves (something like a horse's or cow's) that could be used in walking or resting. There was a small outer finger that could have been used for grasping vegetation. An unusual spikelike bone belonging to *Iguanodon* was, at first, thought to be a nose horn. It turned out to be a large, spikelike thumb. This thumb could have been used as a weapon against meat-eating dinosaurs. It might also have been used during contests between rival *Iguanodon* males— fighting over territory, food and water, or females.

Iguanodon was the second dinosaur (after Megalosaurus) to be named and scientifically described.

This historic picture is what scientists thought *Iguanodon* looked like. We now know its hands were more blunt.

Iguanodon was a large ornithopod. Adults were as long as 33 feet, and they weighed about six tons! At first, scientists thought *Iguanodon* looked like a cross between an iguana and a rhinoceros.

relative size

| 248 | TRIASSIC | 213 | JURASSIC | 144 | CRETACEOUS | 65 MILLION YEARS AGO |

Maiasaura

A hatchling *Maiasaura* had a tall, narrow head and big eyes. Even by today's standards, the babies were cute. As the baby grew, the head got lower and wider from front to back. A wide horny beak developed.

Maiasaura is an important and famous discovery. It was found in the Two Medicine Formation of western Montana in 1978. Scientists had believed that dinosaurs laid their eggs and left them. *Maiasaura* cared for its young.

Maiasaura was a flat-headed hadrosaur (or duck-billed dinosaur). It was a large animal, measuring about 30 feet long. Its face was long and somewhat narrow, and there was a low bony crest over the eyes.

The mother *Maiasaura* laid her eggs in a large nest of dirt or mud that measured about six feet across. The eggs, between 15 and 24, were laid in a circular or spiral pattern. The eggs were about six inches long. The mother covered the eggs with plants. The rotting (or composting) plants gave off heat that incubated the eggs (made them hatch).

Maiasaura hatchlings were about 15 inches long. Unlike some other known dinosaur hatchlings, these babies were not able to take care of themselves. A young *Maiasaura* probably stayed in the nest for a few months. During this time, it grew to about four feet long. When it reached about eight feet, it was big enough to join the herd.

relative size

John Horner and Robert Makela gave this dinosaur its name for a very good reason. *Maiasaura* means "good mother reptile."

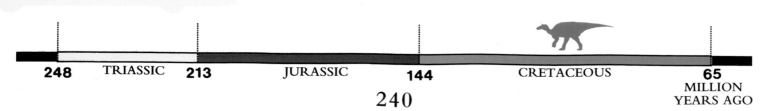

| 248 | TRIASSIC | 213 | JURASSIC | 144 | CRETACEOUS | 65 |

MILLION YEARS AGO

Pachyrhinosaurus

Like other ceratopsians, *Pachyrhinosaurus* had a massive head. (Only the heads of *Pentaceratops*, *Torosaurus*, and *Triceratops* were bigger.) Its face was long and rather flattened. It had a short beak and a short frill. The frill had two large openings (called "fenestrae"). Bony spikes of different sizes ran along the border of the frill. These included two very large spikes toward the top. Most unusual were the structures that stood straight out from the middle of the frill.

Instead of having horns on the face (like *Triceratops* and other large ceratopsians), *Pachyrhinosaurus* had a very thick "boss" (a thick, bumpy pad of bone). This boss ran from the front of its snout back to above the eyes. *Pachyrhinosaurus* means "thick-nosed reptile."

Did *Pachyrhinosaurus* once have a horn that had broken off? Was this boss really what was left of that horn? Was it a scar? The answers came in 1985 when a large bonebed (a place containing a large number of bones of the same kind of animal) with many adult and juvenile *Pachyrhinosaurus* specimens was discovered in Alberta. These specimens proved that the boss was a normal feature.

In 1988, the remains of Pachyrhinosaurus were found on the North Slope of Alaska.

Pachyrhinosaurus may have used its boss to push over trees so it could get to the top leaves.

relative size

The most unusual of all known ceratopsians was probably *Pachyrhinosaurus*. This 25-foot-long animal was quite different from its horned cousins.

248	TRIASSIC	213	JURASSIC	144	CRETACEOUS	65

MILLION YEARS AGO

Segnosaurus

The discovery of *Segno-saurus*, in the Gobi Desert of Mongolia, was one of the most important dinosaur finds of the 1970s. It was found during an expedition by Russian and Mongolian scientists. *Segnosaurus* represents a whole new group of Late Cretaceous dinosaurs.

Segnosaurus, whose name means "slow reptile," was a curious new kind of dinosaur. Although it was a saurischian, its bones showed a strange mix of features.

The small, sharp teeth and long, slender claws were like those of theropods. In some ways, however, these teeth were more like those in prosauropods than theropods. Unlike theropods but like ornitho-pods, there were no teeth in the front of the jaws.

The limbs of *Segnosaurus* were heavy and the feet wide. Where did *Segnosaurus* and its relatives fit in dinosaur classification? Was *Segnosaurus* a theropod, a prosauropod, or something else? Some paleontologists have thought of segnosaurians as being late descendants of the earlier prosauropods. A more recent idea is that *Segnosaurus* and other segnosaurians may have been a group of theropods that had evolved in a special way.

relative size

Unlike theropods, the feet of *Segnosaurus* had four toes instead of three.

Another segnosaurian, called *Erlikosaurus* (AYR-lik-o-SAHR-uhs), seems to have had a prosauropodlike beak. *Segnosaurus* might also have had a beak.

248	TRIASSIC	213	JURASSIC	144	CRETACEOUS	65

MILLION YEARS AGO

Tyrannosaurus

One of the last dinosaurs, and almost everyone's favorite, is *Tyrannosaurus*. *Tyrannosaurus rex* means "tyrant reptile king."

Tyrannosaurus stalked its prey on powerful hind legs. Some paleontologists believe that these legs were made for fast running, and that the animal could have run over 30 miles an hour! Whether running or just walking, *Tyrannosaurus* was one of the biggest and most powerful meat-eating animals that ever lived.

For many years, specimens of this dinosaur were very rare. In recent years, more *Tyrannosaurus* remains have been found. Two almost complete skeletons were collected in 1990—one in Montana, the other in South Dakota.

Tyrannosaurus is famous for its very short arms. These front limbs were much shorter than those of earlier theropods, such as *Allosaurus*. While *Allosaurus* and its relatives had three fingers on each hand, *Tyrannosaurus* only had two.

Some paleontologists thought that these limbs were completely useless. One of the recently found *Tyrannosaurus* skeletons includes a complete front leg and hand. Now we know that the upper arm bone of this dinosaur was quite massive, and that the lower arm bones were very short. Although tiny, the forelimbs of this dinosaur were indeed strong.

Just imagine a meat-eating creature measuring 40 feet long and weighing six tons. Its head, big as an easy chair, was held as high as a split-level house. The mouth, more than a yard long, was filled with sharp teeth, some as long as six inches.

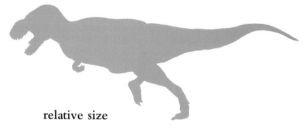

relative size

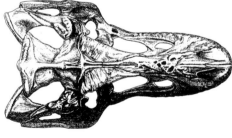

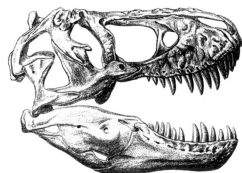

The brain of *Tyrannosaurus* was quite large. *Tyrannosaurus* had the biggest brain of any dinosaur. Its brain was even larger than the brain of a gorilla or chimpanzee.

248	TRIASSIC	213	JURASSIC	144	CRETACEOUS	65

MILLION YEARS AGO

Troodon

Troodon had more teeth than any other known meat-eating dinosaur. Each side of the lower jaw had a total of 35 teeth. Most theropods had about 15 teeth.

Troodon was a small theropod of the Late Cretaceous. Its skeleton was about six feet long.

This was the first dinosaur to be named in North America. It was named in 1856 by Joseph Leidy. *Troodon* means "wounding tooth." The first specimen of *Troodon* found was just one tooth. The specimen was collected in the Judith River area of what was then called the Nebraska Territory (now Montana). Leidy at first thought the tooth was from a prehistoric lizard. Since that original discovery, more and better *Troodon* specimens have been found.

This dinosaur had huge eyes that took up a big part of its skull. With these eyes, the animal could probably have seen in dim twilight. Eyes like these would have let *Troodon* hunt prey that other theropods, with poorer vision, might never even see.

The hands of *Troodon* had slender fingers. The inner finger had a big, thin, pointed, sharp claw.

The second toe of the foot was similar to the toe of *Deinonychus*. It had a large sickle claw for slashing prey. Unlike the "terrible claw" in *Deinonychus*, the claw of *Troodon* was smaller and higher up on the foot. It was also smaller than the very large claw of its hand.

Troodon had a very large brain. The brain would have been about six times bigger than that of a crocodile the same size.

relative size

248	TRIASSIC	213	JURASSIC	144	CRETACEOUS	65

MILLION YEARS AGO

OUR NATURAL WORLD

Perhaps you live in a big city. Or maybe you live in a small town or even on a farm in the country. You and the people around you form a community. You depend on each other, helping each other live in your environment.

The Earth's ecosystems are also communities. The plants and animals that live in each ecosystem depend on each other for survival. Some places seem to us to be rich with life. Others look barren and empty. But even the harshest environment supports its own community of creatures.

Earth's ecosystems, from the driest desert to the ocean floor, show us great contrasts. Each is unique and is home to a unique community of plant and animal life. Studying these communities helps us understand the richness of life on Earth.

The Edge of the Ocean

Waves never stop crashing against the rocky shore. Animals and plants that live there have developed ways to survive the pounding surf.

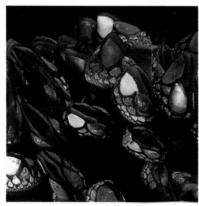

A crab (left) can skitter about the rocks looking for food. Its shell will keep it from being hurt if it is dashed against the rocks by a wave. These gooseneck barnacles (right) are "glued" to the rocks. Pulling their soft bodies inside their shells, they are quite safe from harm.

A sea star might lose a leg as it is tossed by the waves. It can grow a new one, though!

Rocky Shore

The rocky shore is home to the largest variety and the greatest number of seashore creatures. Animals occupy every available space. They are on rocks, under rocks, and in cracks and holes. Animals even live under seaweeds and on the shells of other animals.

All rocky-shore plants and animals must survive the constant pounding of the surf. Animals like limpets and crabs wear hard shells for protection. Others seek a hole or other spot where the surf will not disturb them. To keep from being swept away by the waves, many creatures have ways of clinging to the rocks. A snail's foot lets it move slowly over the rocks or hold fast to one place. Barnacles fasten themselves to the rocks with "cement" they make with their bodies. Mussels attach themselves to rocks with tough, leathery threads. Sea stars have rows of tiny tube feet with suction cups at the tips. The sea star can move around on the rocks as well as cling tightly to the rocks during wave surges.

Some types of seaweed anchor themselves down with strong bases called holdfasts. When the tide goes out, the seaweed stays put. Have you walked over slippery blades of seaweed? Seaweed is slippery because of a coating that helps it hold in moisture and keep from drying out during low tides.

Tide Pool

Tide pools are wonderful places to look for living things when you are exploring a rocky shore. A tide pool is a small pool of water left standing when the tide goes out. It shelters plants and animals that cannot live in the open air during low tides. Every tide pool contains a community of plants and animals. Some are bottom-dwellers, some attach themselves to the rocks, and others swim freely.

Seaweeds clinging to the rocks provide food and shelter for tide-pool creatures. Small animals like hermit crabs often creep under the fronds for protection from the sun and wind. Hermit crabs do not have shells of their own. They live in shells left by other animals.

Sea stars are related to sea urchins. Sea stars usually have five leathery arms. But some have as many as 45 arms!

If you look carefully into a tide pool, you will probably notice colorful "blossoms" clinging to the rocks. They may look like flowers, but they are really animals called sea anemones.

If you see a creature in a tide pool that looks like a giant pincushion, it is probably a sea urchin. A sea urchin wears good armor to protect it against enemies: Sharp spines cover its body. You may find the bleached skeletons of sea urchins—they look like hollow, white pincushions, *without* the pins.

A sea star eats mollusks. It uses the suckers on its tube feet to pull apart the shells. The star pushes its stomach out of its body through its mouth (above). The chemicals in its stomach will digest the fleshy animal inside the shell.

The urchin's mouth is on its underside. It has five sharp teeth that are strong enough to bite into soft rock and coral.

When the hermit crab outgrows its shell, it simply moves into a larger one left behind by another sea creature.

Sea anemones have soft, stinging tentacles. As water flows over the anemones, they wave their tentacles to catch food floating by. When the tide goes out, anemones will pull in their tentacles so they do not dry out.

249

Coral Reefs

After it has anchored itself to a firm surface, a coral polyp builds a skeleton beneath its soft body. The skeleton is cup-shaped. A ship that has wrecked and sunk in warm shallow waters is the perfect place to begin a coral colony.

As new polyps keep building on old skeletons, they form a huge mass that becomes the base of a coral reef. This is Australia's Great Barrier Reef.

The coral skeleton is very hard, but the thin layer of living tissue is easily damaged.

A living coral colony is made up of thousands of tiny animals called polyps. Most coral polyps measure less than an inch across, yet they create some of the largest things on Earth—whole islands and reefs.

A reef begins when the egg of a coral hatches into a larva. This larva drifts with the waves and currents until it settles onto a hard surface. When the coral larva is three weeks old, it becomes a polyp. These polyps divide and form more polyps. Together, the polyps can build huge coral colonies. Some colonies grow to be the size of a car.

If you look closely at coral, you will see tiny holes. Each hole is where a coral animal stuck out its soft body and tentacles to search for food. A polyp is like a tube that is closed at one end and has a mouth at

the other. Its mouth is surrounded by tentacles. These tentacles sting tiny sea creatures as they float by. Once stung, the prey is drawn into the polyp for food. The food on which a polyp feeds is the plankton that drifts with the ocean currents. During the day, most coral polyps stay inside their skeletons. At night, they wave their tentacles to catch food.

Corals have tiny algae living inside them. The algae are single cells, and you would need a microscope to see them. Scientists have learned that the algae supply food for the coral and help the coral produce the chemical it needs to build its limestone skeleton.

The most brightly colored corals are usually the soft corals. Hard corals are often a dull yellow-brown.

There are more than 2,000 different kinds of corals. Some are hard and some are soft. Corals come in many colors—some are pink, some are deep red. Others are violet. Most are yellow-brown due to the algae in their tissues. When photographed underwater with a flash, the colors of corals appear even brighter. The brightly colored corals are not usually the reef builders.

Soft corals have tiny polyps that form branching tentacles that extend into the water. Sea fans are a kind of soft coral. They don't build reefs, though. Instead, their colonies wave gently with the movement of the water, like trees swaying in a breeze. Because sea fans bend, they rarely break when a storm stirs up the water. In some places they even form a protective barrier in front of a reef.

Stony corals, like this staghorn coral, can form huge underwater forests.

Sea fans are a type of soft coral. They do not build reefs, but they may help protect reefs from storm waves.

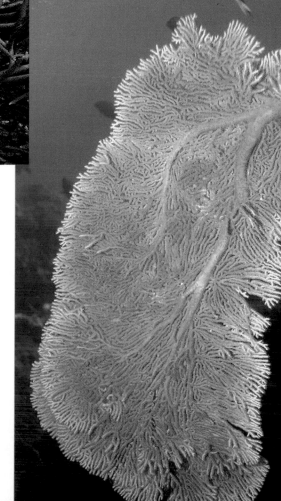

251

Coral Reef Animals

If small fish swim together in a school, they may confuse an enemy and make it think they are really one big fish.

The brilliant colors and patterns worn by reef fish help them to blend with their coral habitat.

Parrotfish have teeth that look like the tip of a parrot's beak. The parrotfish uses its "beak" to graze on algae and coral. Divers may hear a faint crunching sound if a school of parrotfish is grazing nearby.

A moray eel has strong jaws and sharp teeth!

Many fish that live near a coral reef are brightly colored. They flash and shimmer in the shallow waters. Their fancy colors and patterns may help the fish survive by hiding them from enemies. Some fish blend with the colors and patterns of the coral reef. Others wear "warning" colors. For instance, the stripes of the lion fish warn other fish to keep away.

Other fish have poisonous spines to protect them from enemies. The porcupine fish not only has spines but it has another trick that can scare enemies away. The porcupine fish and its relative, the pufferfish, can blow themselves up like balloons by swallowing water. By changing into a bigger fish, they might scare away a hungry enemy!

Some fish have special ways to feed in their coral-reef home. The angelfish and butterflyfish have long snouts with which to reach into cracks and holes for food.

The moray eel is a fish that looks like a snake. It has a long, muscular body and narrow jaws with sharp teeth. Some moray eels may grow to be 10 feet long! The eel looks threatening as it opens and closes its mouth to breathe, passing water over its gills.

A moray eel is more likely to hide in a hole than to swim freely about the reef during the day. At night, however, the eel leaves its cave to search for prey. It feeds on crabs, small octopuses, and a variety of fish.

The octopus is another reef creature that prefers to stay hidden during the day. Like the eel, the octopus will creep out of its cave after dark to look for food. It travels across the ocean floor using its eight long arms. An octopus might be two to three feet long from its head to the tip of its arms. Others are small enough to be found in tide pools along a rocky shore. And a few octopuses can be as much as 26 feet long, but these are not found in the tropics.

Suction cups on the undersides of its arms help the octopus cling to the reef. They also help it catch and pull apart its food. This octopus is eating a crab.

An octopus can escape danger several different ways. It can change its color to blend with its surroundings. It can blast off like a rocket by forcing water very quickly from its gill chamber. It can also "disappear" before an enemy's eyes by squeezing its boneless body into a tiny hiding place. But the most famous trick of the octopus is to squirt an inky liquid from its body. By the time the water clears, the octopus will be gone!

Some reef creatures like sponges, featherduster worms, and anemones look more like plants than animals.

Most people think of sponges as dried plants that are handy for washing the car or for taking a bath. But sponges are really sea animals. Sponges can be as small as a bean or as big as a car. Long, tubular sponges can grow to be six feet high. Others look like giant flower vases. Shrimp and small fish may make their homes in the holes of a sponge. Some sponges produce a chemical that eats away coral to "dig" pits for themselves where they may live undisturbed.

A sponge pumps many gallons of water through its body every day. Plankton in the water is digested as it is pumped through hollow tubes in the sponge's body.

Kelp Forest Animals

A sea otter must take very good care of its fur. Dirty fur does not hold in warmth; a cold otter will probably die.

Playful sea otters are right at home in the tangled fronds of giant kelp.

Before a sea otter goes to sleep in its kelp bed, it wraps itself in fronds to keep from drifting away (above). At mealtime, an otter will often use a rock to help it crack open the shellfish it has found (left).

Sea otters have adapted well to ocean life—and to life in a kelp bed, especially. They are good swimmers, having webbed toes on their hind feet. Otters often swim on their backs. To sleep and eat, the sea otter stretches on its back and wraps itself with kelp to keep from drifting away.

A sea otter has a very thick fur coat that keeps it dry and warm. The fur traps little pockets of air that help hold in body heat. If the fur gets too dirty, it will not hold in the air and the fur will soak up water. The otter will get wet and catch a chill. An otter with a chill will probably die. Therefore, sea otters spend several hours a day caring for their fur. This is called "grooming." The otter rolls over and over in the water to rinse food from its coat. It also cleans its fur by rubbing it with its front paws. Water is removed by licking, squeezing, and rubbing the fur.

Sea otters like to eat the soft meat of clams, abalones, crabs, fish, and sea urchins. An otter usually finds food in shallow water, but sometimes it dives nearly 200 feet to look for food. The otter stays underwater for about a minute while it collects shellfish to eat.

A sea otter may come to the surface with a rock as well as food. It uses the rock as a tool to open shells of the clams and urchins it gathers. The otter floats on its back with the rock on its chest. If the shellfish is hard to open, the otter smashes it on the rock.

The otter eats nearly a fourth of its weight in food every day. California fishermen blame sea otters for eating too much abalone, which brings a high price on the seafood market. In one day, a sea otter can eat 12 abalones, 20 sea urchins, 11 rock crabs, 60 kelp crabs, and 112 snails!

Sea otter mothers and babies—called "pups"—stay together for seven to nine months. The mothers teach their pups how to swim, to hunt for food, and to use rocks as tools.

Sea urchins look like living pincushions. Sometimes they live in large groups that form a prickly carpet on the sea floor. The urchin's mouth is on the underside of its body. It has five teeth that can crush small animals, chew plants, and scrape algae from rocks. The urchin often swallows large grains of sand when it eats. It grinds up the sand and sifts out the tiny bits of food. Then it spits out the sand in much smaller grains.

Urchins chew on kelp fronds that settle on the ocean floor; they also eat the holdfasts that anchor the kelp. Too many grazing urchins can destroy a kelp forest. Urchins are a favorite food of sea otters. Some people believe that sea otters help protect kelp forests by eating large numbers of urchins.

Kelp snail

Snails, limpets, and urchins graze on giant kelp. Too many grazers can harm a kelp bed.

How can anything eat such a prickly creature? Usually, a predator will turn the urchin over and attack its unprotected underside. Otters, however, have tough skin. The spines of the purple urchin (right) do not bother them.

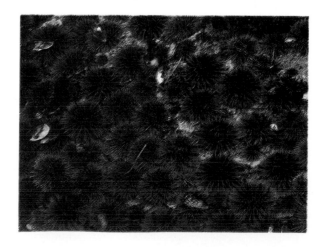

Sea urchins eat not only fallen fronds of kelp, they also eat the holdfasts that anchor the kelp to the ocean floor. A colony of grazing urchins can destroy a giant kelp bed by cutting the kelp loose so that it drifts away.

Kelp Forest Mollusks

The outside of an abalone's shell camouflages it against the ocean floor. The inside of the shell (right) is lined with "mother-of-pearl," which is often used in jewelry.

This luna clam (left) and oyster (right) are examples of bivalves. "Bivalve" means "two valves," or "two shells." The clam has opened to catch food as it floats by.

Colorful nudibranchs are sometimes called the "butterflies of the sea."

"Mollusk" is the correct name for "shellfish" like clams, oysters, and abalone. Some mollusks are experts at clinging to rocks and seaweed. Some, like limpets and abalone, wear a hard shell like a snail. They move around on a sticky muscular foot. Limpets scrape the seaweed, eating any tiny plants and animals that are attached to the fronds. Limpets cling so tightly to a surface that they can be removed only if taken by surprise.

The shell of the abalone is rough and saucer-shaped. Like the limpet, the abalone moves along the ocean floor on its big muscular foot. It scrapes algae off rocks and grazes on kelp. When it senses danger, it uses its foot to clamp to a rock with great force.

Abalones are known for the beautiful pearly colors on the inside of their shells. Many people—as well as sea otters—find the animal inside quite tasty. Today, however, abalones are becoming rare. Too many have been harvested by humans and otters alike.

Nudibranchs are sea snails without shells. They glide along the sea floor among the kelp fronds, sponges, and anemones. Many nudibranchs are brightly colored. Their color is a warning to other sea creatures to stay away. Many nudibranchs are poisonous, stinging, or taste bad.

Kelp Forest Fish and Sea Lions

People who dive in a kelp forest often come nose to nose with many kinds of fish. The garibaldi is a brilliantly colored fish. It can be scarlet red or golden yellow —or any shade in between! Garibaldi fish often lay their eggs among the rocks beneath the kelp.

The garibaldi's brilliant color is a warning to other fish to stay away.

The male garibaldi prepares the nest by first cleaning the algae off a rock. Then he allows certain kinds of algae to grow back. After the female lays her eggs on this algae, the male chases her off. He protects the eggs until the young hatch. Garibaldi fish are fierce guardians of their nests. They may even nip at scuba divers who swim too close.

Rockfish (left) and sheephead (right) are just two of the many fish that live in the cold waters of a kelp bed.

The giant sea bass glides through the kelp. It feeds on small fish and crabs that swim and crawl around the holdfasts of the kelp. The giant sea bass is a big fish—it can grow to be the size of a bathtub!

If you were to scuba dive in a kelp forest, you might see sea lions playing among the ribbons of seaweed. Sea lions belong to the group of sea mammals called pinnipeds. They spend part of their lives in the water and part on shore.

Sea lions swim among the ribbons of kelp, hunting for fish like the ones pictured above.

Like the otter, sea lions are also suited to life in the sea. A layer of blubber just under the skin keeps them warm and stores energy. The sea lion's shape is streamlined, which helps it move through the water with ease and speed. Flippers also help it swim and steer. Sea lions are like acrobats in an underwater circus!

The Open Ocean

Beachcombers should always be on the lookout for jellyfish—especially the Portuguese man-of-war (right)—that may have washed onto the shore. As long as the animal is alive, it can sting you.

Sailfish, swordfish, and some tuna can swim in bursts of speeds up to 70 miles per hour!

Plankton can be any kind of drifting animal or plant. The beach flea pictured above—and shown many times larger than its real size—has been washed out to sea where it may become food for a small fish, like an anchovy (right). These creatures are near the beginning of the ocean food chain.

Away from land, the ocean is almost always clear. The muddy bottom of the ocean is far, far away. Also, there is less plankton to cloud the water. No rivers are near to stir up mud and sand, either.

At the surface of the open ocean are drifters. The giant yellow jellyfish and Portuguese man-of-war dangle their long, deadly tentacles under their soft bodies. Because they drift, they are considered plankton— plankton means "wanderer." Other plankton drift in these sunlit waters, too. Schools of small fish, like herring and anchovies, feed here on the tiniest plankton. These small fish become food for larger fish, like mackerel and bluefish. In turn, these are eaten by sharks and other big fish.

The fish that swim the open ocean have bodies designed to help them move fast through the water. Their bodies are sleek and slippery. Many fish are long and narrow. Their tails sweep from side to side, thrusting their bodies through the water. Fins balance the fish and help them steer.

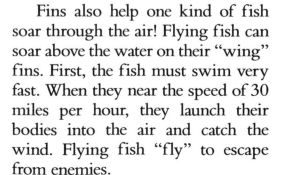

Fins also help one kind of fish soar through the air! Flying fish can soar above the water on their "wing" fins. First, the fish must swim very fast. When they near the speed of 30 miles per hour, they launch their bodies into the air and catch the wind. Flying fish "fly" to escape from enemies.

The sharks that swim the oceans today are much the same as sharks that lived 300 million years ago. They must be perfect for life in the sea. Sharks have long, torpedo-shaped bodies. Their mouths are filled with rows and rows of razor-sharp teeth. They have a keen sense of smell and can also sense the movement of other animals in the water. All these things make sharks expert hunters.

A shark's mouth is a thing of wonder. When attacking, the shark's jaws actually move *out* of its mouth to open wide. Its lower jaw hits first; the upper jaw then snaps down with enough power to bite through a large seal. The shark's teeth lie row upon row, like shingles on a roof. As the front teeth are lost or worn out, the next row of teeth moves up to take their place. Sharks never lose all their teeth.

The great white shark is the shark most feared by humans. A great white shark may grow to be 25 feet long and weigh nearly four tons. Other sharks may grow as long as the great white, but they are not as heavy. The teeth of a great white grow to be two inches long. The great white shark will eat just about anything.

Except for the great whales, the basking shark and the whale shark are the largest animals in the sea. The basking shark can grow to be more than 30 feet long. It got its name because it prefers to bask in the sun, quietly floating on the surface of the water.

The great white shark (above) will sometimes attack humans. But this is probably because the shark has mistaken the person for its favorite food—the sea lion.

Shark skin is rough, like sandpaper. A shark that brushes against you can cause a painful injury.

In spite of its size, which may be 50 feet or longer, the whale shark (right) is a peaceful giant. It feeds only on plankton and small fish.

259

The Abyss

Anglerfish like these wear a glowing "fishing lure" that dangles in front of their mouths. A fish that is drawn to the lure will probably be eaten.

Deep-sea creatures have different ways of surviving in the total darkness.

Lanternfish

In the deep, dark ocean, a faint light flickers. A fish swims toward it. Suddenly, WHOOSH! the fish disappears! What happened?

The light came from the anglerfish. This fish is about five inches long and has what looks like a fishing pole fastened to its forehead! The tip of the "pole" holds bacteria that glow. The light acts as bait to attract other fish to the anglerfish's mouth. When a fish swims near, the anglerfish opens wide and swallows.

The deep sea sparks and winks with lights. The creatures that make their own light are called *bioluminescent*. On land, the fireflies seen on a summer evening are bioluminescent. Bioluminescent light comes from chemicals in an animal's body.

A full-grown lanternfish is only about two inches long, from jaw to tail. But in spite of its size, it may have as many as 100 lights on its body! There are 32 lights on each of its sides, and more on its head, back, and tail.

These lights are not strong enough to light the darkness. They do help the lanternfish see other lanternfish, though. They can all swim together for protection. If an enemy comes near, the lanternfish put out their lights so they can't be seen. Food is scarce in the deep ocean. At night, lanternfish swim to shallower waters to feed.

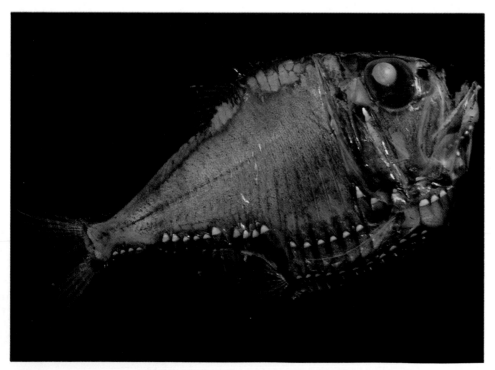

The hatchetfish has big eyes on top of its head. Its eyes can filter light and help it to see prey overhead.

The scaly dragonfish grows to be about 10 inches long. Nearly all dragonfish have a whisker, called a "barbel," attached to the chin. This barbel may be five times longer than the fish itself. It often has one or more lights that give off a faint glow.

Viperfish dangle a glowing lure in front of their mouth to attract prey. This deep-sea fish can unhinge its jaw to eat larger fish. Since food is scarce in the abyss, a meal must sometimes last a long time. Viperfish sometimes swim up toward the surface where food is more plentiful. The fierce-looking viperfish will only grow to be 12 inches long or less.

The bottom of the deep sea is made of ooze. The ooze is millions of years worth of dead plants and animals that have floated down and settled in layers. Most creatures on the sea floor are scavengers. They feel their way along the bottom, finding food as it drifts down. Some animals burrow into the ooze. Still others are rooted in it, like plants rooted in soil.

The tripod fish can rest on the soft ooze without sinking. It has three long fins that support the fish, like a tripod holds a camera. When prey swims near, the tripod fish leaps from its resting place to snatch it.

The jaws of the viperfish unhinge so that it can eat large prey.

Food is scarce in the abyss. Fish must be able to eat whatever they find, even if it is larger than themselves.

Dragonfish

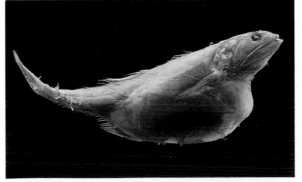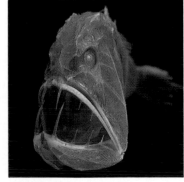

This black swallower's (left) stomach stretches to hold lots of food. The fierce-looking fangtooth (right) can catch prey that is much larger than itself.

261

Survival in the Sea

There are many strange relationships under the sea. Some animals form partnerships with other kinds of creatures. They help each other to find food, shelter, and protection. This partnership is called *symbiosis*.

The anemonefish can swim among the tentacles of a sea anemone without being stung. Scientists are not sure why the anemonefish won't be stung when all others will. It may be because a mucus coating on the fish's body protects it. Scientists think the anemonefish brings food to the anemone and eats the leftovers itself. The anemone protects the anemonefish nestled in its arms—most fish know not to come too close.

The brightly colored clown anemonefish (above) may attract predators to its host anemone. Instead of *having* dinner, the predator *is* dinner —to the stinging anemone.

Anemonefish, like this skunk clown (right), live in family groups with an anemone. The female lays eggs and the male keeps them clean by fanning them with his fins.

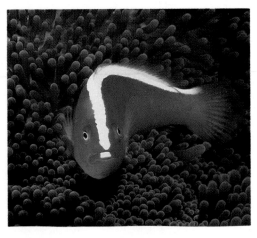

Some sea anemones hitch a ride on a hermit crab or boxer crab. Fastened to the crab's shell, they make it difficult to see the crab. If an enemy of the crab comes near, the anemones sting it with their tentacles. The sting drives away large animals and may kill small ones. What does the crab do for the anemones? When it catches food, the anemones get to eat some of it.

Sometimes a fish needs cleaning, but cannot handle the job itself. Several kinds of small fish—wrasses and gobies—offer cleaning services for larger fish. These little helpers eat bits of dead skin and parasites off the bodies of their "customers." This cleaning service helps both fish. The cleaners get a meal and the large fish will stay healthy.

Neon Goby

The wrasse and goby will even serve customers that would normally eat a small fish. But the big fish hardly ever eat the wrasse or goby—even if the cleaner were to swim into their mouth! This is exactly what the goby does, too. The goby removes food from the teeth of the grouper. The goby gets a meal and the grouper gets a healthy mouth.

These big fish know the cleaners by their colors and by the way they swim. The cleaner wrasse wears bold stripes, and rocks side to side as it swims. Customers will line up for a cleaning by the wrasse. A wrasse may clean hundreds of fish a day!

Some gobies serve as "seeing-eye fish" for a kind of blind shrimp. The shrimp digs a burrow in the sea floor and shares it with the goby. The shrimp will fish for food just outside the hole. If danger threatens, the goby wiggles its body and the shrimp feels the wiggle. Both the shrimp and the goby quickly disappear down the hole to safety!

This cleaner shrimp (left) may signal that it is ready to clean fish by rocking back and forth and whipping its long, white antennae. Even predators will not eat the shrimp while it is cleaning.

The yellowheaded wrasse (below) not only helps other animals by cleaning, but it gets a meal in the process!

Cleaner fish and shrimp are able to swim safely into a predator's mouth to clean—their customers need cleaning more than they need a meal.

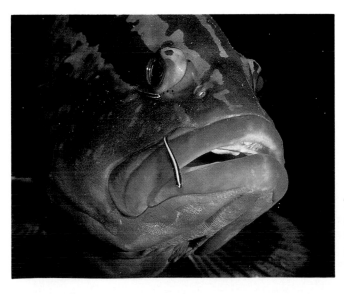

This grouper will be a much healthier fish when the gobies finish the cleaning job!

Survival in the Sea

Like the Portuguese man-of-war and the shepherdfish, some jellyfish have a partnership with fish they might normally eat. These medusa fish are protected by the jellyfish. They lure other fish into the jellyfish's tentacles.

The Portuguese man-of-war and the shepherdfish have a strange partnership, too. The Portuguese man-of-war floats at the top of the water, its "float" acting as a sail. Under the float, hanging far down in the water are dozens of stinging tentacles. Some of the tentacles may be 100 feet long. Few fish will survive the sting of the Portuguese man-of-war. But the small shepherdfish actually makes its home in the tangle. The shepherdfish is not hurt at all! It lures other fish into the tentacles for the man-of-war to eat and then feeds on the leftover bits of food. Without its protector, the shepherdfish would be easy prey for bigger fish.

Remoras "hitch" rides on rays and sharks. These remoras may eat bits of food that this manta ray leaves behind.

This remora is attached to a nurse shark (below).

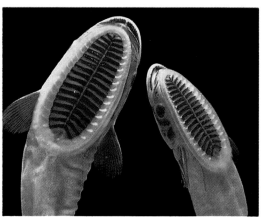

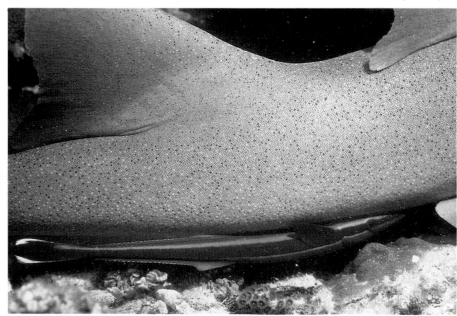

The remora, or shark sucker, hitchhikes on sharks. The remora is long and thin, with a suction cup on its head (above). The remora fastens itself onto a shark for a free ride. Sometimes, the remora gets a free meal, too. When the shark eats, the remora gets the scraps that fall from the shark's jaws. The remora also attaches itself to sea turtles, swordfish, rays, and some whales.

Some sea creatures fool their enemies by wearing disguises. Others wear the colors or patterns of their surroundings. Both of these "tricks" are called *camouflage*.

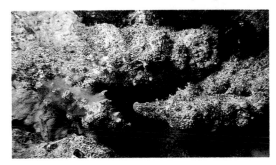

As the decorator crab (above) crawls across the ocean floor, it picks up pieces of seaweed and puts them on its body. It may even pick up sponges or anemones to wear. Can you see the crab in this picture? Its enemies can't see it either.

The octopus is a master of disguise. If the ocean floor on which it is resting is brown, the octopus turns brown. If it is swimming through seaweed, the octopus turns seaweed-green. It may turn coral red, too. Some kinds of octopus can even be several colors at once!

When a ray comes to rest on the ocean floor, it waves its "wings" to stir up the sand around it. The sand settles and lightly covers the ray's body. Hidden like this, the ray will wait for a meal to swim by.

Flounder and other flatfish are experts at disguising themselves against the ocean floor. Rather than arrange the sand over them, they change their skin to match the bottom. They may even become spotted to match a pebbly ocean floor.

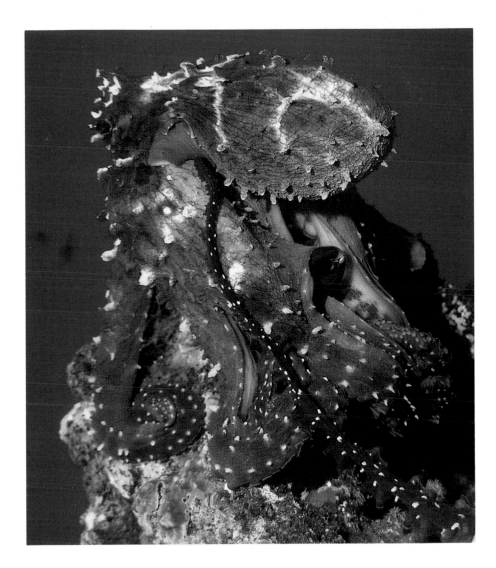

An octopus can change both its color and its skin texture to hide. It can make its skin look like rock!

This **stingray** (left) hides in the sand and awaits its next meal. The **flatfish** (right) hides so it will not be a meal. Can you see it against the pebbly floor?

265

Welcome to the Rain Forest

Some very wet rain forests can get more than 400 inches of rain each year!

In temperate areas like Europe and North America, changes in temperature mark the coming and going of the seasons. In the tropics, rainfall defines the seasons. Most tropical areas have one dry season and one wet season.

True to their name, rain forests receive an incredible amount of rain. About 60 inches of rain falls every year in an average rain forest. Temperatures usually range between 70 and 85°F, but it can get much warmer. The temperature at night rarely drops below 70°F.

The constant moist and warm conditions in the rain forest allow an astounding variety of plants and animals to thrive. On a single acre of rain forest, you may find about ten times as many tree species as in a forest in a temperate region.

Most of the plants and animals that live in the rain forest live nowhere else in the world. Scientists are not even sure how many plants and animals live in the world's rain forests because not all rain forest areas have been studied. There are probably between five million and 30 million rain forest species that we have not discovered yet! Most of these species are probably insects and other *invertebrates,* or animals that have no backbones.

Rain forests are sometimes called green treasure chests because they are so rich with life. People might think that rain forests are very tough and strong because they support so many living creatures. In fact, the opposite is true. The rain forest is a very fragile place. Beneath the thick green layer of trees and shrubs, the soil that supports the rain forest is thin and poor in nutrients. In all forests, water washes away some of the nutrients in the top layer of the soil every time it rains. In the rain forest, it can rain very hard every day.

Most of the nutrients and energy in the rain forest are not free to be taken from the soil. Instead, they are locked up in living plants and animals. When a creature dies or a leaf falls, bacteria, fungi, and tiny invertebrates quickly go to work to break it down. They decompose the debris into nutrients, some of which they use and some of which go into the soil. The plants' roots must absorb these nutrients before the rain can wash them away. This natural process must happen very quickly, or the valuable nutrients will be lost. The cycle of life and death in the rain forest is very fast and very efficient. In the rain forest, nothing is wasted and everything is recycled.

The rainfall has been washing nutrients out of the soil for thousands of years. The rain forest soil has a very thin top layer with few nutrients. Most rain forest plants have very thin roots that grow only in this top layer.

Nutrients return to the soil when a plant or animal dies or when a leaf or a piece of fruit falls to the forest floor. Mushrooms and other decomposers make this system possible.

The World's Rain Forests

The world has three major regions of tropical rain forests: the Amazon basin of South America, Africa's Congo basin, and the Malay archipelago (ar-kuh-PEL-uh-go) in the South Pacific.

South America has the largest rain forest in the world. This region is known as the Amazon basin or Amazonia, named for the mighty Amazon River. Most of the Amazonian rain forest is in Brazil, but large portions also grow in neighboring Peru, Colombia, and Ecuador.

Rain forests also grow in the Caribbean. In Central America, rain forests still grow in Guatemala, Honduras, Nicaragua, Belize, Costa Rica, and Panama.

South American rain forests are home to their own unique animal species. If you are lucky, you might see a slow-moving sloth or a quick, silent jaguar. They each travel through the trees in their own unique way. You might spy a colorful toucan as it gobbles fruit with its huge bill or a tiny hummingbird as it moves from flower to flower and sips nectar.

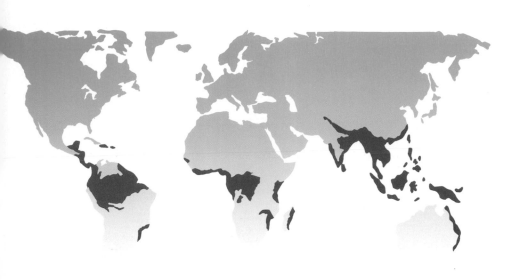

This acrobatic spider monkey will spend its life among the treetops of the Colombian rain forest.

The anteater is one of the Amazon's strange-looking creatures.

In Africa, rain forests occur in two main blocks—one along the south coast of West Africa and one centered in the country of Zaire. Businesses probably value the African rain forests most for the beautiful species of hardwood trees that grow there. Loggers have cut down countless mahogany and ebony trees. These trees are now very rare.

Interesting animals are also native to Africa's rain forests. The okapi (o-KAHP-ee) was first discovered by

Elephants strip leaves and bark from the trees of the West African rain forest.

scientists in 1900. The endangered mountain gorilla and the forest elephant are two of the largest residents of the African rain forest.

The rain forests in Southeast Asia and Australia do not grow in huge areas like they do in South America and Africa. Instead, they are spread out mostly over the many island countries in that region.

Rain forests in Asia are home to Asian elephants, tigers, and orangutans—all endangered species. Rain forests in Asia are also home to some of the most valuable tree species in the world.

The rain forests in Asia are disappearing the fastest. Inhabitants such as the orangutan are disappearing along with them.

Rain Forest Layers

Emergent Layer

Canopy

Understory

Forest Floor

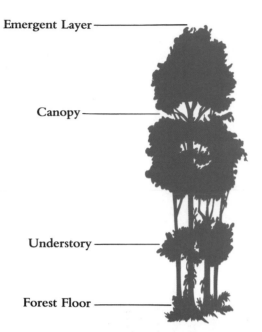

Even with its layers, the rain forest is still one connected system from top to bottom.

At first glance, a rain forest will look like a solid green wall from top to bottom. The boundaries between layers are not clear, and no two sections of rain forest will be the same.

In order to divide a rain forest into layers, scientists start with a small patch. They clear the area of vines and shrubs. Next, they measure the position and height of each plant and identify it by species. They plot this information on a chart as a sample of how plants grow in that area of rain forest. They can then compare and contrast samples from different patches in one rain forest or from patches in different rain forests.

Conditions change from one layer to the next, so the species that live in each layer change too. Each layer provides a special habitat for a wealth of different species. Every layer also has special challenges for survival. Every plant or animal needs special features that will allow it to survive in the layer that serves as its home.

The different layers also have an effect on each other. The top of the forest controls how much light and water reach the lower layers. On the forest floor, insects and other decomposers recycle the nutrients that creatures in the upper layers need to survive.

The layers of a rain forest allow more species to find homes there. Sometimes a single acre of rain forest will have more than 350 different plant species growing on it.

The Emergent Layer

The rain forest usually supports one or two giant trees per acre that tower above all the other plants. The tops of these *emergents* sprout above the dense jungle like huge umbrellas. Emergents are often about 115 to 150 feet tall, but some can reach up to 250 feet, as high as a 25 story building!

Because emergent trees are the tallest, they have a different environment than the rest of the rain forest. These trees get the first share of the strong sunshine that beats down on the equator. They must survive hot and changing temperatures, low humidity, and strong winds.

Many giant trees have unusual root structures. Some species have thick, ridged *buttress roots* that give extra support. These buttresses grow above ground and surround the tree. Buttresses may reach 30 feet up the trunk of the tree and spread even further along the ground.

Animals visit the emergent layer to munch on the leaves, fruits, and seeds that grow there, to escape predators, or even just to sunbathe! Woodpeckers, hawks, and eagles visit the emergent layer frequently. High-flying butterflies also are common.

The emergent trees usually have long, slender branches.

Buttress roots help to keep the tree standing when large gusts of wind pass overhead, and they support the tree in the shallow rain forest soil. The roots may also help by spreading the great weight of the tree over a larger area of ground.

The emergents are the oldest trees in the rain forest, but it is hard to tell their exact ages.

Africa's colobus monkey will sometimes visit the emergent layer.

271

The Canopy

Some trees in the canopy have *stilt roots*. Stilt roots are long and thin. They surround the base of a tree trunk in the form of a triangle. Like buttress roots, they provide extra support.

Orchids are probably the best-known epiphytes. There are around 20,000 species of them.

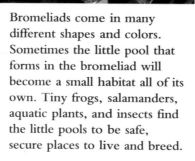

Bromeliads come in many different shapes and colors. Sometimes the little pool that forms in the bromeliad will become a small habitat all of its own. Tiny frogs, salamanders, aquatic plants, and insects find the little pools to be safe, secure places to live and breed.

Beneath the swaying tops of the giant emergents grows a second thick layer of shorter trees. The tops of these trees overlap into what looks like a solid green roof. This is the *canopy* layer.

The trees that form the canopy are usually between 65 and 100 feet tall. Many are still growing, and eventually they may join the emergent layer. Other species will never grow past the canopy no matter how long they live.

Other plants share the canopy layer with these tall trees. *Epiphytes* (E-puh-fytz) are plants that are totally dependent on other plants for support. They attach themselves to a tree or other plant and let their roots drape downward. They get their nourishment from dead leaves and animals that fall from above, get caught in their roots, and decay.

Another group of plants that grows in the canopy is the *bromeliads* (bro-MEE-lee-adz). Bromeliads are another kind of epiphyte, and they are related to the pineapple. Because they have no roots growing in the ground, bromeliads must soak up water and nutrients in another way. Some bromeliads have what look like small cups surrounded by leaves. The cups catch rainwater and falling bits of plants, insects, and other forest litter.

Vines, some of which are called *lianas* (lee-AH-nuhz), grow on the trees in the canopy, too. The dense leaves and branches of the trees overlap with the vines, epiphytes, ferns, and other plants to form a thick roof. This umbrella that tops the canopy limits the amount of sunlight and rain that reaches the forest floor.

Many of the large animals that live in the rain forest make their homes in the canopy. Some spend almost all of their lives there. They hunt, eat, sleep, and even give birth to their babies high in the trees!

Some animals have evolved ways to glide from tree to tree or from the canopy to lower levels in the rain forest. This allows them to escape predators and to search for food over a larger area of the rain forest. Flying squirrels have thick folds of skin that stretch along their bodies from their wrists to their ankles. Wallace's flying frog is the only frog that can glide. It has skin flaps between each toe that open like small parachutes when the frog jumps. These frogs can glide up to 40 feet! Parachute geckos have skin flaps on either side of their heads and along their bodies. They can also sail from tree to tree. Sloths, orangutans, and parrots also make their homes in the canopy.

Some vines begin life at the forest floor, slowly creeping up through the trees. Others start as seeds in the treetops and drop their roots to the ground.

In many places, the canopy is a lush, thick tangle of green.

Parachute gecko

273

The Understory

Many plants that grow in this layer are young trees that will eventually grow high into the canopy layer. Other plants found here are shrubs, miniature trees, dwarf palms, and herbs.

Below the canopy are small trees and shrubs that usually will not grow higher than about 15 feet. The plants that live in the *understory* face a very difficult environment. The canopy layer overhead acts almost like a shield from the sun, the rain, and the wind. The understory is very dim and still. To survive in their shady environment, understory plants have adapted broad, thin, flat leaves that allow them to collect as much light as possible.

Many of the creatures in the understory have become *nocturnal* because they are often the prey of large cats, snakes, and birds. Nocturnal animals are active during the night and sleep during the day. Most nocturnal animals, such as the night monkey or the bizarre aye-aye (EYE-eye), have huge eyes and excellent night vision. Some bats use sound echoes to hunt and to avoid bumping into things in the darkness.

Spotted cats such as the jaguar, the ocelot (AHS-uh-laht), and the clouded leopard also live in the understory. They spend much of their time hunting for deer, rodents, and birds. Other animals that spend much of their time in the understory are emerald tree boas, coatimundis, and lemurs.

Only five percent of the rain forests' sunlight reaches the understory.

Ocelot

Coatimundi

274

The Forest Floor

It is a long way from the top of the tallest tree in the emergent layer to the forest floor—as much as 250 feet. On the forest floor it is very dark and the air is very quiet and still. The plant life growing in the three layers above keeps out almost all of the light, wind, and rain.

Still the forest floor is brimming with life. Along with fungi and lichens, millions of invertebrates—ants, termites, spiders, land crabs, earthworms, and beetles—live on or just below the surface of the forest floor. These are the decomposers that keep the forest clean by recycling debris into life-giving nutrients.

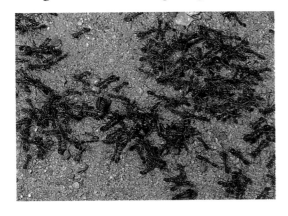

Some mammal species also live on the forest floor. Many of these are specially suited to root out the invertebrates that live just under the topsoil. The giant anteater has an incredibly long tongue and snout to suck out ants and termites from their nests. The white-lipped peccary (PEK-uh-ree) and the Malayan tapir (TAY-pur) use their broad snouts to root out insects and worms. Elephants and gorillas are also common visitors to the floor of the rain forest.

Lichens

Only a few large plants can grow under the harsh conditions of the forest floor—some seedlings, herbs, and ferns.

When one tree dies, many other plant species can begin to grow. They quickly take over the patch of rain forest soil along with its sunlight and water.

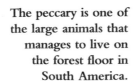

The peccary is one of the large animals that manages to live on the forest floor in South America.

275

Mammals

A sloth's hair grows toward its back so that rain drops will roll off as the animal hangs upside down. Algae grow on the hairs and give the sloth a muddy color that helps it blend in to the trees.

Sloths never move quickly. Their slow pace helps protect them from the keen eyes of predators. Sloths like to hang upside down from branches in the canopy layer, and they almost never go down to the forest floor.

The South American tamandua (tuh-MAN-doo-wuh) is a type of anteater that is very clumsy on the ground. With the help of its prehensile tail, it is very much at home high in the trees. The tamandua specializes in eating termites and ants and finds them with its keen sense of smell. The tamandua itself has a very bad odor, and it has earned the nickname "stinker of the forest."

The okapi is a very unusual hoofed animal that looks like it is half deer and half zebra. It is actually a relative of the giraffe. Scientists first discovered the okapi in 1900 deep in the rain forests of Zaire, a country in Africa. The okapi eats leaves that it strips from trees in the understory. The okapi's tongue is so long—14 inches—that it can even use it to clean its own eyes and ears!

The clouded leopard is one of the top predators in the rain forest of Southeast Asia. This rare spotted cat gets its name from the soft edges it has to its large spots. It has no enemies except humans, who kill clouded leopards for their beautiful coats.

The clouded leopard can run down trees headfirst, climb upside down, and swing by a single hind paw.

The tapir of Southeast Asia uses its long snout to browse on grasses, leaves, and fruits.

276

The capybara (cap-i-BAYR-uh) is a funny-looking mammal that just happens to be the world's largest rodent. This South American resident looks something like a giant guinea pig. Capybaras are usually three to four feet long. They eat grasses that grow in or near water. Some people consider capybara meat extremely tasty. In Venezuela, there are even capybara "ranches" where these giant rodents are raised like cattle!

Howler monkeys get their name from their very loud voices that roar through the rain forests of South America. Howlers live in groups of 20 or so monkeys and will defend their homes from other howler monkeys by shouting and shrieking at them. Their howls can be heard over half a mile away.

The golden lion tamarin (TAM-uh-ruhn) is a bright orange, squirrel-sized monkey that lives in only one small section of the Brazilian rain forest. The golden lion tamarin lives in family groups of two to nine monkeys and eats insects, small lizards, and fruits. Many golden lion tamarins have been captured for pets, and almost all of their rain forest home has been destroyed. The golden lion tamarin is an endangered species and is a symbol of wildlife conservation in Brazil.

Capybaras live in large groups near water. Folds of skin between their toes help make them excellent swimmers.

Howler monkeys spend most of their time in the canopy layer and very rarely come to the ground.

Many of these animals are in danger of becoming extinct.

Today, many zoos are working to save the golden lion tamarin from extinction. Some zoos breed them and then prepare them to live in the wild when they are older.

277

Birds

The harpy eagle is the largest eagle in the world.

The harpy eagle is the top predator in the emergent layer of South America's rain forests. It can streak through the trees at speeds close to 50 miles per hour and then grasp its prey in its deadly sharp talons. The harpy eagle eats monkeys, sloths, opossums, and snakes.

The toucan (TOO-kan) is probably one of the most well-known birds of the rain forest. It spends much of its time in the emergent and canopy layers with as many as 12 others of its kind. The toucan's bill is much lighter than it looks, and the bird uses the tip to snip off small fruits and berries. The jagged edge of the bill helps the bird bite off larger pieces of fruit.

The bowerbird of Australia and Papua New Guinea uses the forest floor in a very unusual way. The male bowerbird builds an elaborate home, called a bower, out of grasses, leaves, and twigs. He will even decorate his bower with brightly-colored berries and feathers. He does all of this to attract a female bowerbird.

Woodpeckers fly through all levels of the forest in search of insects. Their strong bills work like a chisel to dig into tree bark. Their long, sticky, barbed tongues pull out burrowing bugs and larvae. As they pound into a tree, woodpeckers use their tails and long, sharp claws for support.

The male bowerbird is waiting outside while a female inspects his bower.

The toucan sometimes eats insects, spiders, and even small birds.

Reptiles and Amphibians

Poison-arrow frogs are brightly colored to warn predators that their skins are very poisonous. Indians in the Amazon rain forest use their poison to coat the tips of the arrows they use for hunting. Poison-arrow frogs live in the understory.

The poison in this tiny frog is one of the strongest natural poisons in the world—one millionth of an ounce can kill a dog.

Chameleons (kuh-MEE-lee-uhnz) can lighten or darken their skin to blend in to their surroundings in the Asian and African rain forests. They are able to change color with special pigment cells in their skin. Chameleons can look at two things at once because their eyes can move in different directions at the same time! They have long, sticky tongues that can shoot out with great accuracy to snap up insects and spiders.

Freshwater crocodiles, or freshies, live in the rivers and streams that flow through the rain forest in Australia and Papua New Guinea. At night, they wait just beneath the surface of the water for a thirsty animal to come to the water's edge. The crocs knock their prey over with a swing of the tail and drag it underwater with their huge jaws.

The green tree python is a beautiful green snake that blends well with the leaves of the canopy. It is a very deadly predator that feeds on the birds, small mammals, and tree frogs of Southeast Asia. When the snake catches a victim, it wraps itself around the prey and squeezes until the victim suffocates.

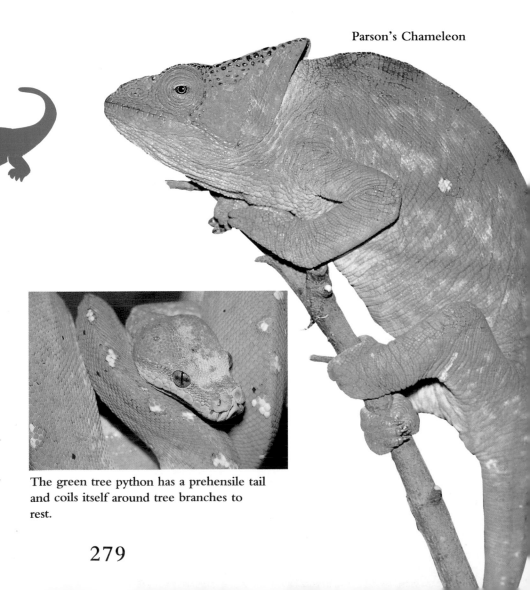

Parson's Chameleon

The green tree python has a prehensile tail and coils itself around tree branches to rest.

279

Insects and Spiders

One to two million leaf-cutter ants may live in one nest, called a colony. A large colony may need seven pounds of leaves per day to keep the fungus garden growing.

Although they look quite scary, bird-eating spiders are actually shy creatures and will only attack a human if they are attacked first. A bite from this spider is very painful but usually not fatal.

Birdwing butterfly

Leaf-cutter ants of Central and South America are the farmers of the insect world. They collect pieces of leaves and flowers and carry them to their underground nest. The ants chew up the bits of plant to create a pulpy material. The material provides food for a layer of fungus to grow. The ants then use that fungus for their own food.

Also known as tarantulas, bird-eating spiders are large enough to attack birds, reptiles, and small mammals. These spiders hunt at night in the South American rain forests. Some hide on the forest floor under leaves and stones, waiting for their prey to walk by. Others live and hunt in the trees. Their thick covering of hair is sensitive to movement and helps them detect their prey.

Birdwing butterflies of New Guinea are some of the largest and most beautiful butterflies in the world. Their wingspan can be as much as eight inches wide. Their brightly colored wings flash in the sun. Their colors are a signal to other animals that they are poisonous. Birdwing butterflies spend most of their time in the upper layers of the rain forest, but they will fly down to the forest floor to find food or to drink from a puddle. Because of their beauty, birdwing butterflies are in great demand by butterfly collectors and are becoming very rare.

Exotic Plants

Lianas are thick, ropelike vines that grow on trees for support. They begin life as seedlings on the forest floor and grow up the trunks of trees. Or, they attach themselves to a small tree and hitch a ride up into the canopy as the tree grows. Lianas do not twine around tree trunks but hang freely down toward the ground.

Strangler figs start life as seeds dropped by birds high on the branch of a tree. A seedling will send long roots down the trunk of the support tree to the forest floor. As the strangler fig grows, more roots are sent down and form a web around the trunk of the tree.

The rafflesia (ruh-FLEE-zhee-uh) plant has the broadest flower in the world—it can grow to three feet across. The rafflesia plant lives on the forest floor in Southeast Asia. It is a parasite that gets all of its energy from other plants and none from the sun. The huge rafflesia flower smells like rotting meat! This attracts certain insects that will pollinate the flowers.

Bird's nest ferns are epiphytes. They attach themselves to other plants but they do not steal nutrients from them. These ferns are found high in the canopy layer and have long leaves that grow in the shape of a cup. Water and falling plant matter from above fall into this cup and are held there. From this pool the bird's nest fern draws water and nutrients.

The rafflesia flower can grow to three feet across, and it smells like rotton meat!

This bird's nest fern is growing on a tree trunk in the rain forest of Malaysia.

Strangler figs can completely surround their host tree and block the sunlight it needs. The tree may die, but the fig will continue to grow.

281

Struggling to Survive

A tiger will usually stay on the ground to stalk and ambush its prey. Its coat has vertical black and dull orange stripes that blend in with the tree trunks and tall shrubs of the forest floor.

In a world of hunters and prey, staying unseen can mean staying alive.

Camouflage is any disguise that helps a creature blend with its background. Many animals use their color, shape, and behavior to hide in the rain forest. This can give them an edge over the animals they hunt and the animals that hunt them.

The large cats that live in the rain forest rely on the patterns of their fur to hide from their prey. A jaguar's bright orange coat with black spots may seem very bold and easy to see. In the rain forest, though, the pattern is a perfect disguise. The colors of its coat blend in with the dappled light that filters down through the leaves of the rain forest canopy.

The South American potoo (po-TOO) is a nocturnal bird that hunts insects by night and rests in trees during the day. Unlike some rain forest birds, the potoo is not very beautiful. It is a dull, brownish color. The potoo rests upright on the branch of a tree, and it blends in with the bark of the tree so well that it seems to vanish.

A jaguar spends much of its time in the trees. The big cat will wait without moving for a deer or tapir to come near.

The grass-green vine snake simply waits quietly in a tree for its prey—young birds, frogs, and insects—to come near. At the same time, the snake remains hidden from predators.

The grass-green vine snake spends all of its time in the trees. The snake is several feet long but only a little thicker than a pencil. Its color and shape look exactly like a young vine. Scientists call this form of camouflage mimicry. The snake will even sway gently in the breeze to mimic the movement of a vine in a soft wind!

Millions of insects live in the rain forests worldwide, and they are probably the most hunted rain forest dwellers. Many species have evolved clever adaptations to help them hide from birds, reptiles, mammals, and other insects. Insects are masters of disguise and imitation. In the rain forest, some insect species mimic leaves, flowers, twigs, bark, or leaf litter. If they do not move, their enemies have a very difficult time seeing them.

Katydids and some mantids look exactly like the leaves in which they hide. They have flat, green wings that are the exact shape and color of young leaves. Their wings even have thin veins that look just like the veins in a leaf!

Other species of leaf insect are also light green, and they look like young, living leaves. Some even have blotches that look like chew marks, as if they were leaves that had been munched on. All of these leaf insects make their disguises more effective by swinging gently from side to side. They look like leaves swaying in the breeze!

The eyed silkmoth has two large markings on its wings that look like the huge round eyes of a large rain forest predator. The sight of the eyes may make a hunter pause long enough for the moth to escape.

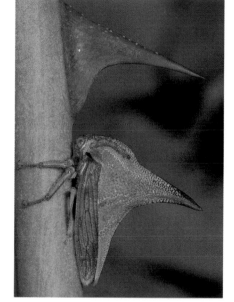

Thornbugs look like the thick, spiny thorns of many rain forest trees that other animals have learned to stay away from.

Leaf mimicry works very well. There are four moths sitting atop these leaves.

Struggling to Survive

The heliconid butterfly (above left) is poisonous. The mechanitis butterfly (above) is not, but predators can't tell the difference.

Camouflage is an excellent tool, but some animals use just the opposite strategy. Instead of trying to blend in with their surroundings, they stand out and call attention to themselves. They avoid being eaten by having bright colors that make them easy to see and identify. These bright colors say loudly, "Don't eat me! I taste bad!" or "Stay away! I am poisonous!"

The Costa Rican caterpillar is bright yellow and green and has clumps of stinging hairs. Predators that try to eat the caterpillar get a painful sting. The next time they are out hunting, the predators remember the bright yellow and green and stay away!

In the rain forests of South America, heliconid (hee-li-KAHN-id) butterflies are black, yellow, and orange. They are also poisonous! Birds and other predators have learned that these butterflies are dangerous to eat, and they stay away from any butterfly that is black, yellow, and orange. Some harmless butterflies also have this color pattern and are protected by their resemblance to their poisonous relatives.

Milesia vespoides is another interesting mimic. This harmless fly has evolved to look exactly like a species of poisonous wasp, *Vespa cincta*. Birds that have learned to avoid the stinging wasp will stay far away from the fly as well.

The bright yellow and green colors are a warning to stay away.

This harmless rain forest fly looks exactly like a wasp, so it gets left alone by predators.

284

Plants that depend on birds for pollination usually produce large, showy flowers that are often red or orange. Bird-pollinated plants often have little or no smell. Many species of birds have a better sense of sight than smell, and they are attracted to red and orange.

There are many species of hummingbirds in the rain forest, and all are important pollinators. As they hover against the flower, they pick up pollen. When they feed at the next flower, they leave some of the pollen behind.

Plants that need insects for pollination usually produce yellow or blue flowers that have a strong scent. Some flowers smell very sweet and others smell terrible! Some plants rely on flies for pollination, and their flowers produce very bad smells. The *Aristolochia grandiflora* smells like rotting meat or animal droppings. Flies are attracted to this odor!

Euglossine bees are the only pollinators of certain species of orchids and other plants in the Amazonian rain forest. The male bee visits orchid flowers to collect fragrance from the petals. The perfumed bee will fly from flower to flower, picking up their scent. Groups of sweet-smelling males gather together, and their combined scent is strong enough to attract female bees. The orchids have helped the bees find mates, and the bees have helped the orchids reproduce.

The pollen of many plants is located deep inside the flower. Hummingbirds use their long thin bills and tongues to reach into the flowers and sip the sweet nectar.

The color of a flower is one thing that attracts pollinating animals— red and orange for birds, blue and yellow for insects.

Euglossine bee

Deserts of the World

The Australian Desert is a harsh place. Few plants grow here because the weather is so dry and hot.

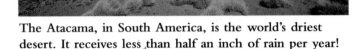

The Atacama, in South America, is the world's driest desert. It receives less than half an inch of rain per year!

The Mohave is one of the North American deserts. The yucca plant grows well in this dry climate.

The world has 12 main desert regions. Three of them are found in Africa. The Sahara stretches across northern Africa, and the Namib (nah-MEEB) and Kalahari (KAHL-uh-HAH-ree) deserts are in southwest Africa.

A fourth major desert covers the center of Australia. The Australian Desert is the world's second largest desert. In fact, most of Australia's lands are *semiarid*. Semiarid lands receive a little more rainfall than a desert.

Five major deserts are scattered across Asia. They are: the Arabian, the Iranian, the Thar (tahr) (in India and Pakistan), the Gobi (in China and Mongolia), and the Turkistan (TUR-kuh-stan) (in central Asia).

South America contains two major deserts. The Patagonian (PAT-uh-GO-nee-uhn) Desert is found in Argentina. The Atacama (AHT-uh-KAH-muh) Desert—the smallest of the 12 deserts—covers parts of Chile and Peru.

One major desert region is found in North America. It is actually made up of four deserts. The region covers the southwestern United States and northwestern Mexico. The four deserts are called the Great Basin Desert, the Mohave (mo-HAHV-ee) Desert, the Sonoran (suh-NOR-uhn) Desert, and the Chihuahuan (chuh-WAH-wuhn) Desert.

Some deserts look very "typical." They have vast stretches of sand and waves of dunes. Much of the Arabian Desert looks like this. So do parts of the Sahara. Some areas of the North American deserts are covered with sand and dunes. Desert sands are many colors, from gray to tan gold, and rose.

Most of the world's deserts are rocky, not sandy. Like sand, desert rocks come in many beautiful colors. They also come in many sizes and shapes, from gravel to snow-capped mountains. Caves, canyons, and strange, twisted rock formations add special beauty to deserts.

Desert landscapes change with the seasons. In some deserts, such as the Mohave, summers are hot and dry. Winters bring milder temperatures and, hopefully, rain. In other deserts, rains visit in summer. Those deserts come to life in early fall. Some, like the Sonoran Desert, have two rainy seasons, one in winter and the other in late summer.

Plants and animals have only a few weeks after rain falls to produce seeds or young before the desert dries again. Deserts look anything but empty during this time. Carpets of flowers add brightness to the desert's earthy tones. Animals come out of hiding.

Sandy deserts look harsh and exotic. It is no surprise most movies and books show deserts this way.

The desert landscape blooms with life after a spring rain.

The world's deserts have many faces. Some are covered with shifting dunes. Others are rocky and have more plants.

Desert Weather

Deserts often go years without rain. In fact, some desert areas have gone 25 years or more without a single drop of it!

All deserts have one thing in common no matter where they are. Deserts are *arid* (AR-uhd), which means they are very dry. Less than 10 inches of rain fall across desert regions each year.

Most deserts are very hot. Daytime air temperatures of 100 degrees Fahrenheit or more are common. The ground itself becomes 30 to 50 degrees hotter than the air! Why do deserts get so hot? Deserts lack many things that normally block the sun's heat. For example, moisture in the air "soaks up" some of the sun's heat. So do bodies of water such as lakes. Desert air and desert surfaces are very dry.

Clouds also block the sun's heat. But few clouds float above most deserts. There is rarely enough moisture in the air above the desert for clouds to form.

Deserts may become quite cold at night. The ground loses its heat once the sun goes down. Without moisture, clouds, or plants to trap the heat at the surface, it escapes. Temperatures can drop 50 degrees in deserts at night.

Some deserts are cooler than the others. They are usually located at higher altitudes or farther from the equator than hot deserts. The Gobi (GO-bee) Desert in central Asia is a high-altitude desert.

Odd as it seems, the frozen lands far to the north and south qualify as deserts. Most of the water there is locked up as snow and ice. So, these polar lands are very "dry." Polar "deserts" are called *tundra* (TUHN-druh).

Desert Waters

The desert has few permanent bodies of water. Rivers and streams do run through some desert regions. But most rivers and streams dry up as they cross the desert.

A few permanent lakes can also be found in arid lands. The Great Salt Lake in Utah and the Dead Sea near Israel are two examples.

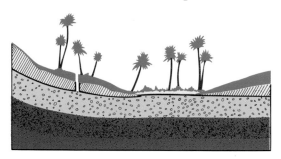

There is actually a lot of water trapped in layers of rock under the desert surface. Water collects in spongelike rocks that are filled with tiny holes and cracks. These rocks are called *aquifers* (AK-wuh-furz).

When rain falls in the desert, some of it sinks down, or seeps, into aquifers. Today's aquifers may hold water that fell as rain thousands of years ago.

Wherever water from an aquifer reaches the desert surface, an *oasis* (o-AY-suhs) forms. The land around an oasis doesn't look very much like a desert. It is green with plant life. And it is busy with the activities of animals and people. An oasis may be large, or it may be little more than a damp spot of sand. Some oases support entire civilizations.

A desert rainstorm can be a beautiful sight. The plants soak up as much water as they can while the storm lasts. They may not receive another rainfall for a full year.

Rainfall in deserts is unpredictable. Some deserts may go many years without it. A desert may get all its rain for the year from a single storm.

The oasis formed by the Nile River in Egypt has supported civilization for thousands of years.

Desert Formations

The famous Grand Canyon in northwestern Arizona is the work of a rare, permanent desert river.

For millions of years, the Colorado River has cut its way into layer after layer of rock, gradually deepening and widening its channel. Now that channel is the Grand Canyon. It is more than a mile deep and almost 20 miles wide in some places!

After the storm, rainwater washes over the desert. It cuts, or *erodes*, channels in the soil and even in layers of soft rock. These channels are called *washes* or *arroyos* (uh-ROY-oz) in North America. Arroyos typically have steep walls and flat floors. Floods gush through these arroyos time and again, cutting deeper and deeper to form canyons.

Desert mountain ranges often have many canyons, carved by the flow of rainwater. As the runoff (water that runs off the mountain) reaches the base of a mountain, it begins to slow down. At this point, the water leaves behind piles of boulders and large rocks it has carried. As the water spreads over the flat land, it dumps its load of sand and other fine bits of soil. The piles of rock and sand that collect at the ends of canyons near mountain bottoms are called *alluvial* (uh-LOO-vee-uhl) fans.

Mesas (MAY-suhz) are another special feature of deserts. Mesas are flat-topped mountains. The word "mesa" means "table" in Spanish. Mesas develop when a flat area of land is cut into sections over time by water erosion. Mesas are topped by layers of hard rock that don't easily erode.

Desert Winds

Deserts are windy places most of the time. Like water, wind is a powerful force in shaping desert surfaces. Blowing winds lift and carry small grains of dry sand and even smaller bits of dust from the ground.

A dune begins to form when moving sand bumps up against an object in its path. The sand forms a pile over the object. More sand blows up one side of the mound and drops off the other.

If the winds that carry the sand blow in more than one direction, star dunes form. They look like stars with many points. Star dunes tend to stay in one place, even up to hundreds of years. The other types of dunes constantly move across the desert like waves. A "sea" of sand is called an *erg* (urg).

Sometimes blowing sand forms spinning cones called *dust devils*. And sometimes strong winds cause sandstorms.

Whenever sand blows, it erodes the surfaces of objects in its path. Many of the rock shapes that dot the desert surface are created by wind erosion. A special combination of wind and water can even carve holes in rocks. The rock then forms a natural arch.

Some sand dunes form a crescent shape around an object that blocks their path. That is, they look a bit like a crescent moon. The wind blows more sand over the dune's outer edges than over its middle—this is how the shape forms. These dunes are called *barchans* (BAR-kuhnz).

If a desert area is covered mostly by sand, the wind blows the sand into rippled patterns and higher mounds called *dunes.*

The longest natural arch is called Landscape Arch. It is located in Utah. This arch is nearly 100 feet high and 300 feet long—about as long as a football field!

Daytime & Nighttime Animals

In deserts as in all places, different animals are active at different times. Some animals come out at night. Others are active during the day.

Animals can be grouped by the time of day they are active. *Diurnal* (dy-URN-uhl) animals are active mainly during daytime. *Crepuscular* (kri-PUHS-kyuh-lur) animals are also active by daylight, but are most active at dawn and late afternoon, or dusk. *Nocturnal* (nahk-TURN-uhl) animals are active mainly during nighttime.

Most desert animals disappear during the heat of the day. They have moved out of the sun to rest in cooler, shadier spots. When the sun sets, the desert will cool. The air may also become a bit more moist, or humid. That's when many animals will come out of hiding to "start their day."

Some desert animals move underground during dry, hot periods. They go into a sleeplike state that is called *estivation* (ES-tuh-VAY-shuhn). When an animal estivates, its body becomes dormant. This means the body's functions slow down. Breathing becomes slower, and the heart beats slower. Energy is burned more slowly, too.

Some desert animals become dormant during winter to escape the cold. This is called *hibernation* (HY-bur-NAY-shuhn). It is very much like estivation. Many desert animals hibernate *and* estivate. Frogs, toads, ground squirrels, and tortoises hibernate and estivate to avoid the desert's hottest and coldest temperatures.

Because bats and snakes hibernate and estivate, they are active mostly in spring and fall.

292

Early Morning

Desert mornings are filled with activity. In the first few hours of light, the desert is still cool. Dawn's arrival is loudly announced by singing birds. They have spent the night resting. Now, they are ready to start their day.

At dawn, birds also move across the ground. A North American bird called the Gambel's quail travels in groups called *coveys* (KUHV-eez).

The roadrunner also covers ground in the early hours. It is a large, striped bird with a long tail and strong legs. Roadrunners are speedy—they run as fast as 15 miles per hour!

The roadrunner and the quail do fly, but only when they have to. Some desert birds cannot fly. They must depend on their legs for escape. One flightless bird of the desert is the ostrich. Ostriches live in the Sahara Desert.

Some birds take to the sky in the morning hours. Eagles and hawks circle overhead. They are watching for rabbits, snakes, ground squirrels, birds, and other small animals.

Birds get most of their water from the food they eat. Seeds, fruit, stems, leaves, and animal flesh contain much moisture. Some birds get enough water from the food they eat. But many birds also need fresh water. So, they must spend their mornings in search of a drink.

You can easily see birds in the desert. They sing from atop shrubs, trees, and cacti.

The quail scratch at the ground, looking for seeds. They may also eat insects, berries, and leaves.

The ostrich is a well-known bird. It is the world's largest bird, standing nearly eight feet tall. Ostriches can run as fast as 40 miles per hour.

Roadrunners hunt insects, baby birds, gophers, mice, and snakes. They are even able to kill rattlesnakes.

293

Early Morning

You may have to look in the branches of a tree to find the Clark spiny lizard. This agile reptile is one of the daytime lizards.

The regal horned lizard blends in with the colors of the desert to make it hard for predators to find.

Early morning is also a busy time for many insects. Insects are not as easily seen as birds. But insects out-number birds and all other groups of desert animals. Insects that are active during the day include ants, cicadas, termites, wasps, beetles, grasshop-pers, and butterflies.

All but a few lizards are active during daylight hours. Lizards are mainly insect-eaters.

Lizards have many enemies. Most lizards can escape when grabbed by the tail—their tails simply break off! New tails grow in later.

Other reptiles also come out in early morning. A few snakes may be on the move. However, most snakes are nocturnal—they wait until dark to come out.

The desert tortoise walks along slowly, feeding on plants. The desert tortoise hardly ever drinks. But it will drink water when it finds some. The tortoise stores water in large bladders inside its body. Desert tortoises grow very slowly. They can live over 60 years!

Lizards are well suited for desert life. Some lizards are able to plug up their nostrils. This keeps sand from blowing into them.

The collared lizard can actually rise on its hind legs and run quickly to escape danger.

Ground squirrels and rock squirrels scurry here and there in search of seeds, fruits, and other plant material. Both of these small, furry creatures are *rodents*.

Rodents are animals that have a special set of teeth for chewing, or gnawing. They are very common in all the world's deserts.

Larger mammals also live in deserts. Some of them are active during the morning hours. In North American deserts, herds of mule deer move carefully and quietly. Sometimes, they travel in small groups.

Desert bighorn sheep also travel in groups. They have beautiful, curling horns. Both deer and bighorn sheep are *herbivores* (HUR-buh-vorz). This means they eat plants.

The camel is one of the most familiar desert animals. Camels are perfect for the desert. They can go a long time without drinking. They have long eyelashes to protect their eyes from blowing sand.

How do camels last without water? Camels eat plants, which contain water. They also have fat stored in their humps. They break this fat down for energy and for water. When camels do drink, they drink a lot—up to 20 gallons at one time!

Many of the animals you see in the early morning seem to disappear by midday. The heat of the afternoon sun is too much for them.

Desert bighorn sheep hide high in the mountains. They can easily run over rocks and across ledges.

There are two species of camels. Arabian camels have only one hump. Bactrian camels, which live in Asian deserts, have two humps.

Midday

The golden eagle keeps cool by soaring high above the desert during the hottest part of the day. Even from a great height, the eagle's sharp eyes can spot its prey on the ground.

The gilded flicker makes its home in a hole it drills in a tree or cactus. In the hottest hours, it cools off in its shady nest.

Most desert birds find places to rest until the sun begins to go down. Birds make their homes in many places, even underground tunnels.

Even thorny plants like the cactus of North America's deserts make good homes for birds. They may build a nest by drilling a hole in the cactus.

An old nest hole often becomes a new home for another animal. The new owner may be another bird, such as the tiny elf owl. Mice, rats, lizards, insects, or even a bat might also use the hole.

Eagles, hawks, and vultures may still be seen overhead at midday. These birds can be active even during the scorching afternoon hours. They soar on rising winds high above the desert. The air up there is much cooler.

It's surprising, but temperatures change quite a bit just inches above or below the desert surface. Many desert animals have long legs. Ostriches, camels, and deer are long-legged animals. They walk along with their bodies high off the ground. This helps keep them cool.

Just inches below the desert surface, temperatures can be much cooler. That's why so many desert animals, like the kangaroo rat, make their homes underground. The air in these homes is also more moist.

Late Afternoon

It is late afternoon in the desert. The sun has started to sink in the sky. The temperature is dropping. Long shadows stretch across the land. Desert life begins to stir once more.

Birds begin to sing again. The ants come out of their nests. Other insects leave their shady hiding places. Lizards are on the move again. Squirrels come above ground. The mule deer and the bighorn sheep search for a last bit of food and water. For all of these animals, the day is coming to an end.

The Gila (HEE-luh) monster is often active at this time of day. It is one of two poisonous lizards in North America.

The Gila monster is a very large lizard. It grows to over eighteen inches long. The Gila monster moves very slowly until it finds food, such as a young mouse. Then the lizard quickly moves to grab it. The Gila monster holds onto the animal with its teeth. Poison flows through grooves in the lizard's teeth.

The Gila monster hibernates in winter and estivates most of the summer. It lives off fat stored in its tail. The Gila monster's tail actually gets smaller as it uses up the stored fat. When the Gila monster builds up a new supply, its tail becomes larger again.

As late afternoon turns to dusk, the desert world changes. Animals of the daytime world seek places to rest and hide from predators.

As the evening approaches, snakes slither out of the rocks.

The Gila monster's bite is painful but not deadly to humans.

Reptiles

Most lizards are active during the daytime. Only the gecko, and sometimes the Gila monster, can be seen in the desert at night.

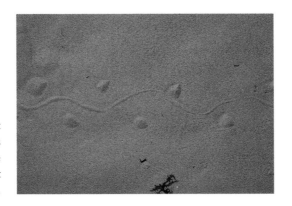

If you explore the desert at night, you might come across tracks left by the daytime animals. These tracks were left by a fringe-toed lizard.

Gila monsters are described as having "leaky" skin. They lose moisture through their skin more easily than other desert lizards. This is why they estivate and become nocturnal during the driest seasons.

Most lizards rest at night, but geckos do not. Geckos are found in many of the world's deserts. They get their name from the squeaky, chirping noise they make. Geckos are the only group of lizards that have vocal chords. Many other lizards hiss, wheeze, or whistle by exhaling air.

Most geckos can walk just about anywhere. They can move up and down smooth walls, and even across ceilings! They have special feet to help them. A gecko's toes are covered by brushy pads. Each pad is covered by tiny hairlike bristles with sticky ends. A gecko's feet also have claws for climbing in rough places.

Many people think the Gila monster is also a nocturnal lizard. As we have seen, this is not always true. The Gila monster is active mostly during the daytime, in the early morning and late afternoon.

So why do people think the Gila monster is nocturnal? Like many desert animals, the Gila monster sometimes changes its habits. At certain times of the year, you can see this lizard roaming the desert at night. When the weather is too hot and dry, the Gila monster cannot stand to be out during the daytime. The hot sunlight would cause it to lose too much moisture and die. So it comes out at night instead. At night, there is more moisture in the air.

298

Most snakes come out in the evening to hunt. Some of them are very poisonous. Coral snakes are dangerous. They have rings of black, red, and yellow. One type of coral snake lives in the North American deserts. Many snakes copy the coral snake's colors so other animals will avoid them.

Rattlesnakes are often nocturnal. They are dangerous desert dwellers. The rattlesnake sends poison, or venom, through the two long hollow teeth in its upper jaw. These teeth are called fangs. The poison forms in glands behind each eye.

In winter, rattlesnakes sometimes hibernate in large groups in underground burrows. Freezing temperatures are dangerous for them because they are cold-blooded reptiles.

There is a way to tell a real coral snake from a "fake" one. Left: A coral snake's bands go all the way around its body. Right: Most harmless snakes have bands just on their backs.

The rattlesnake's tail ends in a rattle. The rattle makes a buzzing sound when the tail shakes rapidly. A rattlesnake rattles its tail when it is alarmed and ready to strike.

The Western diamondback rattlesnake is one of the world's most dangerous snakes. It is to blame for more serious bites and deaths than any other snake in North America. It grows over six feet long!

The sidewinder is a rattlesnake that moves in a very special way. It lives in sandy desert areas. The sand makes it hard for the snake to slither. So, the sidewinder moves by making its body into a loop and "throwing" it sideways.

Mammals

The badger has strong front legs and claws. These make it a good digger. Badgers dig after rodents trying to escape underground.

The jackrabbit has very big ears. Heat escapes through the ears, helping the jackrabbit keep cool. Many desert mammals have big ears.

This is a rare glimpse of a golden mole above the ground. It spends most of its life tunneling under the desert's surface.

Jackrabbits' ears can turn left and right to pick up sounds. Their eyes are sharp, too. Jackrabbits eat cacti, grass, and low-hanging leaves.

The badger is also nocturnal. The badger has a territory it defends from other badgers. The territory is filled with holes. Each hole is a den. In the day, it rests in its den. The badger rarely rests in the same den two days in a row.

The Grants golden mole is a rodent that also has a special way of moving through the sand. The mole lives in the Namib Desert in Africa. It spends its whole life under the sand.

The golden mole hunts at night. The mole "swims" through the sand in search of insects and lizards to eat. It doesn't use its eyes and ears. It doesn't need them. How does the golden mole "see" its prey? It feels vibrations made by nearby animals moving over the sand.

Jackrabbits are also on the move at night. The jackrabbit is actually a hare, not a rabbit, although the two are very much alike.

How are rabbits and hares different? Rabbits are blind and have no fur when they are born. Hares can see and have fur when they are born.

The jackrabbit has long hind legs. These long legs help it run from danger with big leaps. A jackrabbit can reach speeds of 30 to 40 miles an hour.

Just as the jackrabbit is not a rabbit, the ringtail cat is not a cat. Ringtail cats are actually related to raccoons. Ringtails have rings of dark hair on their tails just as raccoons do.

Ringtail cats live in the North American deserts. They have very large eyes to help them see in the darkness. Ringtails eat rodents, birds, reptiles, insects, and plants.

Sometimes ringtails travel in pairs. They make dens in caves, in cracks along cliffs, in hollow trees, under rocks, or in empty buildings. The ringtail's nest is made of bark, grass, leaves, or moss.

The coati (kuh-WAHT-ee) also lives in North American deserts. It is also closely related to raccoons. Its tail is long and has rings. Coatis use their tails to help them balance. They wrap their tails around tree branches when they are climbing down headfirst.

The fat-tailed mouse is not really a mouse. It is actually a tiny *marsupial* (mar-SOO-pee-uhl). A marsupial is a mammal that has a pouch for carrying its young. Kangaroos are well-known marsupials. Kangaroos live in Australian deserts. So do fat-tailed mice. Fat stored in the mouse's tail breaks down into food when it is needed.

Ringtails make their dens in caves, in cracks along cliffs, in hollow trees, under rocks, or in empty buildings.

The coati has a long snout for rooting out grubs and plant roots.

Coatis are active at night. They often run in groups of up to a dozen. They are great climbers and leap easily among desert cliffs.

What do a fat-tailed mouse and a camel have in common? Both of them store fat in their bodies that can be turned into energy when they need it. The camel stores the fat in its hump. The fat-tailed mouse stores it in its tail.

Desert Dogs

The coyote hunts by day or night, depending on the temperature. It moves through the desert in search of prey during the cooler parts of the day.

The jackal is another foxlike hunter that lives in African deserts. Jackals look and act very much like coyotes.

North American deserts are home to the coyote, which looks like a dog. Coyotes spend hot days in a den underground. They eat whatever they can find—rodents, rabbits, snakes, grasshoppers, lizards, even grass. They can sometimes find water by digging holes in soft creek beds. But most of their water comes from the food they eat.

The kit fox is a neighbor to the coyote. The kit fox has large ears to keep it cool. Its den is a sheltered place in the rocks or in a shallow hole.

The kit fox has a close relative in the Sahara Desert. It is called the fennec (FEN-ik) fox. The fennec fox is the world's smallest fox. It's smaller than a house cat.

The fennec fox has very large ears, like the kit fox does. In fact, a fennec fox's ears are bigger than its face! The ears are very good at hearing small rodents on the move.

Australian deserts are home to dingos. Dingos are wild dogs that were brought to Australia by its first people. Dingos hunt as family groups at night. They don't bark, but they do howl. They eat small kangaroos and rabbits.

Dingos look very much like dogs. Most are yellow or reddish brown and have long tails.

Desert Cats

Hunting cats also move across the desert at night. The bobcat is on the prowl. It has a short tail and long legs. Its pointed ears have tufts of hair at the tips.

The bobcat is a good climber. It will spend the night looking for rabbits, birds, mice, rats, and squirrels. Then, it will sleep through the day in a cave, under rocks, or maybe in a hollow tree.

The largest hunter in North American deserts is the mountain lion. These big cats are also called pumas or cougars. The mountain lion hunts deer, bighorn sheep, and smaller mammals. The lion's cry sounds like a human scream.

Mountain lions are uncommon in the deserts of the United States. People have hunted them and forced them to leave their old homes. Now they live mainly in protected areas and in mountains and forest regions outside of the desert. Mountain lions are more common in the Mexican deserts.

Although the mountain lion is strong and fierce, it usually stays away from people. For this reason, it is not thought to be dangerous to humans.

Cats are the largest hunters in the North American deserts. At night, they wander through the desert in search of prey.

303

Metals

Today, silver, gold, and copper are still mined from desert regions worldwide. Surely, people will always admire the beauty of these valuable metals.

Like iron, copper is found in rocks called ore. Miners look for copper ore in the desert. Once it is separated from the ore, copper is one of the desert's treasures.

Thousands of years ago, people began to search deserts for silver, gold, and copper. The people used these metals to make jewelry, tools, and weapons.

Silver and gold are mined from deserts in South Africa and in North and South America. Desert regions in the former Soviet Union also contain gold. The Atacama Desert in South America has silver and copper.

Some of these deserts contain another metal called *iron*. Iron is one of the world's most useful metals. People build mines to find iron. Miners look for iron trapped inside rocks. Iron within rocks is called *iron ore*. The rocks are crushed to powder to separate the iron from the rock.

Uranium is another metal found in deserts. The United States and South Africa have large amounts of it. Uranium is used to make a special form of energy called *nuclear energy*. It is also used for making some kinds of weapons and for medical studies.

The world's largest supply of *bauxite* lies beneath the Australian Desert. Bauxite is used to make a light metal called aluminum. Giant shovels and bulldozers remove the earth that covers bauxite. Then, the bauxite is blasted loose with dynamite. It's loaded up, washed and dried, then shipped to factories.

Most of the time, iron mines are deep pits in the earth. Sometimes, people build tunnels underground to look for iron.

Minerals

Minerals are *inorganic*. This means they don't contain anything that was once alive. That is, they have no material from plants and animals.

The United States collects sand from its deserts. Chemicals, glass, paper, and concrete are made from sand. The United States also collects gravel and salt from its deserts.

Gypsum and soda ash are other minerals found at or near the desert surface. Gypsum is used to make plaster for walls and other building materials. Soda ash contains a form

of salt called sodium. Soda ash is used to make glass, soap, paper, and cleaning materials.

The Atacama Desert is rich in minerals called *nitrates*. Nitrates were once important in making fertilizers. Now, other materials are often used in place of nitrates for fertilizers. Nitrates have other uses. Camera film and some medicines and explosives contain nitrates.

Diamonds are one of the desert's rarest minerals. Only four areas in the world have good diamond supplies. The most important diamond supply is in the deserts of South Africa.

The Australian Desert also contains diamonds, as well as minerals called opals. Opals have many beautiful colors. They are used in jewelry.

The United States is the world's biggest salt producer. Salt is common in many desert regions. It coats the ground in layers of white chunks.

Many minerals are found in deserts. Examples of minerals include sand, salt, water, and stones.

Diamond miners must dig through tons of earth to find one good diamond.

305

Growing Grasses

Grasses can survive climate swings ranging from very hot to very cold weather.

Blades of grass are well adapted for survival in their environment.

The reason grasses can grow so abundantly in so many places is that they have developed a number of valuable *adaptations* (ad-ap-TAY-shuhns) over time. An adaptation is a feature that helps a plant or animal survive in a certain environment. Grass leaves, called blades, are long, thin, and flexible to withstand strong winds.

Grasses are also able to survive periods of flooding as well as long dry spells, called *droughts* (drowts). In fact, grasses are especially well adapted to survive drought, because their blades grow close together, and their stems, called *rhizomes* (RY-zoms), often grow underground. Both of these features help reduce water loss. Grasses also have densely packed roots that trap rainwater and hold it like a sponge before it has a chance to sink into the soil.

Grasses also have the ability to reproduce in two different ways. Sometimes new grass plants are produced directly from the rhizomes of the old plants. Many grasses can continue reproducing in this way for years. However, because they are flowering plants, grasses also have the ability to make flowers and seeds, and they can reproduce when these seeds sprout.

Grass pollen from the flowers is carried off by the wind, sometimes for long distances, from one grass plant to the next. Once it receives the pollen, the flowering head of the grass plant produces a great number of seeds.

The flowering head of one cattail can produce anywhere from 20,000 to 70,000 seeds!

Have you ever seen a grass flower? Many people haven't, because these flowers are small.

Grasses also have the special ability to keep growing even after being nibbled by animals, or grazed. In a perfect example of how plants and animals depend on each other, grasses and grazing animals need one another to stay in balance. The grazers have teeth suited to grinding up tough grass leaves, and special stomachs to digest them. Meanwhile, the saliva of some grazing animals actually makes the grass grow faster!

Believe it or not, fire is also a good thing for grasslands. Grasses are well adapted to these fires. Their rhizomes are protected from fires because they grow underground. Also, grasses are small, thin plants. Dead, dry grass provides much less fuel for fires than dead, dry trees would.

In fact, without occasional fires, the build-up of dead grasses can prevent new grass plants from growing. Fire also releases the minerals and nutrients in these dead grass plants, and returns them to the soil to feed new plants. After a fire, when the rains come, grass seeds will sprout in the nutrient-filled ashes.

Some grasses are even further adapted to living in areas of frequent fires. In the African grasslands, the seed of the red oat grass is pointed at one end. As it expands and contracts with changes in moisture, the pointed seed works its way under the ground. The seed is protected from fires and quickly sprouts when the rains come.

Fires that break out in grasslands are not as hot or as long-lasting as forest fires, and there is less damage to the area.

Fires occur frequently in grasslands because of the long dry spells. Most often, they are started by sparks of lightning.

When grazing animals bite off the tops of the grass blades, more sunlight can reach the lower parts of the plant, and this helps the grass plant sprout even more shoots closer to the ground.

309

America's Great Plains & Prairies

Because the prairies seemed so vast to the early settlers, they came to be known as the "Great Plains."

Above: Grama grass is a common grass of the plains. Right: A variety of plants grow together in the shortgrass prairie of Wyoming.

The shortgrass and tallgrass prairies make up the two major grassland areas of the United States. The shortgrass prairies, or plains, cover parts of ten states: the western parts of Texas, Oklahoma, Kansas, Nebraska, South Dakota, and North Dakota, and eastern Montana, Wyoming, Colorado, and New Mexico. Stretching out for 1,600 miles from north to south and 750 miles from east to west, they total 586,460 square miles.

Rain falls on the plains mostly in May, June, and July, and averages about 20 inches per year. But it is hard to predict: In some years, rain is abundant; in other years it hardly rains at all. This type of climate is called *semiarid* (se-mi-AR-id), or half dry.

The plains are quite flat, with few trees, no high mountains, and no large bodies of water, although they are crossed by major river systems. The most common grass on the plains is *shortgrass*, a group of grasses that can survive the great changes in moisture. Some can even push their roots up to the surface of the ground and draw in the surface water if there is no water to be found underneath the soil. One kind, buffalo grass, can survive long periods of heavy grazing better than almost any other grass. This is lucky, since nearly all cattle like to eat it. Western wheatgrass, named for its wheatlike appearance when it ripens in the fall, grows abundantly in the northern and central plains.

The tallgrass prairies, like prairies throughout the world, are wetter than steppes, but dryer than savannahs. Prairies are known for their deep, dark, fertile soil, which makes good farmland. Tallgrass prairies once stretched from western Ohio all the way to the edge of the Great Plains.

The prairies average 30 inches of rain a year, about a third more than the plains. Tall grasses are the most common prairie plants.

There are about 150 different kinds of prairie grasses. Once, the most common was big bluestem grass, also called turkeyfoot because of the way it branches out on top. Now much of this grass has been replaced by miles of cornfields and seas of golden wheat. But this six-foot-tall plant is still an important pasture grass in Oklahoma, Kansas, and Nebraska. Little bluestem grass, also called prairie beardgrass, is only four feet tall. It grows in the same areas as its larger cousin, and is eaten by cattle.

Nearly all the plants of the prairie are *perennials* (puh-REN-nee-uhls). They retreat under the soil each winter, and flower again each spring. The wildflowers that grow among the tall grasses bring beauty and color each spring. Wild prairie roses bloom in summer. Pasque flowers, coneflowers, phlox, and violets add a touch of purple; goldenrods, trout lilies, dandelions, black-eyed Susans, and huge sunflowers are a splash of sunny yellow.

Today, tallgrass prairies are considered one of the world's most endangered environments.

This prairie is in Illinois. Illinois may still be called the "Prairie State," but it has only one-hundredth of one percent of its original prairie left.

A field of black-eyed Susans is a beautiful springtime sight on the tallgrass prairies of Illinois.

South Dakota has some wide expanses of tallgrass prairie.

Birds

In grasslands and farmlands, the crow is a common sight. When a farmer plows the fields, crows will follow the tractor, picking up the worms, insects, and mice that the plow uncovers. When the corn sprouts, crows will pull up some of the shoots and eat them. They also eat many pesty insects, making up for the crops they destroy.

People who study them think crows are one of the smartest birds in the world. Crows have learned to eat grain that has fallen in the fields; they pick through dumps and garbage cans for scraps of food; and they pick at road-killed animals without getting killed by a car themselves.

The crow has an "all-purpose" bill. It is strong, sharp, and long—perfect for eating whatever food the crow can find.

Crows live in flocks most of the year. As many as 200,000 crows may roost together in one flock! During the breeding season, pairs go off by themselves to build their large stick nests.

Crows are nature's garbage collectors!

The American crow usually lays four to six eggs. Both male and female incubate the eggs for 18 days. The chicks leave the nest in 28 to 35 days. A pair of crows may nest a second time if their first nesting fails for any reason.

The adult red-tailed hawk's rusty tail is its best field mark, but don't expect to always see it. The orange-red color is only on top of the tail; it is invisible when you are looking up at a soaring hawk. Only if a circling hawk tilts to one side will you catch a glimpse of this marking.

High above grasslands and farmlands, the red-tailed hawk watches carefully for movement below. Like all hawks, its eyes are much better than ours at picking out details. A hawk that is hundreds of feet in the air can spot a mouse running through the grass. The red-tailed hawk's diet changes with the seasons, including what is most abundant at that time. These birds mostly eat small mammals, like mice, shrews, voles, rabbits, and chipmunks. As with most predators, they will catch whatever they can, and their diet sometimes includes other birds, snakes, frogs, lizards, and insects.

The undersides of the red-tailed hawk are white. Seen from below, the tail looks slightly pink, especially if the sun is shining through it.

Even though red-tailed hawks hunt over open country, they nest in trees. They build large stick nests high in the branches.

Compared to smaller birds, hawks do not lay many eggs. The normal clutch for a red-tailed hawk is just two or three eggs. The chicks are unable to move at birth, but are not as helpless as songbird babies, for they have their eyes open and are covered with soft down. In a few days, they beg their parents for food. They are growing fast!

The red-tailed hawk eats live prey. Its bill is sharp and curved for shredding pieces of meat.

Animals of the Savannah

Much of the pride's day is spent peacefully conserving energy—adults will sleep or rest in the shade about 20 hours each day!

The African savannah is home to a greater number of animals and more different kinds of wildlife than any other grassland. The Serengeti is the most famous of Africa's savannahs. Here, one of the world's tallest grasses grows over 12 feet high. Because it is tall enough to hide an elephant, this grass is called elephant grass.

The endangered African elephant is the largest of all land animals. It is protected from most predators by its enormous size. Elephants spend most of their time feeding on grasses and even small trees, uprooted with their strong trunks.

Fully grown male elephants, called bulls, can weigh over 11,000 pounds!

Besides the largest animal, Africa also has the world's tallest land animal—the giraffe. Only lions dare to hunt the giraffe for food.

Lions are the only big cats that live in family groups. These groups, called *prides,* average several dozen members. Several animals hunt together, usually at night.

Most graceful of the African grazers is the ever-alert gazelle, which leaps off at the first hint of danger. Gazelles easily outrun most predators. One predator that can catch up to a gazelle is the cheetah, a long-legged cat. At 70 miles per hour it's the fastest-running animal in the world. Other grazing animals include antelopes, wildebeests, and zebras, who are as shy as their stripes are bold.

Giraffes use their seven-foot necks to help them feed on leaves in the very tops of acacia trees, where other grazing animals cannot reach.

Grant's gazelle is found in Tanzania, Africa.

318

Grassland Animals of the World

On the Asian steppe, Saiga antelope, roe deer, red deer, bison, camels, and wild horses once roamed. Today, few of these animals are left. Even fewer of the Indian rhinoceros, the mightiest Asian herbivore, still exist. Not many predators would dare attack this massive, thick-skinned animal—it weighs up to 8,000 pounds!

Rodents include the steppe marmot and suslik. These two creatures are well adapted to the steppe's temperature extremes. They hibernate underground in winter and undergo *estivation* during the summer. Estivation is similar to hibernation, but the animals are inactive in the hottest part of the summer rather than in winter.

The Australian grassland also has some exotic inhabitants. It is unusual because *marsupials* (mar-SOO-pee-uhls)—kangaroos and their smaller cousins, wallabies—are the main native grazers. Marsupials are mammals that have special pouches in which they carry their young. Nowadays, enormous flocks of domestic sheep numbering in the millions compete with the marsupials for grass and water.

Termite mounds are probably the most surprising structures on the Australian savannah. These mounds range from 6 to 16 feet high. Tiny holes in the walls provide fresh air. When the mound is abandoned, the rich soil that remains is spread by the rain, adding nutrients to the soil.

In Southern Asia, tigers, originally forest animals, have been forced out onto the grasslands as more and more forests are cleared.

The foot-long horn of the rhinoceros is considered valuable, so these great beasts, like the elephant, have been hunted to near extinction.

Kangaroos can reach speeds of 25 miles per hour.

Have you ever tried a broad jump? Humans would be no match for red kangaroos (right), which can cover up to 30 feet in one leap! All female kangaroos carry their young in pouches on their abdomens (below).

319

What Is a Temperate Forest?

Vast expanses of land are covered by temperate forests in areas like the Great Smoky Mountains of North Carolina and Tennessee.

It's almost never extremely hot or cold, or extremely wet or dry, in a temperate forest.

You might recognize a conifer by its shiny, dark-green needles and its scaly cones.

Deciduous forests grow in the eastern United States, from Maine down to Tennessee, as well as in Europe and Asia.

Temperate (TEM-puh-ruht) forests grow in milder climates. The weather in a temperate climate changes with the seasons, but compared with other climates, it doesn't change very much. Forest trees help to keep the temperatures mild. In the summer, the trees' leaves block out much of the sun's heat and keep the woods cool. When the trees drop their leaves in winter, the sun's light shines in and warms up the woods.

The trees also soften the effects of wind and rain. They turn strong winds into soft breezes and change driving rain that can erode the soil into droplets that seep gently down into it. Temperate forests generally get 40 to 50 inches of rainfall each year.

Temperate forests are sometimes divided into two categories: *coniferous* (kuh-NI-fuh-ruhs) and *deciduous* (di-SI-juh-wuhs) forests. Coniferous temperate forests have mostly *conifers* (KAH-nuh-ferz), also called evergreen trees, which produce cones instead of flowers. You would recognize a conifer in the winter because it would still be completely green. All Christmas trees are conifers!

Deciduous forests contain mostly deciduous, or hardwood, trees, which lose their leaves each winter. Beeches, maples, oaks, ashes, and birches are all deciduous trees. Deciduous trees produce flowers in the spring, seeds in the summer, and spectacularly colored leaves in the fall.

320

Types of Temperate Forests

The age of a forest has a lot to do with the sizes and types of trees growing there. If the forest has escaped destruction by natural disasters and human effects like timber cutting, it is called an *ancient forest*. Scientists also call these forests old growth forests or primary growth forests. All these terms simply mean a forest whose trees are fully grown and where the plant and animal life is very similar to what it was a century ago. Many tall beeches and maples grow in old growth forests in the northeastern United States; oak and hickory trees can be found in greater numbers in ancient forests that have less moisture.

In some areas, ancient forests have been cleared for timber, farming, or cattle grazing. Or they were leveled by fires or great storms. Newer forests that grow up in these places are called *secondary growth*. As a forest matures, it evolves, or changes, from grasses and flowers, to shrubs, to small trees, and finally to tall trees. The forest actually changes itself as it grows over time.

In some areas that have been cleared for timber, forests have been replanted. However, such forests often consist of a single tree species, or *monoculture*. The trees are planted so that they can be cut down again when they mature in another 70 years or so. The tree planted most often in the western United States is the Douglas fir.

In this greenhouse, Douglas fir seedlings are being grown to be planted in new, monoculture forests.

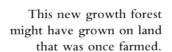

This new growth forest might have grown on land that was once farmed.

Most of the forest left in the United States, particularly throughout the Northeast, is secondary growth.

Ancient, majestic trees shade the old growth forest.

Ancient Forests of the Pacific Northwest

The rufous hummingbird lives and feeds among the giant redwoods.

A single acre of ancient forest contains over 400 tons of wood.

The ancient forests along the coasts of California, Oregon, and Washington contain the most massive living things on Earth—conifers called redwood trees. One of the tallest redwoods in California towers 367 feet tall—as high as 60 tall men all standing on top of each other! One big tree can shelter 1,500 animals.

So many fallen needles and animal droppings may pile up on the high branches of ancient trees, that the "soil" they make may be over an inch thick! In this soil in the sky grow moss and lichens, used as nests by flying squirrels, rufous hummingbirds, and a bird called the marbled murrelet.

The red tree vole lives in ancient Douglas fir trees, eating only the needles, living in a nest lined with more needles, and drinking the raindrops that fall on the needles. In fact, it may live its whole life without ever leaving its "family tree." The endangered spotted owl depends upon the red tree vole as a source of food.

The Pacific yew tree also depends on the shade of ancient forests. This tree takes as long as 50 years to grow one inch in diameter. As we learn more about ancient forests, we are beginning to realize how important it is to protect plants like the yew that may someday prove valuable to us.

The bark of the Pacific yew contains a cancer-fighting chemical called taxol.

These tall trees can pull water out of the sky: Fog condenses on the needles as water and drips down to the forest floor. This can add up to a third of the yearly rainfall.

Deciduous Forests

Each spring as the weather warms, the tree's "blood," or *sap,* begins its journey upward, carrying water and nutrients from the roots to the treetops. The leaf buds of deciduous trees begin to open and flowering trees blossom.

Insects and bats, attracted to the fragrances and colors of these flowers, *pollinate* (PAH-luh-nayt) them by carrying pollen from male flower parts to female flower parts. But trees with small, drab flowers, like oaks and hickories, must depend on the wind to blow the pollen from tree to tree. By midsummer, the trees are in full leaf.

Fall brings a new set of changes. Trees slow down and then stop producing food for themselves from sunlight, water, and air. The leaves stop producing *chlorophyll* (KLOR-uh-fil), the substance that gave them their green summer color.

Now the hidden *pigments,* or leaf colors, that have been covered up by the green chlorophyll, begin to show themselves. Sugar maples, birches, tulip

trees, and hickories have large amounts of a pigment called *carotene* (KAYR-uh-teen). The carotene causes their leaves to turn yellow and orange.

Along with the leaves, the tree seeds also begin to ripen and fall each autumn. A few of these will survive the winter to grow next spring.

In winter, this black oak awaits the springtime, when its leaves will again begin to grow.

When fall arrives, the trees begin to prepare for winter.

In spring, pink cherry blossoms add color to the forest.

When a maple tree stops producing chlorophyll, its bright summer green turns to the reddish orange of fall.

Dead Trees

Woodpeckers drill holes into a tree trunk, making new entryways for still more insects and fungi.

A pioneer Douglas fir seedling may take root in the soft decay.

Honey mushrooms grow on stumps and logs of dead trees.

Dead trees play a vital role in the forest.

Ferns and other plants grow on the dead log, wrapping it in a living blanket.

An old growth tree like a Douglas fir may live for over 500 years and grow to be 300 feet tall. A tree this old has survived centuries of lightning, fires, floods, and blizzards. But finally, some of these lightning bolts may break off major branches from the tree—or even crack off the entire top of the tree itself. Heavy ice and snow piled up on other branches may break them off, too.

These injuries leave open holes, which make good homes for many forest animals. But they also provide a convenient entrance for insects, fungi, and diseases, as well as making it hard for sap to flow freely upward in the spring. Eventually, the giant tree becomes weaker and weaker, and at last it crashes to the forest floor.

But the tree doesn't really die there. Instead, it begins a new phase of life as a log, giving back to the forest the stuff from which it was made. Beetles that chomp through the log's thick bark open up passageways for termites and carpenter ants, who grind the wood into sawdust other insects will eat. Soon, miles of insect tunnels turn the log into a huge sponge. It may, over time, soak up over 1,000 gallons of water! Shelf fungi and honey mushrooms digest the wood from the outside, while millions of bacteria work to break it down from the inside.

The log may lie rotting on the forest floor for decades, protecting the creatures sheltered in its heart.

Layers of Life

Scientists who study plants classify temperate forest plants into five overlapping horizontal layers. Just as your house has a ceiling, so does the forest: This top layer, called the *canopy* (KA-nuh-pee), is made up of tall treetops. The canopy determines the "personality" of the forest. If the tall trees are closely spaced and little sunlight can get through to the lower levels, the forest floor will have little vegetation.

Below the canopy is the *understory*, made up mostly of young trees and trees that don't grow very tall. Next comes the *shrub* layer. Shrubs usually grow only about six feet tall and have many woody stems rather than one trunk.

Next is the *herbaceous* (er-BAY-shuhs) covering made up of nonwoody plants like wildflowers, ferns, grasses, and mosses.

Beneath these, covering and insulating the forest floor itself, is a protective covering of *leaf litter*. This is made of fallen leaves, twigs, flower petals, seeds, fruits, animal droppings, and pine needles. In this layer live *decomposers* (dee-kuhm-POZ-erz) like worms, insects, bacteria, and fungi. Decomposers break down the organic litter and, in a few years, transform it into rich, dark soil called *humus* (HYOO-muhs).

Under the litter is the final forest layer, the *soil*. Here, seeds take root and grow up to produce all the other forest layers.

Plants in the herbaceous layer grow from an inch to several feet tall.

Bushes and saplings, or very young trees, are found in the shrub layer.

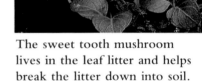

The sweet tooth mushroom lives in the leaf litter and helps break the litter down into soil.

If canopy trees are widely spaced, the vegetation in the lower levels will grow much thicker, providing more habitat for forest animals.

Squirrels visit all the forest layers, from the canopy to the soil. Some animals never leave the layer in which they were born.

Trees & Shrubs

To collect maple sap, people insert a small spout into the tree trunk and hang a bucket on it. The sap, diverted from its upward journey, drips into the bucket.

Deciduous trees provide habitats for many animals, and some also have uses for humans!

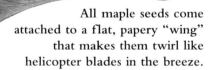

All maple seeds come attached to a flat, papery "wing" that makes them twirl like helicopter blades in the breeze.

Acorns (above), grown abundantly by all oaks (right), are an important food source for squirrels, deer, and many other forest creatures.

Many deciduous trees are well known to most of us. Maples, oaks, and hickories are a common sight in temperate forests.

The sugar maple is famous for its sweet sap, which is made into maple syrup. The sap begins to rise in February, when the tree awakens from its winter sleep. The sap is collected and poured into a large, flat pan, where it is boiled until the sap thickens into syrup. It contains so much water that it takes about 40 gallons of sap to make one bucket of syrup! The red maple tree—named for its bright red flowers in spring and bright red leaves in fall—is related to the sugar maple.

Oak trees are sometimes called the kings of the forest because they are so big. Three types of oaks—white oaks, red oaks, and black oaks—are common in the deciduous forest. Oak leaves are longer than they are wide. All oak leaves contain a lot of tannin, a bitter substance that makes them resistant to fungi and insects. Oaks also have strong wood, valuable for heavy-duty uses like buildings, furniture, and railroad ties.

The shagbark hickory is instantly recognized by its long, peeling strips of bark. Settlers used hickory wood for wagon wheels and axe handles. They "hickory smoked" meat to preserve it, and ate hickory nuts—edible both for squirrels and people!

Conifers grow abundantly in the West and in colder climates farther north, like Canada and Alaska. Their tough, needlelike leaves are better adapted for cold weather than the thin leaves of deciduous trees.

Early settlers cut down large numbers of white pines, using the wood for everything from furniture to ships' masts. However, this tall, graceful tree is still scattered throughout the East. The white pine's long, slender needles grow in "bundles" of five. It's the only conifer with five needles per bundle.

The eastern hemlock usually grows in ravines and along streams, waiting until other trees grow tall enough to provide it with the shade it needs before sprouting.

Shrubs and bushes are also important forest vegetation. Mammals and birds feed on their berries and take cover in their foliage.

One common shrub is the spicebush, which gets its name from the pleasantly spicy smell of its crushed leaves and the bright red berries it produces each fall. This tree is much appreciated by campers because, in an emergency, its wood will burn, even when still green.

Poison ivy grows hairy-looking, tree-climbing vines, flaming red leaves, and white berries in the fall. While its berries may be poisonous to us, they provide an important food source for dozens of bird species in winter.

The white pine's thickly needled branches provide good hiding places for owls and sleeping songbirds.

The white pine was once one of the most common trees in the eastern forest.

Hemlocks have short, flat needles that also grow singly on the twig, with a white stripe on the back of each needle.

Touching any part of a poison ivy plant may give you an itchy rash.

327

Mammals

Fawns are well camouflaged, with white spots that look much like dappled sunlight.

The graceful white-tailed deer has become a symbol of the northeastern temperate forest.

The black bear can weigh up to 600 pounds!

The bright white stripe down the skunk's black back is an example of *warning coloration*. It signals predators to stay away.

The northeastern temperate forests are home to the white-tailed deer. The deers' white-striped brown coat provides excellent *camouflage* (KA-muh-flazh), or protective coloring, that helps them blend in with the sun and shadows in the woods. They are named for the white undersides of their tails, which lift as they run, warning other deer of danger.

Male deer mate with several does, or female deer, in the late fall. Fawns are born in late spring. Fawns keep their spots throughout the summer, until they are old enough to travel and feed with the herd. In winter, deer nibble on twigs and buds or acorns dug from the snow. In the summer

months, they prefer wild fruits, nuts, leaves, grasses, and flowers.

The biggest animal found in temperate forests is the black bear. Long claws make it possible for these animals to eat everything from fish scooped out of a forest stream to mouthfuls of honey scooped out of a hollow tree.

Flying squirrels wait until dark to glide from their homes in tree trunk cavities to the forest floor below, looking for food. A fold of skin stretching from front legs to rear legs catches the air when this rodent jumps from the treetops, and gives it a safe trip down. Because the flying squirrel cannot make an upward flight, it is not considered a true "flier."

Another mammal that is active by night is the black-masked raccoon. It spends many moonlit hours by cool waters, fishing with its paws for crayfish, fish, and frogs, or raiding bird nests to eat the eggs.

Changes in the length of day and colder temperatures trigger *hibernation* (hy-ber-NAY-shuhn), a period of inactivity, in mammals like bears, chipmunks, and woodchucks. The thick, white blanket of snow insulates these hibernating animals and protects them from the icy winds above. Their heartbeat and breathing slow greatly: A hibernating woodchuck's heart may beat only five times per minute, and its body temperature may drop way down to 40 degrees Fahrenheit. In an hour, it may take only a dozen breaths.

Chipmunks, too, head for their underground burrows when the temperature drops. In warmer months, chipmunks are active during the day, filling their little cheek pouches with food to take back to their dens.

The numbers of some animals, like deer, rabbits, and squirrels, have actually increased over the years. With the disappearance of deep forests has come an increase in fields containing the grasses and grains these animals eat. But other creatures, especially many large predators, could not survive the loss of habitat and hunting by humans. Cougars, lynx, bobcats, and wolves disappeared from the northeastern forest nearly a hundred years ago.

Woodchucks are active in the summertime. In the winter, this woodchuck will hiberate beneath the snow.

In the warm months, the yellow-pine chipmunk feeds and harvests seeds and nuts to store for the winter.

Many forest animals are active at night.

Some wolves still live in forests in the northern United States, but they have become rare.

Birds

Great horned owlets hatch at different times. If food is scarce, the oldest owlet will get it all. This way, at least one owlet will live instead of all of them starving to death.

On a frosty January night, the deep *whooo, whooo, whooo* of a pair of great horned owls fills the woods. Even though it is the middle of winter, the owls are beginning their courtship. By February they have chosen their nest, which will probably be an old one once belonging to hawks, squirrels, or crows. The nest may be the top of a broken tree. Either way, the female will add a little down to the nest lining. Otherwise, the owls do nothing to the nest, which will hold two or three eggs.

The adult great horned owl stands about two feet tall. Its wingspan is nearly four feet!

Both male and female great horned owls are feathered in a mix of brown, black, and white. Their large eyes are yellow and the "facial disk" around the eyes is red-brown. The tufts of feathers that look like ears or horns—and that give the owl its name—do several things. First, the tufts show the owl's "mood." Also, their different shapes help other owls to know who's who. Last, the tufts are a kind of defense—they make the owl look like a mammal. The owl's real ears are near its eyes, at the edge of the facial disk. And though its ears are not easily seen, the owl's hearing is very good.

The great horned owl's hearing is so good, it can hunt by sound alone!

The female great horned owl is slightly bigger than the male. You cannot tell them apart, though, unless you see them at their nest.

Great horned owls eat almost any small animal they can catch. They'll even kill skunks and porcupines!

The highlight of a birdwatcher's spring is the sight of a flock of warblers feeding in the treetops, hungry after a night of migrating. No other group of North American songbirds is as beautiful as these feathered gems.

There are more than 50 species of warblers found north of Mexico.

Warblers also nest in the treetops, so we know very little about their habits. We do know that the female lays about four eggs, which she incubates for 11 days. The females are usually drab, to help them hide while they are incubating their eggs.

There are fewer and fewer woodland songbirds these days—especially warblers and thrushes. Ornithologists think one problem is here in North America: By chopping down trees to make way for roads, power lines, and buildings, people have divided the forests into smaller and smaller pieces. Doing this allows predators that usually stay out of the deep woods—crows, blue jays, and raccoons—into the birds' breeding grounds.

Warbler males of most species are brightly marked in yellow, orange, red, green, or blue. The females are not as colorful, perhaps to help them hide while they incubate their eggs.

The warbler's beak is thin and sharp for catching insects.

Importance of Rivers & Lakes

Chicago's famous Buckingham Fountain circulates water at a rate of 15,000 gallons per minute.

Did you know that more than two-thirds of your body is made up of water? Health experts tell us we should drink at least a half gallon of water each day. That's because we have to make up for the pint of water lost from breathing, the pint lost from sweating, and the quart-and-a-half lost in eliminating our waste each day.

Water covers about 70 percent of the Earth's surface. Most of this is ocean salt water. Some water exists as ice, and some is underneath the ground. Lakes and rivers are the only places where we can easily get fresh, flowing water. But these lakes and rivers—along with their smaller relatives, ponds and streams—contain less than one-tenth of one percent of all the water on Earth. That's not very much.

Every plant, animal, and person on Earth needs water to live.

Many of the fun things people do for recreation would not be possible without water.

Dams are used to provide a type of energy called hydropower.

It is important to protect our lakes and rivers because we need water for so many things—drinking, bathing, flushing toilets, watering lawns, washing cars, cooking, and cleaning. In fact, each person in the United States uses about 180 gallons of water each day.

Before cars existed, rivers were the very first highways, transporting people and things from place to place. Today, water is used to manufacture all kinds of useful products, from paper to soft drinks. Not only do plants need water, but so do the trees in the forest and all the wildlife that live there.

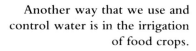

Another way that we use and control water is in the irrigation of food crops.

Where Are Rivers & Lakes Found?

When settlers colonized new lands, many looked for a place where a river emptied into the sea, called the *mouth* of the river, or a place where two rivers came together, called a *confluence* (CON-flew-ents). Some of these early settlements would later become great cities.

One of the world's most famous rivers is Africa's Nile, which, at a length of 4,160 miles, is the longest river in the world. Other famous rivers include Russia's 2,290-mile-long Volga, Europe's longest river, and the mighty 3,900-mile Amazon, which runs through South America's tropical rain forests.

Right here in the United States flows New York's 350-mile-long Hudson River, one of our most important trade routes, and the Colorado River, an important source of power and water in the dry land out West. Our best-known river, the Mississippi, begins in Minnesota's Lake Itasca and runs for 2,350 miles to the Gulf of Mexico.

Famous lakes include Lake Baikal in the former Soviet Union, which holds more water than any other lake, and Lake Titicaca, the largest freshwater lake in South America.

Our own five Great Lakes—Superior, Erie, Michigan, Huron, and Ontario—take up 300,000 square miles. Lake Superior alone has a larger area than any other lake in the world.

When people first began to grow crops for food, they realized that the rich land next to rivers was ideal for farming.

Throughout history, people settled near rivers and lakes because they knew having water nearby would make their lives easier.

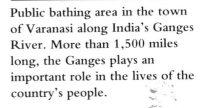

Public bathing area in the town of Varanasi along India's Ganges River. More than 1,500 miles long, the Ganges plays an important role in the lives of the country's people.

Lake Superior as seen from Michigan's Pictured Rocks National Lakeshore. The Great Lakes combined hold about one-fifth of the Earth's supply of freshwater.

Shared by Bolivia and Peru, Lake Titicaca is the largest freshwater lake in all of South America.

The Water Cycle

Water enters the air from evaporating lakes, rivers, and oceans. Some also comes from the "breathing" of plants. The vapor stays in the atmosphere for an average of ten days before it returns to Earth as rain or snow.

The water cycle is the process by which Earth's water supply is continually being recycled by the forces of nature.

Water or snow that lands in a polar region may become part of a frozen ice sheet, or glacier, and remain there for centuries!

Water that evaporates from the surface of the planet returns to Earth as rain or snow, a process called precipitation.

To understand the water cycle, it is important to first know that water can exist in three different forms: as ice, as the familiar liquid that flows from our faucets, and as water vapor, or steam.

One of four things eventually happens to every drop of water in every lake or river in the world: The drop may *evaporate*, it may be *transpired*, it may become groundwater, or it may become runoff.

Transpired water is first taken up by the roots of a green plant. Then, during the plant's transpiration, or "breathing" process, oxygen and water vapor are given off, and the water vapor goes back up into the atmosphere. If the drop of water sinks deep enough under the ground, it may reach an underground river called an *aquifer* (AH-kwi-fer), which contains groundwater.

This groundwater may eventually come back to the Earth's surface in the form of a spring or a wetland area. From there it may flow downhill in tiny streams called *rivulets* (RIV-yew-lets), joining other runoff water to form larger streams, and then even larger rivers. The river may carry the original drop to a lake, where it may again seep into the groundwater below the lake, or it may be carried into the ocean. From either the lake or ocean, it may once again simply evaporate from the surface.

A River's Journey

When a river runs rapidly down a sharp slope like a mountainside, the sediment carves, or erodes, a narrow, V-shaped path in the land underneath and around it, called the river valley.

Over time, the sediments in the river begin to wear away the sides of the river valley. Its shape gradually changes from a "V" to a "U," and it becomes progressively wider. As the slope of the river becomes less steep, the river's current slows down, and it begins to deposit the sediments it has been carrying all along.

Rivers have a lot of power. Each grain of sand in the sand castle you build at the beach was worn  down by a river from a larger pebble; each pebble you find on the sand was once part of a large boulder.

When a river's waters rise so high that it overflows its banks, the land surrounding the river becomes flooded. Along with the water, all the sediment that the river has been carrying is deposited upon this land, called the floodplain. When the water dries up, this sediment is left behind, and the floodplain soil becomes enriched by the nutrients and minerals it contains.

For this reason, floodplains are good places for growing crops. They are not, however, good places to build cities. This lesson was learned the hard way in 1993, when the Mississippi River flooded eight states, temporarily creating a vast inland sea.

The incredible power of some rivers carves through soil and stone to create fantastic formations like the Grand Canyon in Arizona.

Different rivers have different "personalities." Some are quiet and slow-moving; others are loud and wild.

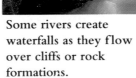

Some rivers create waterfalls as they flow over cliffs or rock formations.

Rivers with strong currents carry large amounts of sediments to the sea. Much of this material is deposited at the river's mouth in areas called *deltas*.

Estuaries

Above: A pair of laughing gulls patrols the coast, searching for food and scavenging on the bodies of cast-up sea creatures. Left: A breeding ground for birds and fish, estuaries like this one in northern England are among the most productive ecosystems on the planet.

All rivers eventually reach the sea. The places where the freshwater of a river meets the salty water of the sea are called *estuaries* (ES-chew-ayr-eez). There are about 900 of them along America's coastlines. One of the largest is Chesapeake Bay, which stretches 195 miles from Maryland to Virginia. Covering three million acres, Chesapeake Bay is fed by about 150 rivers.

Since salt water is heavier than freshwater, a bottom layer of seawater is often pushed by the ocean tides far up into the river. Meanwhile, the upper layer is made up of fresh river water flowing downstream into the sea.

Estuaries are important hatching areas. Ocean fish, like shad, striped bass, and sturgeon, all swim into estuaries to lay their eggs in large numbers, a process called *spawning*. Other fish, like bluefish, only swim into estuaries to feed.

Estuaries are also home to crabs, oysters, and scallops. They are important feeding grounds for shorebirds like egrets, herons, terns, and gulls—and, indirectly, for humans as well.

In fact, half of all seafood animals caught along the Pacific Coast spend at least part of their lives in estuaries. Simply put, these are among the most productive ecosystems on Earth.

One acre of estuary can produce ten tons of plant and animal life each year.

Some fish, like perch, spend their entire lives in estuaries.

A least tern confronts a crab as both look for food along the shoreline.

The Life of a Lake

A lake may form at the bottom of a valley, in a place where many small streams flowing down nearby slopes finally meet. If one end of such a valley is blocked off by leaves and twigs, a natural dam is formed.

Dams are also built by beavers. They chew down trees up to two feet thick with their razor-sharp teeth, then drag and float the fallen branches and logs to the dam site, where they are packed together with rocks and mud. Eventually, the water flowing in will back up.

These are examples of how lakes can be formed naturally. Artificial lakes are made when people dig out large areas and fill them with water, or build concrete dams across a river.

Life comes to a newly formed pond or lake when animals begin to crawl, swim, or fly into it. Insects and birds stop by, attracted by the reflections on the water. Streams carry in microscopic animals, insects, fish, and tiny floating plants.

Younger lakes tend to be deep and clear, with few plants living in them. These are called *oligotrophic* (ah-li-go-TRO-fic) lakes. In time, as the aquatic plants die and decay, sediments build up on the bottom of the lake, and the lake becomes shallower and full of nutrients, with many plants present. Such lakes are called *eutrophic* (yew-TRO-fic) lakes.

Have you ever heard the expression "busy as a beaver"? Because beavers need lakes to live in, they work hard at creating them.

Lakes have a quieter life than rivers, which must do all the moving and carrying of water and soil.

Aerial view of Lake Powell, located in Arizona's Glen Canyon National Recreation Area.

339

Plants

Blue-green algae were among the first forms of life to appear on Earth more than 3,000 billion years ago.

The tiny plants found in rivers and lakes are the foundation of a very important food chain.

In rivers and lakes, the tiniest plants, algae, and other *phytoplankton* (FIE-to-plank-tun) have a very important role. They are eaten by tiny animals, called *zooplankton* (ZOH-oh-plank-tun), which are then eaten by larger animals, like fish, which are then eaten by still larger animals, like eagles and other birds of prey.

These tiny plants are very important in another way. Although they are microscopic, they are able to photosynthesize, or make their own food from sunlight, water, and nutrients, as all green plants do. They produce oxygen as they undergo photosynthesis, and this oxygen is used by every animal in the lake or river.

Many people who try to cross a stream by jumping from rock to rock often find themselves sitting in the stream instead! That's because tiny algae plants will coat anything in the water, including stems, twigs, and rocks. If you sat there long enough, they would coat you, too!

Some grasses, called cordgrass, or spartina, grow along the saltier estuary waters. Spartina is one of the few rooted plants that can survive in saltwater. It provides shelter from the tides, wind, and sun for numerous estuary animals.

Rushes and sedges are grasses that grow by freshwater lakes and slow-moving rivers. They can be woven into beautiful mats and baskets.

Sedges growing at water's edge.

Cordgrass is a common sight in the coastal regions of Europe, northern Africa, and the Americas.

Floating Flowers

Some flowers bloom on a lake's surface. White and yellow water lilies, which can grow to be more than a foot wide, are a common and lovely sight on many North American lakes.

Another unrooted floating flower, the water hyacinth, grows in warmer places like Florida. Like many other plants that are not native to North America, water hyacinths have taken over in some areas, replacing the native plants that once grew there.

Another floating plant, called duckweed, is the world's smallest flowering plant. As you might guess, duckweed is a favorite food of ducks!

If you visit an estuary, you may see widgeon grass, coontail, or eelgrass waving in the tides. Although it is not really a grass, eelgrass has similar long, narrow leaves, which are eaten by worms, shellfish, and crabs. These underwater plants provide shelter and food for all kinds of animals. As they carry out photosynthesis, these plants bubble dissolved oxygen through the water, which nourishes fish, young aquatic insects, and amphibians. The waste from these animals, in turn, fertilizes the plants.

Riverbank plants include water plantain, sunny yellow marsh marigolds and irises, and the orange-flowered jewel weed, also called "touch-me-not."

Duckweed looks much like a green mat on still water, but if you look closely, you can see the tiny round plants that make up the mat.

When aquatic plants die, the nutrients they contain feed the next generation of plants. In nature, nothing is wasted.

A giant water lily found in the Amazon region of South America grows to be more than six feet across.

The water hyacinth's ability to clog up waterways has earned the plant its nickname: the beautiful nuisance.

Aquatic Insects

Dragonfly larvae often hide in the mud at the bottom of a lake or pond, feeding on insects or worms that swim by. In the spring, they crawl out of the water and change into winged adults.

A water strider can glide around on the surface of quiet water as if it were ice-skating.

Many people dislike insects, but most birds and many small fish depend upon them for food.

Adult caddis flies swarm around a comfrey plant.

Caddis fly larvae construct cylinders of tiny pebbles or pieces of wood around their bodies. Inside this cylinder, they are both protected and camouflaged.

Aquatic insects that live in fast-running water are different from those that live in quieter water.

Mayfly larvae are very well adapted to life in fast-running streams. Water flows easily over their flat bodies, as they cling to the undersides of rocks with their strong claws.

During the spring and summer, their bodies will change a great deal. They will lose their gills, grow wings, and fly away. Adult mayflies live for just a few days. During this time, they mate and lay their eggs in the water.

Another lake insect, called the water boatman, gets its name from its long, paddle-shaped back legs. They stick out from its body like a pair of miniature oars, and they are used in much the same way.

Small, black insects, called whirligig beetles because they swim around and around in circles, carry their own "oxygen tank" with them as they search underwater for food. They hold a bubble of air between their front legs as they swim!

Female mosquitoes are attracted to still water, where they lay masses of eggs that hatch within just a few hours. Out come the wrigglers (mosquito larvae), which float near the surface, feeding on green algae. The wrigglers turn into large-headed *pupae* (PYOO-pee) that grow into winged adults. The entire process takes only two weeks.

Because trout can only live in fast-running, clear, cold, unpolluted water, they are considered an "indicator species." Their presence indicates that the water is fairly clean. In quieter freshwater you'll find large fish like bass, carp, pickerel, and bluegills, as well as some of the smaller varieties, like killifish and minnows. These smaller fish often end up being eaten by the bigger fish.

Smaller rivers contain smaller fish, while larger rivers contain larger fish. The world's biggest freshwater fish, the arapaima, can grow to a length of 12 feet and weigh 300 pounds! This red-scaled giant lives in the Amazon River.

Salmon have an unusual lifestyle among fish. Young salmon hatch in freshwater streams, where they spend several months feeding and growing as they make their way downstream. Only five inches long when they enter the sea, they can weigh up to 100 pounds by the time they return several years later. But unlike most other fish, they continue upstream, past the estuary, leaping over waterfalls and swimming against strong downstream currents, until they reach the very same stream where they were born. Only there will they spawn, as their parents did before them.

Many salmon "runs," as these routes are called, have been blocked by dams. Eventually, salmon will no longer be found in these rivers.

The mighty paddlefish, found in the Mississippi River, can grow to be six feet long and weigh 200 pounds.

The range of fish that live in our rivers and lakes is enormous. In different ways, all have adapted to their watery environments.

These pink salmon have light-colored stomachs and dark-colored backs so they are hard to see from below and above.

This bluegill is spawning. Bluegills are sought both for food and sport.

343

Amphibians

Although adult salamanders can breathe through their noses, they still get some of their oxygen through their moist skin. Drying out could be fatal for them.

Amphibians have existed for millions of years and are found everywhere but Greenland and Antarctica.

Most members of this cold-blooded group of animals have aquatic larvae, so they need to live near water.

Salamander eggs are laid upon stones in or near the water. When the young salamanders hatch, they breathe the dissolved oxygen in the water through their gills. When they mature, their gills close, they develop lungs, and they begin to breathe through their noses.

Amphibian eggs are fertilized by the males after spawning. The eggs are surrounded with a clear, jellylike substance that swells up as it absorbs water. This clear jelly traps the sun's heat like a greenhouse, so the eggs stay warm as they develop.

While peepers lay their eggs one by one, toads lay strings of eggs that look like black beads on a necklace, and wood frogs lay eggs in masses, often surrounding a submerged blade of grass. But the female bullfrog lays the most eggs of all—as many as 30,000! More than 90 percent of these eggs will not make it to adulthood.

In a good example of a working food chain, tiny fairy shrimp will feed on green algae. Then, water striders and water boatmen will eat the fairy shrimp. Tadpoles will then feed on the water striders and boatmen, and will themselves be eaten by fish, birds, snakes, and turtles. All the plants and animals living in a lake or river depend upon one another to survive and to keep the ecosystem in balance.

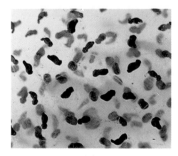

Frog eggs hatch into tadpoles. These small, plump creatures with large heads and tails feed on tiny animals. Eventually, their legs grow out, their tails disappear, and they develop lungs. Soon, they hop out of the water as adult frogs.

Mallards

When you think of a wild duck, you probably picture a mallard. With its green head, chestnut-brown chest, and orange feet, the male mallard—or "drake"—is one of the best-known birds in the world. It is no wonder: The mallard is found all over the northern hemisphere and in Africa.

Mallard drakes are unmistakable. But the females, called hens, are less colorful and may be confused with females of other species. The mallard hen is brown, with a pale head. Her bill is orange with a large black splotch. Her legs and feet are orange, too. The hen and drake both have large, shiny blue patches on their wings; the wing edges are striped with thin bars of black and white. No other puddle •duck has this combination.

Mallards pair up in winter while snow is still on the ground. The hen does all the work of raising the chicks. She finds a quiet, hidden spot for the nest, sometimes very far from water. The nest itself is built on the ground. It is a shallow bowl of grass lined with feathers the hen plucks from her breast. The chicks hatch with a fluffy coat of down. Their eyes are open, and they can walk and feed themselves right away.

As soon as her chicks have hatched, the hen leads them to the water for their first swimming lesson.

Mallards belong to the group of birds known as puddle ducks. They prefer shallow ponds, marshes, and lakes.

345

What Is a Wetland?

Wetlands can develop where water collects, such as the bottom of a hill, or where the land forms a bowl-shaped basin.

A puddle is not a wetland. An ocean is not a wetland either.

Wetlands are home to plants adapted, or suited, to living in wet conditions.

The Everglades, in Florida, is a wetland that covers many miles.

That's simple, you might think. The name says it all: wet...land. But don't be fooled by the simple name. There's much more to wetlands than wet.

The only simple thing about a wetland is its name. "Wetland" is the basic name for a kind of *ecosystem* (EE-ko-sis-tuhm) that forms where land gives way to water. (An ecosystem is a community of plants and animals and the environment they live in.) For example, wetlands form along the edges of rivers, lakes, and ponds. They form along coastlines, where the ocean meets the shore.

No two wetlands in the world look exactly alike. Some wetlands are small enough to fit into a backyard. Others cover many miles. Some stay wet all year. Others have no water part of the year, or even years in a row. But no matter what their differences, all wetlands share certain features that set them apart from other ecosystems. Scientists identify wetlands as places that, at least some of the time, are covered by a shallow layer of water or have waterlogged soils.

Wetlands receive their water from a number of sources. They collect rain, melted snow, and runoff—surface water that drains off the higher land around them. Wetlands may be fed from below: Groundwater stored in the earth may rise to the surface. Wetlands also fill with water that overflows the boundaries of nearby rivers, lakes, and oceans.

346

Wetlands are found around the world. In the United States, wetlands are thought to cover about five percent of the land in the lower 48 states. More than half of Alaska is covered by wetlands.

Living in a watery place like a wetland offers special challenges. The biggest challenge is getting enough oxygen. Oxygen is sparse in water and in soils that contain lots of water.

Wetland plants have special ways of getting as much oxygen as possible. For example, many have tiny openings on leaves that are above water. These openings draw in oxygen from the air. Others have openings in bark or roots to pull in oxygen.

Getting around in water offers another challenge. Plants don't have to move, but animals do. Some animals swim, such as fish and frogs. Others have webbed feet for paddling through water, such as ducks and beavers. A number of insects have bodies shaped to let them float, or even walk along the water's surface.

Scientists have a very complicated system for identifying different wetland types. The most basic way to group wetlands is based on whether they are freshwater or saltwater wetlands. Freshwater wetlands are found inland and mainly include marshes, swamps, and bogs. Saltwater wetlands are found along coastlines and mainly include salt marshes and mangrove swamps.

Beavers have webbed feet to help them move through water.

Horseshoe crabs live in saltwater wetlands.

Getting enough oxygen to survive is one of the greatest challenges for wetland plants and animals.

The diving beetle is one wetland animal that takes its own supply of oxygen underwater with it. The beetle traps air under its wings before it dives.

347

Some wetland birds have long legs to help them walk in shallow water.

Marshes

In general, prairie potholes measure a few acres in size. They fill with rainwater and snowmelt in the spring. The shallow waters soon are filled with insects and other water creatures. Frogs thrive on the rich plant life in prairie potholes and other marshes.

Marshes are believed to support as much life, acre for acre, as rain forests.

Above: Water lilies are floating-leaved marsh plants. Right: Waterfowl, such as ducks, geese, and swans, flock to the marsh.

About 90 percent of wetlands in the United States are marshes. Freshwater marshes may contain a few inches to several feet of water.

Most plants in marshes are soft-stemmed, nonwoody species. They mainly include grasses and grasslike plants such as cattails, bulrushes, and sedges. Floating-leaved plants may grow in deeper water. They are rooted in the marsh bottom. Their topmost parts float on the water's surface.

Submergent (suhb–MER–juhnt) plants such as coontail grow completely underwater. The rich plant life found in marshes provides plenty of food and shelter for animals such as muskrats, beavers, mink, fox, moose, deer, frogs, turtles, dragonflies, spiders, skunks, and snakes…to name a few!

Birds are very common in marshes. Smaller birds, such as blackbirds, sparrows, and warblers, feed and nest there. Wading birds, such as herons, rails, and bitterns, walk the marsh.

The prairie pothole is a special kind of marsh. The prairie pothole region covers parts of the northern United States and Canada. Potholes are depressions in the land that have filled with water and developed into marshes. Nearly seven million ducks visit the prairie potholes each year. They come to feed in the marshes and nest in the surrounding prairies. As a result, this region is nicknamed North America's "duck factory."

Swamps

Swamps are freshwater wetlands where trees and shrubs grow. Swamps form along lakes and rivers and in low-lying areas. They contain a few inches to a few feet of water.

Swamps usually flood during the growing season. The water may dry up during late summer, or remain year round. Swamp waters tend to be dark and still. They are patterned with floating plants and shadows from tall, mossy trees above.

Swamps exist in both the northern and the southern United States. In the north, some common trees are red maple, black willow, white cedar, and cottonwood. In the south, water oak, tupelo, and bald cypress trees are common.

Shrub swamps have mostly shrubs, rather than trees. These types of swamps are usually found near lakes, marshes, and streams or next to tree-filled swamps. Some common swamp shrubs include pussy willow, buttonbush, and leatherleaf.

Depending on their location, swamps may contain such exotic animals as panthers, alligators, and black bears. Swamps shelter ducks and wading birds, which paddle or pick their way through the shallows in search of fish and snails.

Cottonmouth snakes and snapping turtles lurk in the water. Higher up, pileated woodpeckers drill the trees during the day.

Bald cypress trees have very knobby roots, which look like knees sticking up from the water. The roots pull oxygen in from the air.

In the Florida Everglades, you might spot an alligator lying in wait for its prey.

Some swamps do have poisonous snakes, quicksand, or thick vegetation. But a typical trip through the swamp is exciting, not dangerous.

Barred owls boom from the treetops at night, joining the chorus of swamp dwellers.

349

Bogs

The pitcher plant "catches" insects as they fall into its slippery, cuplike leaves and cannot get out.

A person can actually walk across the squishy, shaky surface of a bog.

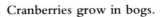

Cranberries grow in bogs.

Sphagnum moss helps form the solid, matted surface of a bog.

Bogs are freshwater wetlands that form in cool areas, where little water flows in and out and where the soil is especially low in oxygen. Most bogs formed thousands of years ago.

The combination of coolness, poor drainage, and low oxygen creates some unique conditions in the bog. For example, dead plants and animals break down very slowly. Over time, layers of dead plant material build up in the bog. These layers pack together to form an acidic material called *peat*.

Plants often grow on top of the peat, or spread across the bog's open water. The most common plants are tiny, carpetlike mosses called sphagnum moss. Networks of tiny water plants weave with the moss to form a floating mat. As the mat thickens, it supports larger plants, even trees.

Oxygen and food are in short supply in bogs. As a result, only a few specially adapted plants and animals live there. The black spruce is commonly found in bogs. It has special roots that pull in extra oxygen.

Orchids, which have beautiful, showy flowers, grow in bogs. A number of meat-eating plants are also found in bogs. The floating bladderwort sucks tiny water animals into special sacs. The sundew traps insects that land on its sticky leaves.

Bogs are visited by a number of animals, though few live there full-time. Moose, deer, bears, and cranes are just a few of these visitors.

Salt Marshes

Salt marshes develop in coves, bays, inlets, and *estuaries* (ES-chuh-wer-ees)—places where rivers meet the sea. All of these low-lying areas are protected from the full force of tides. They are places where grasses have been able to take root and grow.

Salt marshes cover nearly 10,000 square miles of the coastline of the United States. Almost half of them are found between Maine and Florida, along the Atlantic coast.

Salt marshes receive salty water from the ocean. Often, they also receive freshwater from rivers. The more salty the water, the fewer the number of plants and animals that make their homes there.

Salt marshes usually have tall, hardy grasses. A few of these are pickleweed, cordgrass, spike grass, and saltgrass.

Farther from the shore, the marsh may be *brackish,* containing a mix of saltwater and freshwater. More plants are often able to grow here.

Muddy or sandy stretches called *tidal flats* often form between the salt marsh and open ocean waters. Here, the force of incoming and outgoing waves and tides is very strong. Plants cannot take root and grow. The flats are exposed during low tide and covered with water during high tide.

Salt marshes are in tune with the tides. Twice daily, the ocean tides rise and fall. As water washes in and out, the marsh environment changes.

Salt marshes can form where a river meets the ocean.

Usually, only one or two types of grass grow in one salt marsh.

Beneath this tidal flat, a clam squirts out water after the tide washes out.

Cordgrass (left) and pickleweed (right) are common salt-marsh grasses.

351

Mangrove Swamps

Like the salt marsh, the mangrove swamp is washed by ocean tides.

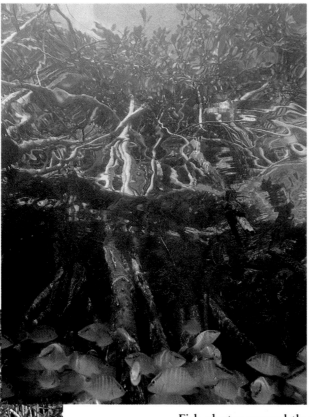

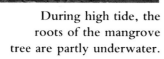

During high tide, the roots of the mangrove tree are partly underwater.

Fish cluster around the submerged roots of mangroves to take shelter and look for food.

The white ibis digs for crabs and other small sea animals with its long, sturdy bill.

Another type of saltwater wetland is the mangrove swamp. Just as the salt marsh is known for its sea of grass, the mangrove swamp is known for its tightly woven stands of mangrove trees.

Mangrove swamps are found in warm tropical and subtropical regions of the planet. In the United States, mangrove swamps line parts of the coast along southern Florida.

Mangrove trees send tough, fingerlike roots deep into the mud. The roots keep the trees firmly in place. For some species of mangroves, the roots pull in extra oxygen. They also keep the tree's trunk above water.

Oysters attach themselves to the mangroves' roots. Sea horses may be found hanging by their tails. Blue crabs, fish, and shrimp climb and swim among the roots.

The mangrove snapper knows it will find a good meal among the roots. The snapper swims slowly along, looking for shrimp and crabs. The turtle may pass an American crocodile in its search for food.

A bit higher up, just inches above the water, green-backed herons make their homes in the mangroves' roots. The branches above are home to spiders, snakes, frogs, and crabs.

The long-legged white ibis nests in groups, called colonies. When the tide flows out, the ibis wings its way to the tidal flats.

The Value of Wetlands

Wetlands are important in many ways. For example, they make good homes for wildlife. More than 5,000 plant species grow in wetlands. More than 600 kinds of animals live in wetlands or need them in some way for survival.

Wetlands shelter many rare plants and animals. Nearly one out of every two endangered animals and three out of four endangered plants in the United States depend on wetlands.

Wetland plants are also gathered for food and other purposes. Peat is collected from bogs and sold as burning material. Wild rice is another plant that makes its way from marshy waters to grocery stores and restaurants.

More than half the seafood caught in the United States comes from wetlands. Animals such as fish, crabs, shrimp, oysters, and clams all live in wetlands.

Wetlands are also important in pollution control. Water that flows into wetlands usually carries "hitchhikers" with it—materials that wash in or are dumped in somewhere else. They may be natural materials, such as dirt, or chemicals used by humans.

Natural or artificial pollution in water makes it hard for living things to breathe or grow. Wetlands can act as natural water cleaners. When water flows into a wetland, it slows down. Pollutants settle to the wetland bottom. They collect around roots and stems of plants. The water flows on out of the wetland, cleaner than when it entered.

The Florida panther is an endangered species that depends on a wetland for survival.

Many people don't realize that wetlands are natural water cleaners.

The survival of the American crocodile is endangered by the shrinking of its wetland habitat.

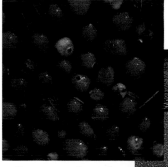

Some people make their living by growing and selling bog plants such as cranberries and blueberries.

The Icy Polar Lands

Islands in the Arctic can be covered by layers of ice that are hundreds of feet thick. This icy scene is on Ellesmere Island.

Polar regions are the lands and seas at the northernmost and southernmost points on Earth. If you have ever written a letter to Santa Claus at the North Pole, you were actually sending your letter to the middle of the Arctic Ocean, because that's where the North Pole is located! The South Pole, on the other hand, is located on Antarctica, a huge frozen continent.

Polar regions are the coldest areas on Earth— the places where it is hardest for humans to live.

In the wintertime, when the Antarctic seas freeze, the size of the Antarctic continent doubles!

In the wintertime, the poles are not only cold, they are dark, too. From September to March, the North Pole tilts away from the sun as the Earth revolves around it, and this movement places the Arctic in darkness for these six months. Meanwhile in Antarctica, on the other side of the world, the sun rises in September and doesn't fully set until March. Then, as the Earth moves in its orbit to the other side of the sun, the polar seasons are reversed.

Why are polar regions so cold? Because the Earth is round, the sunlight that falls at the North and South Poles consists of weaker, more slanted rays. These rays are spread out over a larger area than direct sunlight, which is concentrated into a smaller area. The sun's rays must also pass through a thicker layer of atmosphere at both poles. This absorbs their heat, so there is less heat left in the rays by the time they reach Earth.

The aurora borealis, or the northern lights, is often seen in the Arctic on winter nights. Explosions on the sun's surface send out particles called photons. When the photons hit the air molecules in the atmosphere above the North Pole, the collision produces light.

Have you ever noticed that you stay cooler in the summertime when you wear light-colored clothing? That's because light colors reflect the sun's rays back into the sky, rather than absorbing them as dark colors would. In warmer climates, the dark soil, trees, and grasses soak up most of the heat from the sun's rays. But the white snow covering polar lands reflects the sun's rays back into the sky, so the sea and land become even colder.

The average thickness of the ice on Antarctica is 6,600 feet—higher than most mountains in warmer regions. In some areas on Antarctica, the ice covering is 14,000 feet thick! Antarctica alone contains 90 percent of the world's ice. Scientists estimate that if the ice on Antarctica ever melted, the planet's sea level would rise by 212 feet, flooding coastal areas and low-lying lands around the world.

Antarctica holds the record for being the driest, windiest, and coldest place on Earth. The highest wind speed ever recorded was also in Antarctica—200 miles per hour. And while Antarctica's average annual temperature in the interior of the continent is a very chilly 80 degrees below zero Fahrenheit, the lowest temperature ever recorded was 128.6 degrees below zero Fahrenheit. At such temperatures, metals can shatter like glass and an unprotected person can freeze solid in minutes.

Mount Erebus, an active volcano, stands tall on Antarctica.

The coldest temperature ever recorded was taken on Antarctica.

Ice-covered polar lands and seas reflect the sun's rays, helping to make the polar regions the coldest places on Earth.

On one part of Antarctica, called the Dry Valleys, no rain has fallen for at least two million years!

357

Plants

Some lichens are able to grow for only two or three days each year!

Lichens are organisms that consist of an alga and a fungus living together. The alga and the fungus rely on each other to survive.

Sunny yellow Arctic poppies have fuzzy stems that trap air and prevent moisture loss.

Above: Cotton grass takes advantage of the southern Arctic's short summer growing season. Right: The bunchberry produces its colorful berries in autumn, before the harsh Arctic winter closes in.

Due to the cold temperatures and the short growing season, the most successful polar plants are small, simple ones like algae (AL-jee), lichens (LY-kuhns), and mosses. Some hardy flowering plants also live in polar areas, especially in the Arctic.

The *tundra* (TUHN-druh) is a vast polar plain that covers the Arctic areas of North America and Siberia. Only the top 20 inches of frozen earth thaws out each summer; the ground below never does. This ground that remains frozen all year round is called *permafrost* (PER-muh-frost).

Many seed-producing plants of the Arctic have developed special adaptations to survive the cold weather. Their roots spread out horizontally because the permafrost keeps them from growing farther

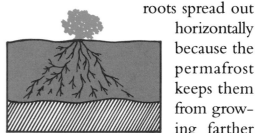

down into the soil. Some plants have chemicals like antifreeze in their sap to prevent their stems from freezing. The mountain saxifrage (SAX-uh-frayj) provides a splash of purple during the Arctic summer. Colorful blossoms like these help plants keep warm by absorbing more of the sun's heat than the white snow around them.

On Antarctica, only two flowering plants are found—the Antarctic hair grass and the Antarctic pearlwort. Otherwise, there are algae, mosses, and some 350 species of lichen!

Animals

Like polar plants, animals that live in polar areas have special *adaptations*—characteristics that help them survive the cold. You may recognize many of these: They are similar to some things humans do in the winter!

Heavy coats: We have to buy and wear heavy coats, but polar animals can grow their own. In fact, many mammals in polar regions grow two layers of fur. Musk oxen are protected by a dense undercoat that is eight times warmer than sheep's wool. On top of that, they grow a thick winter coat so long it almost touches the ground.

Protective coloring: White animals are very hard to see in the snow. Camouflage, or protective coloring, helps prey animals hide from their enemies. The same coloring also helps predators, like white-coated Arctic foxes, weasels, ermines, and snowy owls, to creep or fly up on their meal without attracting its attention. The snowy-white polar bear is an especially effective Arctic hunter.

Layers of fat: Have you ever noticed that you eat more food during the winter? Humans seem to naturally put on a little extra weight in cold weather, but polar mammals need to put on a lot of weight to get them through their winter! A thick layer of fat, called blubber, grows under the skin of polar mammals each winter.

The Arctic fox has a short undercoat that works like long underwear. Above this lies the "outerwear"—an outer coat of long hairs called guard hairs.

The coats of many polar animals turn white in the wintertime.

Arctic hares (above) and ermines (left) use their white color to blend in with snowy landscapes.

Blubber provides walruses with the extra insulation and energy they will need to get through the winter.

Animals

If a musk ox is disturbed and has to flee, the energy drain may prove to be fatal.

Elephant seals are the largest of all seals. The males can weigh four tons!

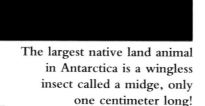

The largest native land animal in Antarctica is a wingless insect called a midge, only one centimeter long!

Weddell seals dive to depths of 1,800 feet to hunt seabed fish.

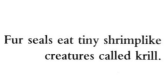

Fur seals eat tiny shrimplike creatures called krill.

Migration: Does your family head for a warmer climate when it's time for a winter vacation? Some polar animals also migrate to avoid the Arctic winter. Next spring, these animals will return to breed and feed on tundra plants, fish, and newly hatched insects.

Staying still: Are you less active in the winter? Polar animals, too, keep their activities to a minimum in order to conserve energy. Musk oxen, for example, simply stand still for long periods of time.

Staying small: Small size is a real advantage in the very coldest areas. In fact, most animals that live in Antarctica are microscopic! Small *invertebrates* (in-VER-tuh-bruhts)—animals without backbones—like threadworms, mites, flies, and jumping insects called springtails, also live there. Since these tiny animals are cold-blooded (their body temperatures are the same as the surrounding environment) they don't have to spend the extra energy needed to keep their body temperatures high. No warm-blooded vertebrate animal spends its life on Antarctica.

Streamlining: The sleek shape of seals is a big advantage in the Antarctic oceans they inhabit, for it lets them swim quickly and gracefully to catch food and escape danger. The seal species that swim off the Antarctic shores each inhabit different *niches* (NICH-uhs). That is, they eat different things and have different habits.

Birds

Some hardy birds live year-round in the Arctic and Antarctic regions. The rock ptarmigan (TAR-mi-guhn) and its close relative, the willow ptarmigan, are found in Arctic tundras around the world. A third species, the white-tailed ptarmigan, lives high in the Rocky Mountains. Ptarmigans are masters of disguise, for they live on the ground. Their nest is nothing more than a small scrape on the ground lined with feathers and grass. Living in trees would do them no good, for the trees of the tundra are only a few inches tall!

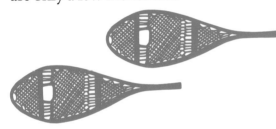

Ptarmigan chicks are able to move and feed themselves soon after hatching. This way, they are not helpless on the ground if an enemy were to show up.

In the summer, the ptarmigan's feathers are brown. When the days grow shorter, its feathers begin to turn white for winter. For a while, though, the ptarmigan looks like it has been spattered with white paint.

Ptarmigans prefer to walk or run rather than fly. However, if a ptarmigan is in danger, it will take off in a roar of flapping wings that will confuse the enemy. Once it is in the air, the ptarmigan will lock its wings and glide a long way. It will probably land far from where its nest is hidden. If forced to move south for food, ptarmigans will migrate on foot.

When the temperature drops dangerously low, ptarmigans may spend the night under a snow drift. The snow drift will block the winds and actually holds in the bird's body heat. If the ptarmigan simply walked into a drift, an Arctic fox or wolf could follow its scent. So instead, the ptarmigan flies—headfirst—into the snow, disappearing in a puff of white!

The ptarmigan wears snowshoes! Feathers on its feet help it to walk on top of the snow.

361

Birds

Like the emperor penguin, king penguin males also hold their eggs on their feet. A special flap of belly skin keeps the egg warm.

These emperor penguin chicks live in a creche, where they are watched by a few adults. This frees both the parents so they can fish for food.

Penguins are not like any other birds in the world. They have completely given up on flight. Instead, they live their lives by—and in—the ocean, where they swim and fish for their food. There are 18 species of penguins, all found in the southern hemisphere. They are not all found in Antarctica, though, as many people think. There are penguins in Australia, New Zealand, Africa, South America, and on many south Atlantic islands. Even though many of these places are far from Antarctica, most have cold ocean currents just off their shores.

The emperor penguin is the largest penguin. It weighs more than 80 pounds and stands almost four feet high. That's almost as tall as a cow! The emperor is found only on the coast of Antarctica, where it nests in huge colonies. Unlike the other penguins, emperor penguins lay their eggs at the beginning of the southern hemisphere winter, when the sun never fully rises and the temperature may drop to −60 degrees Fahrenheit.

The female emperor penguin lays a single egg, but if that egg were to touch the ground, it would instantly freeze. The male emperor penguin stands for six weeks without moving, holding the egg on his feet. A special flap of belly skin covers the egg and keeps it warm. The male eats

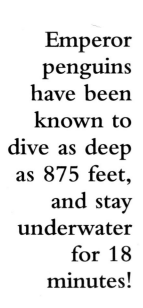

Emperor penguins have been known to dive as deep as 875 feet, and stay underwater for 18 minutes!

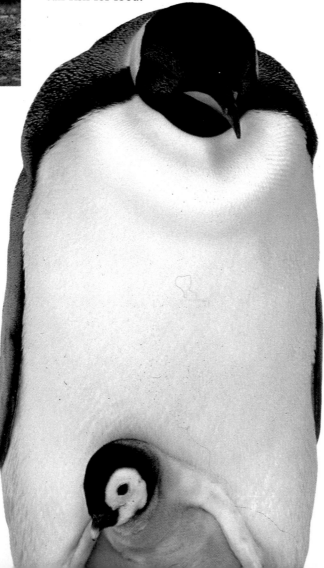

Penguin wings have evolved—changed over the years—into strong "flippers" that help penguins swim.

nothing during this time; he lives off his body fat. When the egg finally hatches, the male leaves the chick in the care of its mother, who has been away all this time, feeding. The male goes off by himself for a well-deserved meal.

The Adélie penguins of Antarctica nest during the South Pole's summer. Millions of these little penguins cover the beaches. Because the weather is a little warmer—reaching 30 degrees Fahrenheit some days—the Adélie can build a crude nest of stones in which to lay their two eggs. The male still does the incubating, though. He sits for seven to eleven days without eating before the chicks hatch and his mate takes charge of them. The Adélie chicks stay in the nest for 22 days. Then they join others their age in a huge creche. With their young in a creche, the parents can both fish for food. Also, there is safety in numbers; the young penguins are less likely to be harmed by an enemy.

To leave the water, a penguin builds up its speed until it can "fly" out of the water and land on its belly or feet!

The little Adélie is the best known of the penguins.
It adapts well to captivity.

The Polar Marine Food Chain

An estimated 1,000 million tons of phytoplankton are produced annually in the ocean surrounding Antarctica.

Krill provide the only food source for the world's largest animals— blue whales.

Walruses rake shellfish from the seabeds with their ivory tusks.

Polar bears are at the top of the polar marine food chain.

Packs of killer whales, among the most skilled hunters of the polar seas, eat mainly fish and squid, but also hunt for seals and other whales.

Polar lands may be barren, but their waters teem with life. Great quantities of microscopic plants called *phytoplankton* (FY-to-plank-tuhn) bloom in the spring and summer sunlight in the surface water—the top 30 to 165 feet of ocean—at both poles.

These phytoplankton are the main food source for the tiny krill. Swarms of krill color the ocean red by day and make it glow at night.

Blue whales, which can grow to lengths of 100 feet and weigh 130 tons, swim open-mouthed through swarms of krill, straining them from the Antarctic seawater with the dense fringes of hairy bristles inside their mouths, called *baleen* (buh-LEEN). Antarctic krill also provide the main food source for four other species of whales, three types of seals, 20 species of fish, three species of squid, and many birds, including penguins.

In the Arctic, land creatures must put up with temperatures of 40 degrees below zero Fahrenheit. The waters, however, rarely fall below 32 degrees Fahrenheit. Phytoplankton in Arctic waters are grazed upon by tiny floating animals called *zooplankton,* which are then eaten by small fish, which are then eaten by larger fish like the polar cod and Arctic char, which are then eaten by white whales and seals. The seals may then be eaten by polar bears.

GLOSSARY

Abyss (uh-BISS): The deepest, darkest part of the ocean.

Acceleration (ik-se-luh-RAY-shuhn): A change in speed. Acceleration can mean that an object is speeding up or slowing down.

Acoustics (uh-KOO-stiks): The science that studies sound.

Adaptation (ad-ap-TAY-shun): A change in a behavior, physical feature, or other characteristic over time that helps an animal or plant survive and make the most of its habitat.

Air mass: A large body of air in which conditions such as temperature, pressure, and humidity are generally the same.

Air pressure: The force created in an area by the weight of all the air above that area. Changes in air pressure are good clues about what kind of weather is coming.

Algae (AL-jee): Simple living things composed of one or more cells. Most algae are plants, but without roots or flowers. Seaweed is a form of algae. One single organism is called an alga (AL-guh).

Amphibians (am-FIB-ee-uhnz): A group of cold-blooded animals that tend to have moist skin and larvae that live in water. Frogs, toads, and salamanders are amphibians.

Amplitude (AM-pluh-tood): The height of a wave's crest above its center.

Aquatic (uh-KWAH-tik): A plant or animal that lives in the water.

Aquifer (AH-kwuh-fer): An underground layer of rock, sand, or gravel in which freshwater collects.

Arachnids (uh-RAK-nuhdz): A group of animals with eight legs, closely related to insects. Spiders, scorpions, mites, and ticks are arachnids.

Arid (AR-uhd): Land that is very dry. Deserts are arid lands that receive less than ten inches of rain a year.

Asteroid (AS-tur-oid): A small body, less than half a mile wide to as much as 630 miles wide, that revolves around the sun. Most are in the asteroid belt between Mars and Jupiter.

Atmosphere (AT-muhs-feer): All the gases, moisture, and dust surrounding a planet.

Atom (A-tuhm): The smallest particle of an element that can exist alone.

Axis (AK-suhs): The center of a planet, from the South Pole to the North Pole.

Bacteria (bak-TEER-ee-uh): Tiny living cells that can only be seen through a microscope. Some bacteria cause diseases, but others do useful things like making soil richer.

Blade (blayd): The long, thin, flexible leaf of a grass plant.

Blubber (BLUHB-bur): A thick layer of fat that grows under the skin of polar mammals each winter and provides them with extra insulation and energy.

Bog (bawg): A freshwater wetland that forms in cool areas. Water in bogs drains poorly and soils are low in oxygen. Bogs contain thick layers of tightly packed plant remains called peat.

Boss (baws): A blunt, raised pad or bump, usually on the head of an animal.

By-product (BY-prah-duhkt): Something that is produced by a process but that is not the goal of the process. Heat is a by-product of the process that transforms a car's fuel into energy.

Caldera (kahl-DAYR-uh): A very large crater that forms when the upper part of a volcano collapses.

Camouflage (KAM-uh-flahj): A way of blending into the surroundings to hide from predators or prey.

Canopy (KA-nuh-pee): The uppermost layer of a forest, composed mostly of treetops and the animals that live there.

Carnivore (KAR-nuh-vor): An animal that eats meat. Lions and eagles are examples of carnivores.

Cartilage (KAR-tuhl-ij): The connective tissue that composes most of the skeleton of vertebrate animals at a certain stage before they are born. Cartilage is more elastic than bone. Even after the animals are born, they still have some cartilage.

Cell (sel): The very small, basic unit of living matter. All living things are made of cells.

Chemical energy (KE-mi-kuhl E-nur-jee): Energy that comes from making or breaking chemical bonds that link atoms and molecules together.

Chemical sedimentary rock (KEM-i-kuhl sed-uh-MEN-tuh-ree rahk): Atoms and molecules floating in water clump together to form tiny crystals of minerals. These tiny crystals may get large enough to sink to the bottom and form thick layers that eventually become rock.

Chlorophyll (KLOR-uh-fil): The green substance in plants that absorbs energy from sunlight. Plants use chlorophyll to change carbon dioxide and water into food and oxygen.

Chloroplast (KLOR-uh-plast): A tiny green structure inside a plant's leaf cells that contains chlorophyll and functions like a solar panel.

Chrysalis (KRIS-uh-lis): The stage during which a caterpillar forms a shell and turns into a butterfly inside it.

Cirrus clouds (SEE-ruhs klowdz): Clouds that have a feathery, wispy look. Cirrus clouds are made mostly of ice crystals, and they form high in the atmosphere.

Cleavage (KLEE-vuhj): A mineral property that describes the way a crystal breaks along certain planes.

Climate (KLY-muht): A description of the average weather conditions in an area over many years.

Coalescence (ko-uh-LES-uhnts): The process of many water droplets in a cloud striking each other and joining together to form a larger droplet. If this happens enough times, a raindrop will form.

Cold-blooded (kold BLUH-duhd): Term used to describe an animal that is not able to maintain a constant body temperature itself. Amphibians, fish, insects, and reptiles are cold-blooded animals.

Cold front (kold fruhnt): The edge of a cold air mass that is advancing against a warm air mass. Weather conditions across a front are usually changing.

Colony (KAH-luh-nee): A group of animals that live close to each other. Some kinds of birds and bats live in colonies.

Comet (KAHM-uht): An object in the sky that usually has a large head and a tail of glowing gas and shining dust when it is close enough to the sun to warm up a little.

Community (kuh-MYOO-nuh-tee): A group of plants and animals living in the same area and depending on each other for survival.

Compound (KAHM-pound): A substance that contains more than one element chemically joined together.

Condensation (kahn-den-SAY-shuhn): The process by which water vapor changes to water droplets high in the atmosphere and down on Earth.

Confluence (CON-floo-ents): A place where two rivers come together.

Coniferous (ko-NI-fuh-ruhs): A type of forest in which conifers, also called evergreen or softwood trees, are the most common. Coniferous temperate forests grow mainly in the northern and northwestern United States.

Conifers (KAH-nuh-furz): A group of plants that includes mostly evergreen trees and shrubs.

Constellation (kahn-stuh-LAY-shuhn): A group of stars named for a shape they were thought to have formed, such as Cancer the crab. There are 88 constellations.

Core (kor): The innermost part of the Earth, surrounded by the mantle and crust. The outer part of the core is liquid. Its inner part is solid.

Crater (KRAY-tur): The hole at the top of a volcano where the main vent brings magma to the surface.

Crust (kruhst): The outermost layer of the Earth. The crust lies beneath the continents and the ocean floors.

Crystal (KRIS-tuhl): A regular pattern that repeats itself throughout a solid substance. The size and shape of a crystal depend on the size and shape of the atoms and molecules that make it up and the strength of the chemical bonds between them.

Cumulus clouds (KYOO-myuh-luhs klowdz): Clouds that have a bulging, bumpy look. Cumulus clouds usually form in air that is rising quickly.

Decibel (DE-suh-bel): A scale used to measure the loudness of sounds.

Deciduous (di-SI-joo-uhs): Term used to describe trees that drop their leaves in the fall.

Decomposers (dee-kuhm-PO-zurz): Animals and plants that break down dead organic material and convert it to soil. Decomposers can be worms, insects, bacteria, or fungi.

Den (den): A sheltered place an animal lives in. Examples of dens include holes dug in the ground and protected spaces between rocks.

Diurnal (dy-UR-nuhl): An animal that is active during the daytime.

DNA: A kind of acid found in the cells of all living things that serves as a blueprint. DNA determines what every plant and animal looks like.

Doppler effect (DAH-plur i-FEKT): A change in the frequency of light or sound waves that is observed when the wave source moves.

Drought (drowt): A long period of little or no rain.

Earthquake (URTH-kwayk): A sudden movement of Earth's crust, usually along a crack, or fault.

Echolocation (e-ko-lo-KAY-shuhn): The way some animals such as bats locate objects by sending out high-pitched sounds that bounce off the objects and then return to the animals.

Ecosystem (EE-ko-sis-tuhm): An entire community of species and the surrounding soil, air, minerals, and water that interact with each other. Examples of ecosystems are rain forests and deserts.

Efficiency (i-FI-shuhn-see): A term used to describe how much useful work is done compared to the energy used.

Electrical energy (i-LEK-tri-kuhl E-nur-jee): Energy carried by electrons in wires.

Electromagnetic waves (i-lek-tro-mag-NE-tik wayvz): Waves of energy that are put out by electric or magnetic vibrations in matter or electrical circuits. Light, radio waves, X rays, microwaves, and gamma rays are electromagnetic waves.

Electron (i-LEK-trahn): A particle of an atom that orbits around the nucleus.

Element (E-luh-muhnt): A substance made up of just one kind of atom. An element cannot be broken down into simpler materials.

Emergent layer (ee-MUR-juhnt LAY-ur): The highest area of a rain forest, above the canopy. The emergent layer is usually between 100 and 250 feet above the ground.

Endangered species (in-DAYN-jurd SPEE-sheez): A plant or animal that is in danger of becoming extinct. The black rhinoceros is an endangered species.

Energy (E-nur-jee): The capacity or ability to do work.

Environment (in-VY-ruhn-muhnt): All the things found in an area and the way they act together and affect each other. The environment includes the air, land, water, weather, plants, and animals of an area.

Epicenter (EP-i-sent-ur): The point at the surface of Earth's crust directly above the focus; the spot within the crust or mantle where an earthquake begins.

Erosion (i-RO-juhn): The wearing away of bare soil or rock, usually by wind and water.

Estivation (ES-tuh-VAY-shuhn): Going into a sleeplike state during times of heat and drought. Estivating animals burn energy slowly, so they don't need food and water.

Estuary (ES-chuh-wayr-ee): The place where the freshwater of a river meets the salty water of the sea. Estuaries are also called harbors, sounds, bays, or fjords.

Eukaryotes (yoo-KAYR-ee-ots): An organism made up of one or more cells that contain visible nuclei.

Eutrophication (yoo-tro-fih-KAY-shuhn): The building up of sediments and nutrients in a lake. This process can be caused by either natural aging or water pollution.

Evaporation (i-va-puh-RAY-shuhn): The process by which liquid water drys up and changes into a gas called water vapor.

Evolution (e-vuh-LOO-shuhn): A process that results in changes in a plant or animal over time.

Extinct (ex-TINKT): A species that no longer exists. Dinosaurs and the dodo bird are extinct.

Fault (fawlt): A crack in the Earth's crust. Movement along a fault causes earthquakes.

Fission (FI-juhn): A nuclear process that produces energy by breaking apart the nuclei of atoms.

Floodplain (FLUHD-playn): The land surrounding a river, which becomes flooded when the river overflows its banks.

Fluid (FLOO-uhd): Substance that can flow from place to place and change its shape whenever a force acts on it.

Focus (FO-kuhs): The point within Earth's crust or mantle where a fault movement starts an earthquake. It lies below the epicenter.

Food chain (food chayn): A process in nature in which food energy is transferred from one living thing to another. An example of a simple food chain is a plant-eating deer that is eaten by a wolf.

Forest floor (FOR-uhst flor): The area of a forest below the understory.

Fossil (FAH-suhl): The preserved remains of long-dead animals or plants that are made by the process of fossilization.

Frequency (FREE-kwuhn-see): The measure of the number of wave cycles that pass by a certain point in one second.

Freshwater wetlands (FRESH-wah-tur WET-landz): Wetlands that are found inland and contain freshwater.

Friction (FRIK-shuhn): A force produced when objects rub against each other or against the air.

Fungus (FUHN-guhs): A nongreen plant, like a mushroom.

Fusion (FYOO-juhn): A nuclear process that produces energy by forcing the nuclei of atoms to combine. Fusion makes the stars shine.

Galaxy (GAL-uhk-see): A large grouping of solar systems, stars, nebulae, and interstellar space. There are billions of galaxies in our universe.

Germinate (JUR-muh-nayt): To sprout; to begin growing from a seed.

Gills (gilz): The breathing organs of fish and snails.

Grassland (GRAS-land): Area where grass is the main type of vegetation. Like forests, which are wetter, and deserts, which are dryer, grasslands are one of the Earth's main vegetation zones, found on every continent except Antarctica.

Gravitropism (gra-vuh-TRO-pizm): The response of plants to the force of gravity. Even if a potted plant is laid on its side, gravitropism makes sure that its stem will gradually bend around so that it is growing upward again.

Gravity (GRA-vuh-tee): The attractive force between any objects. Gravity makes objects fall toward the Earth and keeps the Earth revolving around the Sun.

Graze (grayz): To continually feed upon grasses and herbs; this is usually done by hoofed mammals called grazers.

Groundwater (GROWND-wah-tur): Freshwater found deep under the ground.

Habitat (HA-buh-tat): The area or natural environment in which a plant or animal normally lives.

Hatchling (HACH-ling): A newly hatched animal.

Hemisphere (HE-muh-sfeer): Half of a sphere. Earth is divided at the equator into the northern and southern hemispheres.

Herbaceous (her-BAY-shuhs): Term used to describe plants that have the texture, color, or appearance of a leaf. Also, the horizontal layer in a temperate forest containing non-woody plants like wildflowers, ferns, grasses, and mosses, which grow from an inch to several feet tall.

Herbivore (HER-buh-vor): An animal that eats plants. Deer and elephants are herbivores.

Hibernation (hy-bur-NAY-shuhn): A period of time, usually during the cold winter months, when an animal is inactive.

Hot spot (haht spaht): A part of Earth's surface above an extra-hot part of the mantle. At hot spots, blobs of hot magma force their way from the mantle up through the crust and form volcanoes at the surface.

Humidity (hyoo-MI-duh-tee): The amount of water vapor in the air compared to the amount of water vapor that the air can hold.

Humus (HYOO-muhs): The rich, dark soil formed by decomposed dead plants and animals.

Hurricane (HUR-uh-kayn): A large tropical storm with winds of over 74 miles an hour. Hurricanes can be hundreds of miles wide.

Hyphae (HY-fee): The threads that make up the mycelium of a fungus. Typically, they snake unseen for miles through soil and wood.

Incandescence (in-kan-DES-uhns): The emission of visible light by an object, caused by high temperature.

Incubate (IN-kyoo-bayt): To sit on eggs in order to hatch them by the warmth of the body.

Indicator species (IN-duh-kay-tur SPEE-sheez): A species of plant or animal highly sensitive to pollution.

Interference (in-tur-FEER-uhnts): The effects of two waves combining.

Internal energy (in-TUR-nuhl E-nur-jee): The energy of vibrating atoms and molecules.

Interstellar space (INT-ur-stel-ur spays): The area between two stars.

Intrusive rocks (in-TROO-siv rahkz): Rocks that are formed when magma cools inside the Earth.

Invertebrate (in-VER-tuh-brayt): An animal without a backbone. Insects are invertebrates.

Kinetic energy (kuh-NE-tik E-nur-jee): The energy of motion.

Krill (kril): Tiny shrimplike creatures that are eaten by many larger polar animals.

Larva (LAR-vuh): The immature stage of an animal that will go through a complete metamorphosis to become an adult. Some insects and amphibians begin life from an egg as larva. More than one larva are called larvae (LAR-vee).

Laser (LAY-zur): A device that produces a special beam of light by causing atoms to emit energy in regular waves, rather than randomly, as in ordinary light.

Lava (LAH-vuh): Molten rock erupted by volcanoes.

Leaf litter (leef LI-tur): The horizontal layer within a forest composed of fallen leaves, twigs, flower petals, seeds, fruits, animal droppings, and pine needles. It covers and insulates the soil, and provides shelter and moisture for the plants and animals that live there.

Lichen (LY-kuhn): A plant made up of an alga and a fungus living together. Lichens are often flat and crusty-looking and grow on rocks or tree trunks.

Light-year (LYT-yur): The distance light travels in one year, or about 5,878,000,000,000 miles.

Longitudinal wave (lawn-juh-TOOD-nuhl wayv): A wave that moves by compressing, then stretching out the substance through which it travels. Sound waves are longitudinal when they move through air.

Luminescence (loo-muh-NE-suhns): The emission of light that is not caused by incandescence and that occurs at low temperatures.

Magma (MAG-muh): Molten rock from the mantle or crust of the Earth. When magma reaches the surface through eruptions, it becomes lava.

Magnetic force (mag-NE-tik fors): The force that attracts certain metals to other metals.

Magnitude (MAG-nuh-tood): A measure of the amount of energy given out by an earthquake. Magnitude is measured on the Richter scale.

Mammal (MA-mul): Warm-blooded vertebrate animal that has hair or fur and feeds its young with milk produced by the female's mammary glands.

Mangrove swamp (MAN-grov swahmp): Saltwater wetland that develops in tropical and subtropical coastal regions. Mangrove trees are the main plants.

Mantle (MAN-tuhl): The part of the Earth that separates the core from the crust. The mantle is solid rock, but because it is under extreme pressure, it can flow like putty.

Marsh (marsh): Freshwater wetland that is found inland. Marshes usually hold a few inches to a few feet of water and support soft-stemmed, nonwoody plants. They support the widest variety of life of any ecosystem in North America.

Marsupials (mar-SOO-pee-uhlz): Mammals such as kangaroos, wombats, and opossums whose offspring do not develop a true placenta, but which are temporarily carried in a pouch on their mother's abdomen.

Mass (mas): The amount of matter contained in an object.

Mechanical sedimentary rock (mi-KAN-i-kuhl sed-uh-MENT-uh-ree rahk): Pieces of weathered rock that are cemented or pressed together in a lake, streambed, or ocean.

Metabolism (muh-TA-buh-lizm): All the chemical and biological changes that take place in a living thing.

Metamorphic rock (met-uh-MOR-fik rahk): Rock formed when the heat and pressure within the Earth melt and squeeze older rocks, which then take a new form.

Meteor (MEE-tee-ur): A piece of comet or asteroid that lights up in the sky because of friction with Earth's atmosphere. A meteorite is a part of a meteor that falls to Earth.

Microorganism (my-kro-OR-guh-nizm): An organism of microscopic size.

Migrate (MY-grayt): To move from one area to another, sometimes over long distances. Gray whales, salmon, and many species of birds all migrate.

Mimicry (MI-mi-kree): A type of camouflage in which a plant or animal looks like something else. Species use mimicry to hide from predators or prey or to make themselves look dangerous or poisonous.

Mineral (MI-nuh-ruhl): A naturally occurring element or compound that forms crystals. Every mineral has a unique combination made of certain atoms and a particular crystal structure.

Mixture (MIKS-chur): A substance made up of elements that are not chemically joined together. Each element in a mixture can be removed without chemically changing the element.

Molecule (MAH-li-kyool): A particle made up of more than one atom chemically joined together.

Mollusk (MAH-luhsk): A soft-bodied animal surrounded by a hard shell. Snails, clams, and oysters are mollusks.

Mouth (mowth): The place where a river empties into the ocean.

Mycorrhizal (my-kuh-RY-zuhl): Type of fungus that has a cooperative relationship with the roots of a seed plant.

Nebula (NEB-yuh-luh): A huge cloud in interstellar space that can be seen in the light of the stars nearby. A nebula can be a star's birthplace, and what is left after a star dies.

Neutron (NOO-trahn): A particle that makes up part of an atom's nucleus.

Nocturnal (nahk-TUR-nuhl): Term used to describe an animal that is active during the night.

North Pole: The permanently fixed point at 90 degrees North, around which the Earth rotates.

Nucleus (NOO-klee-uhs): The center of an atom, made up of particles called protons and neutrons. More than one nucleus are called nuclei (NOO-klee-y).

Newton's Laws of Motion: Laws discovered by Sir Isaac Newton that describe the ways in which force, matter, and motion are related.

Nutrient (NOO-tree-uhnt): A substance absorbed or eaten by plants and animals that contributes to their growth and development.

Ocean ridge (O-shuhn ridj): A range of undersea mountains that stretches across the sea floor. Ocean ridges grow where new tectonic plates are formed by magma coming up from the mantle.

Oligotrophic (ah-li-go-TRO-fik): A lake, usually younger, that tends to be deep and clear, with few plants living in it.

Orbit (OR-buht): The path of a planet or other object around a larger object, such as the sun.

Ore (or): A mineral that is mined for a part of its chemical makeup. For example, copper ore is mined because the metal copper can be extracted from it.

Organic (or-GA-nik): A substance derived from a once-living creature.

Organism (Or-guh-nizm): An individual living being. The smallest bacterium and the largest whale are organisms.

Ornithischia (or-nuh-THIS-kee-uh): One of the two major groups of dinosaurs, the "bird-hipped" group. All dinosaurs in this group were plant-eaters.

Oxygen (OHK-si-juhn): A gas found in air and water, and which all plants and animals need to fuel life processes.

Parasite (PAYR-uh-syt): A plant or animal that lives on or in a "host" plant or animal. A parasite can harm or kill its host.

Peat (peet): A layer of tightly packed, partially broken down plant material that builds up in bogs and is very acidic. Peat may be up to 40 feet thick in some places and is firm enough to support humans and even trees.

Permafrost (PUR-muh-frawst): The permanently frozen land beneath the surface of the tundra.

Photon (FO-tahn): A quantity of light energy put out by an atom when certain changes take place inside the atom.

Photosynthesis (fo-to-SIN-thuh-suhs): The process by which green plants make their own food from sunlight, water, and nutrients.

Phototropism (fo-to-TRO-pizm): The process by which plants adjust to changing light by turning their stems and leaves to follow the source of light.

Phytoplankton (FY-toh-plank-tuhn): The tiniest aquatic plants, often microscopic.

Planet (PLA-nuht): A body that is in orbit around a star and is not large enough to glow with its own light.

Plankton (PLANK-tuhn): Tiny floating plants and animals that drift in the ocean and form the basis of many food chains.

Plate boundary (playt BOWN-duh-ree): A place where tectonic plates meet. Plates may crash into each other, move away from each other, or move alongside each other at plate boundaries.

Plate tectonics (playt tek-TAH-niks): The process of tectonic plates moving across the Earth. Plate tectonics is probably driven by movements of the mantle below.

Polarization (po-luh-ruh-ZAY-shuhn): The effect of causing light waves to vibrate in the same direction. Polarized sunlight can cause a harsh glare.

Pollen (PAH-luhn): A yellowish powder found in flowers. Pollen is made up of the male cells of flowering plants.

It fertilizes the female cells so they can form seeds that will later grow into plants.

Pollination (pah-luh-NAY-shuhn): The fertilization process that happens when pollen is carried from one flower to another. Once pollinated, the flowers of grasses and other plants "go to seed."

Potential energy (puh-TEN-shuhl E-nur-jee): Energy that is stored in fuels, batteries, chemicals, or other sources. Also, the energy in a compressed spring or a suspended weight that, when released, can do work.

Prairie (PRAYR-ee): The temperate grasslands of central North America. In the United States, there are two types: the drier shortgrass prairie, or plains, and the wetter tall-grass prairie.

Precipitation (pri-si-puh-TAY-shuhn): The process by which condensed water droplets fall to Earth as rain or snow.

Predator (PRE-duh-tur): An animal that hunts, kills, and feeds on other animals.

Prehensile (pree-HEN-sil): Designed to grab or hold onto things. Sea horses and chameleons have prehensile tails.

Prey (pray): An animal that is eaten by a predator.

Primates (PRY-mayts): A group of mammals made up of humans, apes, monkeys, and related forms, such as lemurs and tarsiers.

Prokaryote (pro-KAYR-ee-ot): A cellular organism (such as a bacterium or blue-green alga) that does not have a distinct nucleus.

Protists (PRO-tists): The kingdom of living things that includes simple organisms, such as amoebas and most algae, that live mainly in water.

Proton (PRO-tahn): A particle that helps form the nucleus of an atom.

Pupa (PYOO-puh): In an animal that undergoes metamorphism, the stage of development between larva and adult, during which the animal often remains very still.

Radiation (ray-dee-AY-shuhn): Energy released by an object in the form of waves and particles. Light is a form of radiation that we can see.

Reef (reef): An underwater ridge built by the skeletons of hard corals.

Reflection (ri-FLEK-shuhn): The return of light or sound after it bounces off a surface.

Refraction (ri-FRAK-shuhn): The bending of a wave as it moves from one substance to another, such as from air to water or from warm air to cold air. Refraction of light can create rainbows.

Reptiles (REP-tuhlz): Cold-blooded animals with scales that lay eggs on land. Living reptiles are turtles, snakes, crocodiles, and lizards. Dinosaurs were reptiles, but may have been warm-blooded.

Resonance (REZ-uhn-uhns): A larger-than-normal vibration that takes place when a vibrating object, such as a musical instrument, receives pulses of energy at its natural frequency.

Revolution (rev-uh-LOO-shuhn): The movement of a planet along its path or orbit. One complete revolution is a planetary year.

Riming (RYM-ing): The process of water droplets in a cloud striking a snowflake, freezing, and becoming part of the snowflake.

River valley (RI-vur VA-lee): The rich land along a river, often good for farming.

Rivulet (RIV-yoo-luht): A tiny stream that may join with others to form a larger stream, and even a river.

Rock (rahk): Rocks are made of one or several minerals. Silicates are the main rock-building materials.

Rodents (RO-duhnts): A group of sharp-toothed, plant-eating mammals that includes the smallest members of the mammal family.

Rotation (ro-TAY-shuhn): The movement of a planet turning on its axis. One complete rotation is a planetary day.

Runoff (RUN-awf): Water traveling downhill, sometimes carrying sediments or pollutants.

Salt marsh (sawlt marsh): A saltwater wetland that forms along protected shorelines, often at estuaries. Salt marshes are washed daily by ocean tides, may contain some freshwater, and mainly support a limited number of grasses.

Saltwater wetlands (SAWLT-wah-tur WET-landz): Wetlands that form along the coast and receive salt water from the ocean.

Saurischia (so-RIS-kee-uh): One of two major groups of dinosaurs, the "lizard-hipped" group. This group includes both meat-eating and plant-eating dinosaurs.

Savannah (suh-VA-nuh): Tropical grasslands that, in Africa, feature scattered trees, sharp-edged grasses, and an unusually wide variety of animals.

Scavenger (SKA-vuhn-jur): An animal that feeds on dead animals or trash. Vultures are scavengers.

Secondary growth (SE-kuhn-dayr-ee groth): The new forest that grows after an older forest has been destroyed.

Sediment (SE-duh-muhnt): The loose soil, sand, and stones carried and deposited by a river or glacier.

Semiarid (se-mee-AR-uhd): A climate that is dry but not as dry as an arid climate.

Shrub layer (shruhb LAY-ur): The horizontal layer within a temperate forest composed of bushes, saplings, and shrubs.

Solar system (SO-lur SIS-tuhm): A star, such as our sun, and the planets, asteroids, moons, and comets that are held by gravity around the star.

South Pole: The permanently fixed southern end of the Earth's axis of rotation.

Spawn (spawn): To deposit large numbers of eggs in the water, as do fish and many amphibians.

Species (SPEE-sheez): A group of animals and plants that are closely related. Only members of the same species can produce offspring that itself can reproduce.

Spectrum (SPEK-truhm): A grouping of light or sound waves by frequency or wavelength. The electromagnetic spectrum is the colored band of visible light wavelengths (red, orange, yellow, green, blue, indigo, and violet) produced by a prism, together with invisible extensions (radio, infrared, ultraviolet, X rays, etc.). The sound spectrum humans can hear is the range of frequencies between about 20 and 20,000 Hz.

Star (star): A ball of gas that is visible in the night sky. Our sun is a medium-size star.

Stomates (STO-mayts): Tiny pores on leaves that allow a plant to take in air or evaporate water.

Stratus clouds (STRAYT-uhs klowdz): Clouds that have a layered, sheetlike appearance. Stratus clouds usually form in air that is rising slowly.

Subduction (suhb-DUHK-shuhn): When two tectonic plates crash into each other, one dives beneath the other, back into the mantle. This process is called subduction. It causes earthquakes and volcanoes.

Swamp (swahmp): A freshwater wetland where trees and shrubs grow. A few inches to a few feet of water flood swamps all or part of the year. The water tends to be dark and still, or slow-moving.

Symbiosis (sim-bee-OH-suhs): A give-and-take relationship between different kinds of living things, in which both creatures benefit.

Tectonic plate (tek-TAHN-ik playt): A piece of Earth's crust that moves across Earth's surface, bumping into or scraping against other plates.

Temperate (TEM-puh-ruht): Having a mild climate that usually includes four yearly seasons of different temperatures.

Temperate forests (TEM-puh-ruht FO-ruhsts): Forests with colder winters and less rain than rain forests, but in which the climate is neither extremely cold nor hot, neither very wet nor very dry.

Temperate grasslands (TEM-uh-ruht GRAS-landz): Grasslands growing in places with hot summers and cold winters. About 10 to 30 inches of rain falls each year, mostly during the spring and summer months.

Tidal flat (TY-duhl flat): A muddy or sandy area that lacks plant growth and is found between salt marshes and open ocean waters. Tidal flats are exposed during low tide and drowned during high tide.

Tornado (tor-NAY-do): A violent, local storm of whirling winds often accompanied by a funnel-shaped cloud. Tornado winds can reach 250 miles an hour.

Transpiration (trans-pi-RAY-shun): The "breathing" process all green plants go through, during which they take in carbon dioxide and give off water and oxygen.

Transverse wave (trans-VERS wayv): A wave that moves at right angles to its direction of travel. Light waves are transverse waves.

Tropical (TRAHP-uh-kuhl): A word that describes a region that is warm all year because it is near the equator.

Tropical grasslands: Grasslands growing in areas where the climate is hot all year. There is usually a "rainy season," where up to 40 inches of rain may fall, followed by a long dry period.

Tsunami (soo-NAHM-ee): A large ocean wave caused by a fault movement or a volcanic eruption on the ocean floor.

Tundra (TUN-druh): The vast, cold grasslands covering the Arctic areas of North America, Europe, and Asia. The tundra makes up 15 percent of the Earth's land surface.

Turbine (TUR-buhn): A machine with turning blades that converts the energy of motion of the moving blades into electricity.

Understory (UN-dur-sto-ree): The horizontal layer within a forest below the canopy, made up mostly of young trees and trees that don't grow very tall.

Universe (YOO-nuh-vurs): All the stars, galaxies, solar systems, and interstellar space.

Vascular (VAS-kyoo-lur): Term used to describe the largest group of plants. Vascular plants have tubes and similar structures to carry water from the ground upward through their stems.

Vertebrate (VUR-tuh-bruht): An animal with a backbone. Fish, birds, amphibians, reptiles, and mammals are all vertebrates.

Volcano (vuhl-KAY-no): A place on Earth's surface where lava, ash, and steam erupt onto the surface and into the atmosphere. Volcanoes can be quiet or very explosive.

Warm-blooded (warm-BLUH-duhd): Term used to describe an animal that is able to maintain a constant body temperature on its own. Birds and mammals are warm-blooded animals.

Warm front (warm fruhnt): The edge of a warm air mass that is advancing against a cold air mass. Weather conditions across a front are usually changing.

Water vapor (WAH-tur VAY-pur): The gaseous form of water.

Wavelength (WAYV-length): A measure of the distance a wave travels during a single cycle.

Wetland (WET-land): The basic name for an ecosystem that contains shallow water or waterlogged soils at least part of the year, and supports plants adapted to wet living conditions. Wetlands form in areas where land gives way to water.

Work (wurk): Effect that takes place when a force moves an object in the direction of the force.

Zooplankton (ZOH-oh-plank-tuhn): The tiniest animals, often microscopic, found in a body of water.

Contributors:

Isaac Abella is Professor of Physics at the University of Chicago and is a member of the National Academy of Sciences Committee on Undergraduate Science Education and K-12 Science Standards.

Joel E. Arem holds a Ph.D. in mineralogy from Harvard University. He has served as the director of the geology program at the Brooklyn Children's Museum.

Lynne Hardie Baptista has written numerous articles and award-winning education programs on wildlife conservation and the environment. Previously with the World Wildlife Fund, she is Director of Education at the American Zoo & Aquarium Association.

Richard Block has served as the Director of Public Programs at the World Wildlife Fund and Curator of Education at Zoo Atlanta. He has lectured at the School of Natural Resources at the University of Michigan.

Bruce A. Bolt, Ph.D. is Professor of Seismology at the University of California. He has been president of both the International Association of Seismology and the Seismological Society of America.

Jennifer Boudart holds a Bachelor of Science degree in wildlife ecology and agricultural journalism from the University of Wisconsin-Madison. She has written for *Ducks Unlimited* magazine and was editor and contributing writer for *Puddler,* a wetland wildlife magazine for children.

Todd A. Culver is the Education Specialist at Cornell Laboratory of Ornithology at Cornell University. He contributes to the nationally aired radio program *Birdwatch.*

Peter Dodson, Ph.D. is a widely recognized expert on dinosaurs and has consulted on many publications. He is an Associate Professor of Anatomy at the School of Veterinary Medicine of the University of Pennsylvania, where he also teaches courses and lectures on paleontology, evolution, and geology. He received his doctorate from Yale University.

Gary Dunn has served as extension entomologist at Michigan State University, where he worked in the entomology youth education program. He has also served as the advisor for the Young Entomologists Society and as executive director and editor of the society's magazines, *Insect World, Y.E.S. Quarterly,* and *Flea Market.*

Toni Eugene has worked for National Geographic Society for many years, and is the managing editor of their Special Publications Division. She has authored three children's nature books: *Creatures of the Woods, Strange Animals of Australia,* and *Hide and Seek.*

Betty Lane Faber holds a Ph.D. in entomology from Rutgers University. She has taught children's workshops for the American Museum of Natural History and has participated in the New York Academy of Sciences' Scientists-in-Schools program.